Tizen Cookbook

Over 100 hands-on recipes to develop, deploy, and debug
applications using the exciting Tizen platform

Leon Anavi

BIRMINGHAM - MUMBAI

Tizen Cookbook

First published: October 2014

Production reference: 1081014

Published by Packt Publishing Ltd.
Livery Place
35 Livery Street
Birmingham B3 2PB, UK.

ISBN 978-1-78398-190-8

www.packtpub.com

Cover image by Leon Anavi (leonanavi@gmail.com)

Credits

Author
Leon Anavi

Reviewers
Philippe Coval
Victor Galindo
David King
Oytun Eren SENGUL

Commissioning Editor
Usha Iyer

Acquisition Editor
Rebecca Youé

Content Development Editor
Dayan Hyames

Technical Editors
Shruti Rawool
Anand Singh

Copy Editors
Roshni Banerjee
Sarang Chari
Janbal Dharmaraj

Project Coordinator
Harshal Ved

Proofreaders
Maria Gould
Ameesha Green
Paul Hindle

Indexers
Hemangini Bari
Mariammal Chettiyar
Monica Ajmera Mehta
Rekha Nair
Tejal Soni

Production Coordinator
Nilesh Mohite

Cover Work
Nilesh Mohite

About the Author

Leon Anavi is a professional software engineer and an open source enthusiast focused on mobile applications and platforms. He is a regular contributor to Qt for Tizen, Tizen projects, and various other open source projects. He is the founder of the open source project Tizen-sunxi, which ports Tizen to devices with Allwinner SoCs. He has won several awards and earned honorable mentions from competitions organized by Samsung, Intel, Nokia, BlackBerry, and maemo.org.

He earned a Bachelor's degree in Computer Systems and Technologies from Technical University of Sofia in 2008; a Master's degree in Information Technologies from Technical University of Sofia in 2010; and a Master of Business Administration degree from New Bulgarian University, Sofia, in 2011.

He was a speaker at the following conferences:

- Mobile Monday Sofia in January 2011
- Openmobility Conference 2013, Bratislava, in April 2013
- PlovDev 2013, Plovdiv, Bulgaria, in October 2013
- OpenFest 2013, Sofia, Bulgaria, in November 2013
- FOSDEM 2014, Brussels, Belgium, in February 2014
- Tizen Developer Conference 2014, San Francisco, U.S., in June 2014

He was also a co-founder of and speaker at TuxCon 2014, Plovdiv, Bulgaria.

About the Reviewers

Philippe Coval has been a Free/Libre Open Source Software (FLOSS) enthusiast ever since the late '90s, when he discovered UNIX at university and replaced his Amiga with a GNU/Linux system at home. He has since contributed to various communities such as Debian, Openmoko, Maemo, and Qt, and is currently focused on Tizen.

After a decade of working as a software engineer in different contexts (a research lab, Telco, the CE industry, and a start-up), he had the opportunity to join the Tizen project in an open source department of a larger French company known as Eurogiciel. For the past couple of years, he has been maintaining some parts of the Tizen distribution and actively supports community contributions.

Feel free to contact him online at `https://wiki.tizen.org/wiki/User:Pcoval`.

I would like to thank my friend Leon for his faithful dedication to sharing his research with the FLOSS hacking scene.

Victor Galindo is a software engineer at CBG Konsult in Barcelona. The company develops and sells high-tech translation solutions for customers such as Volvo and General Motors. He works with cutting-edge technologies to deliver the best solutions to customers. Prior to that, he worked in other tech fields such as materials research at Diopma. He also likes to get involved and collaborate with open source projects; you can find him on GitHub.

When he is not wired to a computer, he likes to spend time outside in the mountains with his family and cross-country running with his dogs.

David King studied Chemistry at the University of Bath, earning his Bachelor's degree in 2005 and his PhD in 2011. Then, he started software development at Openismus GmbH, a small open source consultancy in Berlin, Germany, specializing in mobile and desktop development with Qt and GTK+. He now works for Red Hat and is focused on desktop applications and libraries for GNOME. He maintains EasyTAG and Cheese, among other applications.

I would like to thank my wife for looking after our (increasingly large) flock of chickens during the review process.

Oytun Eren SENGUL is interested in everything related to mobile, community, operating systems, and kernels. However, he's currently working on mobile UX projects and is the community manager of Smartface Inc., mostly writing developer documents and managing content, public speaking, and conferences.

He had started with Maemo and MeeGo, but now he is developing for iOS, Android, Windows Phone, and Tizen.

He is a proud member of the Linux Foundation and is a contributor to Intel software projects. He is one of the developers of Automotive Grade Linux. Currently, he is working on SLP and presents his studies at various conferences. He has participated in various Nokia and Turkcell projects as a community manager.

I would like to thank my wife, Seval, for her support and patience throughout this project. Now, she knows everything related to mobile operating systems such as Tizen, iOS, and Android even though her background is Turkish literature.

www.PacktPub.com

Support files, eBooks, discount offers, and more

You might want to visit www.PacktPub.com for support files and downloads related to your book.

Did you know that Packt offers eBook versions of every book published, with PDF and ePub files available? You can upgrade to the eBook version at www.PacktPub.com and as a print book customer, you are entitled to a discount on the eBook copy. Get in touch with us at service@packtpub.com for more details.

At www.PacktPub.com, you can also read a collection of free technical articles, sign up for a range of free newsletters and receive exclusive discounts and offers on Packt books and eBooks.

http://PacktLib.PacktPub.com

Do you need instant solutions to your IT questions? PacktLib is Packt's online digital book library. Here, you can access, read and search across Packt's entire library of books.

Why Subscribe?

- Fully searchable across every book published by Packt
- Copy and paste, print and bookmark content
- On demand and accessible via web browser

Free Access for Packt account holders

If you have an account with Packt at www.PacktPub.com, you can use this to access PacktLib today and view nine entirely free books. Simply use your login credentials for immediate access.

Table of Contents

Preface   **1**

Part 1 – Getting Started with Tizen

Chapter 1: The Tizen SDK   **9**

Introduction   9

Installing the Tizen SDK   10

Installing the Tizen SDK on Windows   12

Installing the Tizen SDK on Mac OS   13

Installing the Tizen SDK on Ubuntu   14

Managing extension packages   19

Customizing the Tizen IDE   20

Setting the Active Secure profile   22

Tizen Web Simulator   24

Tizen Emulator   25

Getting started with Smart Development Bridge   28

Using Smart Development Bridge   30

Chapter 2: Introduction to the Tizen Ecosystem   **33**

Introduction   33

The Tizen app life cycle   34

Tizen web app programming   36

Tizen web APIs   39

Localizing Tizen web apps   41

Packaging Tizen web apps   44

Tizen native app programming   45

Packaging Tizen native apps   49

Becoming a Tizen Store seller   51

Publishing apps to Tizen Store   52

Part 2 – Creating Tizen Web Applications

Chapter 3: Building a UI   **57**
    Introduction   **57**
    An overview of widgets   **57**
    Creating buttons   **60**
    Creating list views   **63**
    Showing pop ups   **66**
    Using the Tizen Notification API   **69**
    Customizing the look and feel   **73**
    Drawing and writing text on a canvas   **76**
    Creating 3D objects with WebGL   **79**

Chapter 4: Storing Data   **89**
    Introduction   **89**
    Writing files   **90**
    Reading files   **92**
    Creating a simple text editor   **95**
    Downloading files   **100**
    Using web storage   **105**
    Creating Web SQL Database   **109**
    Executing queries in Web SQL Database   **111**
    Retrieving data from Web SQL Database   **112**
    Using IndexedDB   **116**

Chapter 5: Creating Multimedia Apps   **121**
    Introduction   **121**
    Playing local audio files   **122**
    Playing local video files   **124**
    Launching video in an external player   **129**
    Taking a photo   **132**
    Generating linear barcodes   **135**
    Scanning linear barcodes   **137**
    Generating QR codes   **140**
    Scanning QR codes   **143**

Chapter 6: Developing Social Networking Apps   **147**
    Introduction   **147**
    Developing Facebook apps in Tizen   **148**
    Fetching a Facebook news feed   **152**
    Obtaining Facebook friends list   **154**
    Accessing Facebook profile information   **156**
    Reading Facebook messages   **158**

Retrieving Facebook notifications	**162**
Updating a Facebook status	**164**
Filtering a Tizen news feed from Twitter	**166**
Developing a LinkedIn app in Tizen	**169**
Retrieving LinkedIn updates	**173**
Chapter 7: Managing the Address Book and Calendar	**175**
Introduction	**175**
Retrieving all contacts	**176**
Adding a new contact	**178**
Deleting a contact	**182**
Exporting a contact to vCard	**185**
Retrieving all tasks	**187**
Creating a new task	**190**
Deleting a task	**194**
Creating a new event	**195**
Deleting an event	**196**
Retrieving all events	**197**
Setting an alarm	**199**
Chapter 8: Communication	**201**
Introduction	**201**
Sending SMS messages	**201**
Sending e-mail messages	**204**
Receiving and displaying e-mail messages	**206**
Browsing call history	**210**
Using Bluetooth	**212**
Using NFC and detecting other devices	**218**
Sending NDEF messages	**221**
Receiving NDEF messages	**222**
Receiving push notifications	**225**
Chapter 9: Using Sensors	**229**
Introduction	**229**
Using location-based services to display current location	**230**
Getting directions	**235**
Geocoding	**239**
Reverse geocoding	**241**
Calculating distance	**243**
Detecting device motion	**245**
Detecting device orientation	**247**
Using the Vibration API	**250**

Part 3 – Porting and Debugging

Chapter 10: Porting Apps to Tizen   **255**
  Introduction   255
  Porting web apps   256
  Installing the PhoneGap or Cordova SDK   258
  Creating Tizen web applications with PhoneGap or Cordova   259
  Deploying Cordova and PhoneGap applications to the Tizen device
  or Emulator   261
  Bringing Android apps to Tizen   262
  Porting an Android UI to Tizen UI Framework   264
  Setting Qt for Tizen   267
  Deploying Qt applications on Tizen   271

Chapter 11: Debugging Apps in Tizen   **273**
  Introduction   273
  Running an application in Tizen Web Simulator   274
  Running an application in Tizen Emulator   276
  Running an application on a device   278
  Debugging in Tizen Web Simulator   279
  Debugging in Tizen Emulator   280
  Debugging on a device   281
  Using Samsung Remote Test Lab   283
  Tracking JavaScript bugs   285
  Unit testing with QUnit   288

Chapter 12: Porting Tizen to Hardware Devices   **293**
  Introduction   293
  Setting up a platform development environment   294
  Installing development tools in Ubuntu or Debian   297
  Installing development tools in openSUSE   299
  Installing development tools in Fedora and CentOS   300
  Building Tizen platform images   302
  Flashing a Tizen image to mobile devices   306
  Enabling 3D acceleration and OpenGL   308
  Booting Tizen on Intel NUC   311
  Booting Tizen on Allwinner devices   313
  Hacking a tablet and booting Tizen on it   320

Index   **323**

Preface

The story of Tizen begins on February 11, 2011, when Nokia announced a partnership with Microsoft, which led to the end of MeeGo. Shortly after that, Intel and Samsung joined forces and started the Tizen project. Tizen is a trademark of the Linux Foundation, and as of today, more than 40 leading companies are directly involved in the project.

Nowadays, the mobile market is under the control of the duopoly between Android and iOS, who make up about 90 percent of all mobile devices. The control of the other 10 percent of devices is spread primarily between other corporations such as Microsoft and BlackBerry. Innovations are slowing down because of patent wars, proprietary APIs, closed application stores, and billing platforms. As an engineer, I have had to communicate many times that some requested features of a mobile application cannot be implemented because of restrictions of the operating system or just because of missing APIs.

Tizen is here, and it is bold enough to try to change the status quo. It is an innovative open source project that provides new opportunities on the mobile marketplace to application developers, hardware vendors, and telecommunication operators. To guarantee transparency and to prevent any single entity from taking control of the whole platform, Tizen is under open source governance. The objective is to establish a sustainable community of both companies and individuals, to put it at the center of the development process and to create a competitive alternative to the Android-iOS duopoly. Community members are encouraged to contribute and know what to expect from Tizen. Even smaller companies can get involved in the development of the platform, and their contributions can be accepted alongside the contributions of large corporations. Every contributor can participate in defining the future of Tizen. The main benefit for operators and OEMs is that they can customize the software and the services of the platform to match their own requirements and goals.

Tizen targets different computer architectures and form factors: from smartphones, tablets, personal computers, TVs, and photo cameras to home appliances and vehicles. The world and its technologies are moving forward, and the number of Internet-enabled devices is growing fast. New solutions are required to improve the communication between all these devices and to make our life easier. Tizen is here to fill the gap by providing flexibility and standardized solutions through open source software.

The main purpose of this book is to support you in your open source journey and to help you in your quest to develop user-friendly and innovative mobile applications and services.

What this book covers

Part 1 – Getting Started with Tizen

Chapter 1, The Tizen SDK, offers an introduction to the Tizen software development kit and its tools, a step-by-step installation guide for Windows, Mac OS, and Linux, as well as an SDB user guide.

Chapter 2, Introduction to the Tizen Ecosystem, gives an overview of the Tizen web and native application development process as well as guides for publishing and selling applications through the Tizen store.

Part 2 – Creating Tizen Web Applications

Chapter 3, Building a UI, is dedicated to graphical user interfaces. Tutorials for building applications with jQuery Mobile and other Tizen UI components are included. This chapter also contains guides for drawing 2D and 3D objects on an HTML5 canvas.

Chapter 4, Storing Data, contains articles about storing data in files, local storage, and web SQL databases, as well as a tutorial on downloading files over the Internet.

Chapter 5, Creating Multimedia Apps, contains programming examples for playing audio and video files, capturing images, streaming video, barcode generation, and scanning.

Chapter 6, Developing Social Networking Apps, includes tutorials for developing a client web application for the most popular social networks (Facebook, Twitter, and LinkedIn).

Chapter 7, Managing the Address Book and Calendar, includes articles about management of tasks, events, and alarms on the calendar, as well as management of the contacts from the address book.

Chapter 8, Communication, is dedicated to the usage of different communication channels such as SMS, Bluetooth, NFC, and push notifications.

Chapter 9, Using Sensors, contains recipes related to hardware sensors such as the GPS, accelerometer, and gyroscope sensor. The main focus of this chapter is on location-based services, maps, and navigation.

Part 3 – Porting and Debugging

Chapter 10, Porting Apps to Tizen, includes options and hints for porting existing web, Android, or Qt applications to Tizen. Tutorials for running Android applications on Tizen using a compatibility layer as well as for complete porting of Android applications to HTML5 are included. Details about the community-driven port Qt for Tizen, which allows deployment of existing Qt mobile apps for Android, iOS, MeeGo, Symbian, SailfishOS, and BlackBerry 10 on Tizen devices, are also revealed.

Chapter 11, Debugging Apps in Tizen, contains tutorials for running and testing Tizen web applications as well as for JavaScript unit testing.

Chapter 12, Porting Tizen to Hardware Devices, is a getting started guide for building embedded control systems powered by Tizen. Brief tutorials for building Tizen platform images and booting them on ARM and x86 devices are included. The information in this chapter is useful for the development of new systems or porting existing embedded control systems such as IVI or home automation to the Tizen software platform.

What you need for this book

Basic knowledge of general programming in web development is required. To follow the tutorials and experiment with the examples, you will need a decent development computer with Windows, Mac OS X, or Ubuntu.

Who this book is for

This book is suitable for:

- ▶ Mobile application developers
- ▶ Web developers who are interested in developing mobile applications
- ▶ Developers interested in porting existing web, Android, and/or Qt applications to Tizen
- ▶ Tizen developers who would like to improve their skills and knowledge

The main focus of the book is Tizen web application development. It does not contain any tutorials on basic HTML5, JavaScript, or CSS programming; so, a decent knowledge of these technologies is required. The book is also suitable for developers without any experience in Tizen or any other mobile platform but who have basic knowledge about web technologies.

The third part of this book is more advanced, and it might attract the attention of people developing embedded control systems, IVI (In-Vehicle Infotainment), or home automation systems and applications. This part of the book might also be useful to QA (Quality Assurance) engineers as it contains guidelines for both manual and automatic application testing.

Conventions

In this book, you will find a number of styles of text that distinguish between different kinds of information. Here are some examples of these styles, and an explanation of their meaning.

Code words in text, database table names, folder names, filenames, file extensions, pathnames, dummy URLs, user input, and Twitter handles are shown as follows: "Our example inherits UiApp and overloads several methods including `OnAppInitializing()` and `OnAppInitialized()`."

A block of code is set as follows:

```
<link rel="stylesheet" href="tizen-web-ui-fw/latest/themes/tizen-
white/tizen-web-ui-fw-theme.css" name="tizen-theme"/>
<script src="tizen-web-ui-fw/latest/js/jquery.js"></script>
<script src="tizen-web-ui-fw/latest/js/tizen-web-ui-fw-libs.js"></
script>
<script src="tizen-web-ui-fw/latest/js/tizen-web-ui-fw.js" data-
framework-theme="tizen-white"></script>
<script type="text/javascript" src="./js/main.js"></script>
```

When we wish to draw your attention to a particular part of a code block, the relevant lines or items are set in bold:

```
helloWorldFrame* phelloWorldFrame = new (std::nothrow)
helloWorldFrame;
TryReturn(phelloWorldFrame != null, false, "The memory is
insufficient.");
phelloWorldFrame->Construct();
phelloWorldFrame->SetName(L"helloWorldNative");
AddFrame(*phelloWorldFrame);
```

Any command-line input or output is written as follows:

```
sdb devices
```

New terms and **important words** are shown in bold. Words that you see on the screen, in menus or dialog boxes for example, appear in the text like this: "Launch the Tizen SDK Install Manager and click on **Next**."

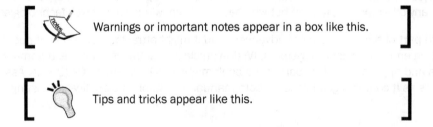

> Warnings or important notes appear in a box like this.

> Tips and tricks appear like this.

Reader feedback

Feedback from our readers is always welcome. Let us know what you think about this book—what you liked or may have disliked. Reader feedback is important for us to develop titles that you really get the most out of.

To send us general feedback, simply send an e-mail to `feedback@packtpub.com`, and mention the book title through the subject of your message.

If there is a topic that you have expertise in and you are interested in either writing or contributing to a book, see our author guide on `www.packtpub.com/authors`.

Customer support

Now that you are the proud owner of a Packt book, we have a number of things to help you to get the most from your purchase.

Downloading the example code

You can download the example code files for all Packt books you have purchased from your account at `http://www.packtpub.com`. If you purchased this book elsewhere, you can visit `http://www.packtpub.com/support` and register to have the files e-mailed directly to you.

Errata

Although we have taken every care to ensure the accuracy of our content, mistakes do happen. If you find a mistake in one of our books—maybe a mistake in the text or the code—we would be grateful if you would report this to us. By doing so, you can save other readers from frustration and help us improve subsequent versions of this book. If you find any errata, please report them by visiting `http://www.packtpub.com/support`, selecting your book, clicking on the **errata submission form** link, and entering the details of your errata. Once your errata are verified, your submission will be accepted and the errata will be uploaded to our website, or added to any list of existing errata, under the Errata section of that title.

Piracy

Piracy of copyright material on the Internet is an ongoing problem across all media. At Packt, we take the protection of our copyright and licenses very seriously. If you come across any illegal copies of our works, in any form, on the Internet, please provide us with the location address or website name immediately so that we can pursue a remedy.

Please contact us at `copyright@packtpub.com` with a link to the suspected pirated material.

We appreciate your help in protecting our authors, and our ability to bring you valuable content.

Questions

You can contact us at questions@packtpub.com if you are having a problem with any aspect of the book, and we will do our best to address it.

Part 1

Getting Started with Tizen

The Tizen SDK

Introduction to the Tizen Ecosystem

1
The Tizen SDK

In this chapter, we will cover the following recipes:

- ▶ Installing the Tizen SDK
- ▶ Installing the Tizen SDK on Windows
- ▶ Installing the Tizen SDK on Mac OS
- ▶ Installing the Tizen SDK on Ubuntu
- ▶ Managing extension packages
- ▶ Customizing the Tizen IDE
- ▶ Setting the Active Secure profile
- ▶ Tizen Web Simulator
- ▶ Tizen Emulator
- ▶ Getting started with Smart Development Bridge
- ▶ Using Smart Development Bridge

Introduction

This chapter offers an introduction to the tools required for the development of Tizen applications. Detailed descriptions of the steps required for the installation of the SDK on three supported operating systems (GNU/Linux, Windows, and Mac OS) are provided. Furthermore, this chapter contains an overview of the development environment, the Web Simulator, the device Emulator, and the user manual for **Smart Development Bridge** (**SDB**).

Those of you who are eager to start coding might be slightly disappointed to find out that this chapter does not contain any code snippets. Nevertheless, please keep calm and carefully explore all the recipes because they will help you understand how the tools work. After you have done that, you will be able to develop Tizen applications more efficiently.

Installing the Tizen SDK

The first step of starting Tizen application development is to download the Tizen SDK and install it. The installation is similar on all supported operating systems. This recipe explains the basics of the installation process of Tizen SDK 2.2.1. Details and notes of each of the supported operating systems are discussed in the subsequent recipes of this chapter.

Getting ready

The SDK contains all the tools required for the development of both native and web Tizen applications. It consists of an IDE based on Eclipse, Emulator, Simulator for web applications, a tool chain, several sample applications, and full documentation. The Tizen SDK is compatible with the following platforms:

- Ubuntu (32-and 64-bit)
- Windows 7 (32-and 64-bit)
- Mac OS X

The minimum hardware requirements of the development systems are as follows:

- Dual-core CPU at 2 GHz
- At least 2 GB of RAM
- At least 6 GB spare disk space

The Tizen SDK can be downloaded for free from the Tizen Project website at https://developer.tizen.org/downloads/tizen-sdk.

More details about the hardware requirements for the Tizen SDK are available at https://developer.tizen.org/downloads/sdk/installing-sdk/prerequisites-tizen-sdk.

Although officially Ubuntu is the only supported Linux distribution, some people have managed to make it work on other distributions such as Fedora and Arch Linux.

Several Tizen SDK installation options are available. You can choose between network, image, or a command-line installation without GUI.

How to do it...

For network installation, please perform the following steps:

1. Begin by downloading the **Tizen SDK Install Manager**.

2. Launch the downloaded file and then click on **Next** on the first screen, as shown in the following screenshot:

The Tizen SDK Install Manager screen

3. On the second screen, accept the terms and conditions and again click on **Next**.

4. Select the components you want to install and click on **Next**. Finally, specify the directory where the SDK will be installed and click on the **Install** button.

 During the installation process, you might be asked to provide administrative privileges. The Install Manager will download approximately 1.5 GB.

If you prefer offline installation, then please follow these steps:

1. Download the SDK Install Manager.

2. When the download finishes, launch the downloaded file.

3. Select **Advanced**.

4. Go to the **Advanced Configuration** window. Click on the corresponding radio button for **SDK Image**.

5. Browse to the SDK image file, click on **OK**, and after that, click on **Next**.

6. On the next screen, the terms and conditions will be displayed. Click on **Next** after accepting them.

7. Select the components you want to install and click on **Next**.

8. Finally, choose the directory where the SDK will be stored and hit the **Install** button.

How it works...

The Tizen IDE is based on Eclipse. Most of the source code of Eclipse is written using the Java programming language. In general, the main advantage of applications created with Java is that they are compatible with different platforms, and this is the main reason why the Tizen IDE and SDK work fine on several desktop operating systems.

See also

▸ For details about the installation on Windows, Mac OS, and Ubuntu, please refer to the subsequent recipes of this chapter.

Installing the Tizen SDK on Windows

Tizen applications can be developed on Microsoft Windows even though Tizen is a Linux-based operating system. This recipe will reveal details of the installation process of the SDK on Windows.

Getting ready

It is recommended to ensure that your development system matches the requirements of the Tizen SDK before proceeding with the installation. The Tizen SDK is compatible with the 32-bit and 64-bit versions of Windows 7, as well as with the 32-bit version of Windows XP. Although Windows 8 is not officially listed among the supported platforms, the version for Windows 7 should be compatible with it.

Please note that the 64-bit version of Windows requires the 64-bit JRE
even if the 32-bit version has already been installed.

How to do it...

The installation of the Tizen SDK on Windows is straightforward. The simplest way to complete
it successfully is to rely on the network installation procedure described in the previous recipe.

See also

▶ After the installation, it might be convenient to register the Tizen SDK installation
directory in the environmental path of Windows so that you will be able to directly run
SDB from any location. Please refer to the recipes related to SDB for instructions on
how to do this.

Installing the Tizen SDK on Mac OS

One of the reasons a lot of mobile application developers use Mac OS is that it is required
for the development of iOS applications. Unlike iOS, the development tools for Tizen do not
have such limitations, and they can be installed on Mac OS as well as other popular desktop
operating systems.

Getting ready

The network installation manager of the Tizen SDK for Mac OS is distributed as a standard
disk image with the `dmg` extension.

How to do it...

Download the `.dmg` file and launch it by following the provided instructions in the recipe
Installing the Tizen SDK.

If you plan to develop native Tizen applications on Mac OS X, install command-line tools
following the Apple guidelines for the version of Mac OS X that you are using (`https://
developer.apple.com/library/ios/technotes/tn2339/_index.html`).

On Mac OS X 10.7.5 (also known as Mac OS X Lion) or later, the Install Manager might fail due to the security settings of the operating system. These settings have to be modified to temporarily prevent the Mac OS X Gatekeeper from blocking the Install Manager and to allow you to proceed with the Tizen SDK installation. Please perform the following steps to configure Gatekeeper on Mac OS X and to solve the issue:

1. Click on the **Apple Menu** button in the upper-left corner of the main screen of the Mac OS X interface.

2. Select **System Preferences.**

3. Click on **Security & Privacy**.

4. Select the **General** tab.

5. To configure the settings, click on the locker icon in the lower-right corner, enter the administrative user's password, and click on **Unlock**.

6. Set **Allow apps download from** to **Anywhere** and confirm the change.

7. Launch the **Tizen Install Manager** again and complete the installation.

After successful installation, the security settings can be reverted to their previous configuration. Alternatively, you can exempt the installer as a single application from Gatekeeper. For more details, please visit Apple's support page at http://support.apple.com/kb/HT5290.

See also

▶ If you are interested in adding SDB to the environment path after successful installation of the Tizen SDK, refer to the recipes related to SDB.

Installing the Tizen SDK on Ubuntu

Ubuntu is the only Linux distribution that is recommended and fully supported by the Tizen SDK. Additional software has to be installed prior to launching the Tizen SDK Install Manager on Ubuntu.

This recipe contains four major steps to install all the required software components and successfully complete the SDK installation on Ubuntu. Before you start, make sure that at least 6 GB free space is present on the computer.

Getting ready

Officially, Tizen SDK 2.2.1 is compatible only with two versions of Ubuntu: 12.04 and 12.10. Despite this, it is absolutely possible to install and run the SDK on newer versions too. This is applicable to the following versions of Ubuntu:

- ▸ 12.10 32-bit
- ▸ 13.04 32-bit
- ▸ 13.10 64-bit

Although Ubuntu 13.10 is not officially supported, the Tizen SDK can be installed successfully on it as well, but a workaround related to `libudev.so.1` should be applied to run SDB. Please check the troubleshooting section of the recipe for more information about fixing SDB on Ubuntu 13.10.

How to do it...

The full installation process can be divided into four milestones:

1. Downloading the Tizen SDK.
2. Installing Oracle Java Runtime Environment (JRE).
3. Installing dependencies.
4. Installing the Tizen SDK.

Visit `tizen.org` to get the Tizen SDK or just execute the following commands to download Tizen SDK 2.2.1 using your web browser or command-line tool such as `wget`. For example, if you have a 32-bit version of Ubuntu, then you can run the following command in the terminal:

```
wget https://cdn.download.tizen.org/sdk/InstallManager/tizen-sdk-2.2.1/
tizen-sdk-ubuntu32-v2.2.71.bin
```

The URL of the installation file for the 64-bit version is slightly different, so it can be downloaded by executing the following command:

```
wget https://cdn.download.tizen.org/sdk/InstallManager/tizen-sdk-2.2.1/
tizen-sdk-ubuntu64-v2.2.71.bin
```

 Any of these URLs might change over time. To download another version of the SDK, please check the available links at the download page at `https://developer.tizen.org/downloads/tizen-sdk`.

Oracle JRE must be installed before launching the Tizen SDK. Make sure that OpenJDK is not supported. Please follow these steps if you do not have Oracle JRE installed:

1. Visit the Oracle website and, depending on the version of Ubuntu that you are using, download the 32-bit or 64-bit JRE 7 for Linux as a `tar` archive available at `http://www.oracle.com/technetwork/java/javase/downloads/jre7-downloads-1880261.html`.

2. Decompress all files from the downloaded `archive.tar -xzf jre-*.tar.gz` file.

3. Create a directory for the JRE files. After that, move the extracted files into the directory by executing the following command:

    ```
    sudo mkdir -p /usr/lib/jvm/jre1.7.0sudo mv jre1.7.0_45/* /usr/lib/
    jvm/jre1.7.0/.
    ```

> The names of the JRE files and directories may be different depending on the version that you have downloaded.

4. If Java is not present, please install it. Otherwise, it is recommended that you update it by using the following command:

    ```
    sudo update-alternatives --install /usr/bin/java java /usr/lib/
    jvm/jre1.7.0/bin/java 0
    ```

Furthermore, Java can be enabled for the Mozilla Firefox web browser that is shipped as the default web browser for Ubuntu. A couple of additional steps must be executed:

1. Create a directory to store the Mozilla plugin for the current user by executing the following command:

    ```
    mkdir ~/.mozilla/plugins
    ```

2. Create a symbolic link of Java that points to the directory that was made in the previous step:

    ```
    ln -s /usr/lib/jvm/jre1.7.0/lib/i386/libnpjp2.so ~/.mozilla/
    plugins/
    ```

> Create a symbolic link of the plugin to `/usr/lib/firefox/plugins/`, or `/usr/lib/firefox/browser/plugins/` for Ubuntu 13.10 to enable it for all users of the system. The web browser must be restarted after enabling Java.

We are almost ready to launch the Tizen SDK installer, but before that, some dependencies must be installed.

Ensure that the following packages are installed:

- ► `expect`
- ► `gtk2-engines-pixbuf`
- ► `libgnome2-0`
- ► `qemu-user-static`
- ► `gettext`
- ► `module-init-tools`
- ► `gksudo`
- ► `libwebkitgtk-1.0-0`

If you are wondering whether a package has already been installed on your development platform, please check it by executing the command `dpkg -s` followed by the package's name or the list of packages. To install any of the packages from the preceding list, open a terminal and execute `sudo apt-get install` followed by the name of the package, as follows:

```
sudo apt-get install expect gtk2-engines-pixbuf libgnome2-0 qemu-user-
static libwebkitgtk-1.0-0 gettext module-init-tools libudev-dev
```

Users of Ubuntu 12.10 or any older version should install the package `gksudo` as well by executing the following command:

```
sudo apt-get install gksudo
```

Please note that if you are using Ubuntu 13.04 or a newer version, you will not be able to install this package as it is not available any more. Instead, you should install package `gksu` by executing the following command:

```
sudo apt-get install gksu
```

Finally, it is time to proceed with the installation of the Tizen SDK. Make sure that the binary file of the Install Manager has executable permissions and launch it. Please note that `<version>` and `<bits>` must be replaced with values that match the file downloaded at the beginning of the tutorial:

```
chmod +x tizen-sdk-ubuntu<bits>-v<version>.bin
```

```
./tizen-sdk-ubuntu<bits>-v<version>.bin
```

When the Install Manager launches, follow the instructions from the *Installing the Tizen SDK* recipe to complete the installation.

If you are unsure which install type is appropriate for your needs, it is recommended that you select **Typical**.

There's more...

In this section, you will learn how to troubleshoot your GNU/Linux installation of Tizen.

▶ Unable to launch the Tizen IDE due to missing or incompatible version of JRE (**SDK runs on Eclipse, which requires JRE, JRE 6, or a newer package is required**).

If you encounter such a problem, please make sure that an appropriate JRE version has been installed on the development system before launching the installer of the Tizen SDK.

▶ Unable to run the installation due to missing packages (**Missing "expect" "gtk2-engines-pixbuf" "libgnome2-0" "qemu-user-static" "libwebkitgtk-1.0-0" package(s)**).

If you encounter such a problem, please install the missing packages using the shell command `apt-get`.

▶ Problem with installing Oracle Java on an Ubuntu machine.

If you encounter such a problem, install `java-package`. Then, convert the downloaded Oracle JDK/JRE archive into a `.deb` file.

▶ Exception when Eclipse is launched (**Exception in thread "main" org.eclipse.swt. SWTError: No more handles [Unknown Mozilla path (MOZILLA_FIVE_HOME not set)] error pops up**).

If you encounter such a problem, please install the `libwebkitgtk-1.0-0` package using `apt-get`.

▶ The Tizen IDE does not display the **Event Injector**.

If you encounter such a problem, make sure that the **Ajax Tool Framework** plugin for Eclipse is installed.

▶ Vertical scroll bars are not shown properly.

To disable the overlay scrollbar in the latest versions of Ubuntu, execute the following command:

```
>gsettings set com.canonical.desktop.interface scrollbar-mode
normal
```

▶ SDB not working on Ubuntu 13.10 64-bit (**sdb: error while loading shared libraries: libudev.so.0: cannot open shared object file: No such file or directory**).

If you encounter such a problem, apply the following workaround for Ubuntu 13.10 64-bit *at your own risk* to temporarily solve the issue until an update of the SDK is available:

```
sudo ln -s /lib/x86_64-linux-gnu/libudev.so.1.3.5 /lib/x86_64-
linux-gnu/libudev.so.0
```

Please note that `libudev.so.1` is essential for Ubuntu 13.10, and if you accidentally delete it or mess with its file permissions, the operating system will not be able to start properly after reboot!

See also

▸ Please refer to the *Getting started with Smart Development Bridge* recipe about SDB if you are interested in registering SDB as a global command.

▸ For up-to-date information, please refer to the Tizen wiki article *Install Tizen SDK on Ubuntu*, which has been maintained by the author of this book since March 26, 2013 at `https://wiki.tizen.org/wiki/Install_Tizen_SDK_on_Ubuntu`.

Managing extension packages

Tizen is an open source software platform and it is very flexible. Third-party individual developers or companies can develop extension packages for the Tizen SDK. Other developers can use and abuse third-party packages in their applications using specific repositories. Some extensions for the Tizen SDK are available at `https://developer.tizen.org/downloads/add-on-sdks`.

How to do it...

Please perform the following steps to add extra repositories and install additional packages:

1. Launch the Tizen SDK Install Manager.
2. Click on **Next** to proceed.
3. Select **Extra Repository** to open a dialog.
4. Click on **Add**.
5. Set an external server as well as the name of a repository and click on **OK**. The repository information will be displayed in the previous window. Click on **OK** again.
6. Select the required packages and click on **Install**.

Perform the following actions to remove an extra repository and all packages installed from it:

1. Launch the Tizen SDK Install Manager.
2. Select **Install or update Tizen SDK** and click on **Next**.
3. Click on **Extra Repository**.
4. Select the repository that you want to delete and after that click on **Remove**.

How it works...

Each repository contains additional packages that are optional and can be added or deleted by the developer at any time. A repository is specified by a URL, so it is mandatory to have a network connection to the repository's server to download any of its packages. If you are experiencing issues connecting to a repository using **HTTP Secure** (**HTTPS**), you can try using the same URL with HTTP.

A proxy has to be used if you want to access repositories from a computer behind a firewall. To configure a proxy, launch Install Manager and click on the **Proxy settings** button.

Customizing the Tizen IDE

The default and recommended IDE that is included in the Tizen SDK is based on Eclipse. Eclipse is an open source software, and through the years it has become a de facto standard for the development of applications for mobile platforms. Developers with experience in Android, Bada, Symbian, and BlackBerry 10 are already familiar with Eclipse as it, or IDEs based on it, is used for application development for these platforms.

 Android developers should note that there is a difference in the way Eclipse is provided for Tizen compared to Android. **Android Development Tools** (**ADT**) is a plugin for Eclipse that can be downloaded and installed. Unlike ADT, the Tizen IDE is provided in the Tizen SDK bundle, and at the moment, a separate plugin is not available.

Getting ready

The first step of the journey into application development for Tizen starts with the launch of the Tizen IDE. It is based on Eclipse, so it is not a surprise that the Tizen IDE also asks you to select a workspace. If you do not want to be asked to select the workspace every time you start the IDE, just check the option **Use this as default and do not ask again**. To change the workspace when the Tizen IDE is running, just navigate to **File | Switch Workspace**.

A welcome screen will be displayed on the first start screen of the Tizen IDE. Click on **Workbench** to open the Tizen Web perspective and start developing applications. If you want to have a look at the documentation, select any of the other three options. You can get back to the home screen at any time by navigating to **Help | Welcome**. If you are searching for Tizen's official development documentation, just navigate to **Help | Help Contents**.

How to do it...

For a lot of developers, the look and feel of their IDE is a key factor for their productivity. Tizen IDE supports all customization options provided by Eclipse. This recipe contains only a few hints for customization of the background and text colors. For more information, please have a look at Tizen IDE and Eclipse documentation or just delve into the preferences.

Execute the following actions to change the background color of the text editor:

1. Navigate to **Windows** | **Preferences** and a dialog box will appear.
2. Navigate to **General** | **Editors** | **Text Editors**.
3. Adjust the background color from the list of **Appearance color** options.
4. Change the text colors.

Text colors depend on the syntax coloring of the programming languages. Tizen web applications are developed using HTML, CSS, and JavaScript, while the development of native mobile applications relies on C++. Follow these simple steps to change the syntax coloring:

1. Navigate to **Windows** | **Preferences** and a dialog box will appear.
2. Select the desired programming language and navigate to **Editor** | **Syntax Coloring**.
3. Adjust the colors.

Perform the following steps if you want to change the fonts:

1. Navigate to **Windows** | **Preferences** and a dialog box will appear.
2. Navigate to **General** | **Appearance** | **Colors and Fonts**.
3. Select a programming language from the list and click on **Edit**.

There's more...

These are the most popular and important views in the Tizen IDE:

- ▸ **Project Explorer View**: This view shows all resources in the current workspace. From the **Project Explorer View**, you can manage projects, open and edit files, and execute operations such as building packaging and signing and validating widgets or applications. Right-click inside this view to open a context menu with all options. If the **Project Explorer View** is missing from the current perspective of the Tizen IDE, you can add it by selecting **Window** | **Show View** | **Other...** | **General** | **Project Explorer**.

- ▸ **Properties View**: This view shows the name and the basic properties of a selected resource. To view more details about a resource, right-click on it and select **Properties**. To add it to the current perspective of the Tizen IDE, navigate to **Window** | **Show View** | **Other...** | **General** | **Properties**.

▸ **Log View**: This is a vital tool to track bugs and investigate the behavior of applications running on the Tizen Emulator or a device connected to the development system. Log messages are displayed within **Log View** while an application is running. The following message types are supported: verbose, debug, info, warning, error, and fatal. The log output can be configured to filter only specific message types using the *V, D, Z, I, W, E*, and *F* software buttons. Next to them are situated the buttons for additional tabs for logging with more filtering options that can be added, edited, and removed. An option to export logs is also available. If **Log View** is not visible, enable it by activating the following option, **Window | Show View | Log**.

▸ **Console View**: This view offers several types of consoles that are useful during the deployment and debugging of Tizen applications. If the console is not visible, navigate to **Window | Show View | Console** to add it to the current perspective of the Tizen IDE. To change the settings of the console, go to **Window | Preferences | Run/ Debug | Console**.

▸ **Connection Explorer View**: The list of connected devices and emulators is displayed at this view. It provides options for exploring their filesystems and transferring files. Select an item from the list and right-click on the item to see a menu with all available actions. To add the Connection Explorer to the current perspective of the Tizen IDE, navigate to **Window | Show View | Other... | Tizen**.

Setting the Active Secure profile

It is mandatory to create and set a **secure profile** in order to successfully deploy and debug applications on a Tizen device. My personal observation is that a lot of developers experience issues due to the secure profile when they are deploying an application on a device for the first time. This recipe explains a couple of ways to generate a certificate and set it on the Tizen IDE.

Getting ready

If an Active Secure profile is not set, the following error message will be displayed on the screen when you try to run an application on a device or emulator from the Tizen IDE:

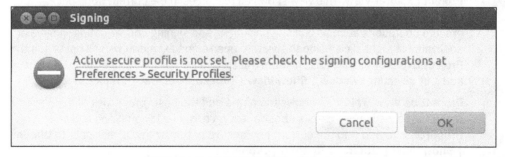

Signing issue due to missing Active Secure profile

Please set up a secure profile before launching any applications from the Tizen IDE to avoid this annoying warning.

How to do it...

The Active Secure profile can be created manually through the command line or using the integrated graphical user interface from the Tizen IDE.

The recommended way is to generate a certificate through the Tizen IDE. The steps are as follows:

1. Launch the Tizen IDE.
2. Navigate to **Window | Preferences**.
3. Navigate to **Tizen SDK | Security Profiles**.
4. Click on the **Add** button.
5. Enter a name for the profile.
6. Click on the **Generate** button to fill the author's details.
7. Click on **OK** to save the profile settings.

An alternative approach is to create a certificate using the command line and set it as **secure profile** on the Tizen IDE. Perform the following steps if you prefer to use a terminal:

1. Launch a terminal and navigate to the directory `<Tizen SDK install directory>/tools/certificate-generator/`.
2. If you are working on a Unix-like operating system, such as Mac OS or Linux, execute `certificate-generator.sh`. If you are using Windows, you should run `certificate-generator.bat`.
3. You will be prompted to type the information about the certificate. After filling in all details, the certificate will be generated.
4. Launch the Tizen IDE because the generated certificate has to be set in it.
5. Navigate to **Window | Preferences**.
6. Navigate to **Tizen SDK | Security Profiles**.
7. Click on the **Add** button.
8. Enter a name for the profile.
9. Type in the path to the certificate's file.
10. Finally, click on the **OK** button to save all settings.

How it works...

The creation process of the certificate is similar no matter which approach or operating system you prefer to use. Both the batch file for Windows and the bash script for Linux and Mac OS run `CertificateGenerator.jar` through the `java -jar` command. This tool is written in Java and its file format is **Java archive (JAR)**. The advantage of using Java for these kinds of applications is the multiplatform compatibility of Java, as the same code works on any of the operating systems supported by the Tizen SDK: Linux, Mac OS, and Windows.

Tizen Web Simulator

Tizen Web Simulator is a simplified tool to test and debug web applications. It is included in the Tizen SDK. Web Simulator is available under Apache Software License v.2.0 because it is based on the **Ripple-UI Framework**, which was initially developed by BlackBerry (known in the past as *research in motion*) to test BB10 HTML5 WebWorks applications. Web Simulator offers the following features:

- ▶ Guest modifications that provide a JavaScript backend that simulates Tizen Web APIs
- ▶ Configuration panes to emit events and messages related to the geolocation, sensors, acceleration, and messaging capabilities of the Tizen software platform
- ▶ Customization of the behavior of the simulator via a variety of preferences

The Google Chrome web browser must be installed because it powers the Tizen Web Simulator. This actually means that HTML5 applications that run on Google Chrome will also be running on Tizen. Another benefit is that all development features of the Google Chrome browser are available in the simulator, including the Remote Inspector tool that can be accessed by pressing *F12*.

Getting ready

It is mandatory to download and install Google Chrome on the development system if you intend to test applications on Tizen Web Simulator. The installation path of the Google Chrome browser can be specified in the **Preferences** of the simulator.

How to do it...

Three options are available to launch an application inside the Web Simulator:

1. Click on **Run** on the toolbar of the Tizen IDE.
2. Navigate to **Run | Run Configurations** from the menu of the Tizen IDE and click on **Tizen Web Simulator Application**.
3. Select a project at the **Project Explorer View** and right-click on it. After that, navigate to **Run As | Tizen Web Simulator Application**.

How it works...

Google Chrome will be started automatically with the Web Simulator. Adjust the orientation and zooming of the simulator by editing the configurations from the panel on the left-hand side of the browser.

Please note that the Web Simulator is compatible only with HTML5 web applications and it is useless for native applications. The simulator loads the HTML file specified at `config.xml` when the web application is launched. By default, the name of the file is `index.html`.

See also

> ▸ Please refer to the recipes in *Chapter 11, Debugging Apps in Tizen*, to learn how to simulate events and debug applications using the Web Simulator.

Tizen Emulator

Although it is highly recommended to deploy and debug applications directly on a real Tizen device, it is not mandatory to have a Tizen device in order to develop applications. A virtual device Emulator is delivered along with the other tools of the Tizen SDK. Developers can create virtual machines with custom hardware specifications that match their requirements for testing.

The device Emulator is a virtual machine based on the open source project **Quick Emulator (QEMU)**. It provides full stacks of the Tizen platform. **Emulator Manager** and **Event Injector** are also provided among the Emulator tools of the SDK. Unlike the simulator, the emulator provides strict implementation of the device specifications and there are no guest modifications. Please note that Tizen SDK 2.2.1 supports only the x86 machine architecture for guests.

QEMU, the engine behind the Tizen Emulator, is an open source project for a visualization machine that allows you to run a separate operating system as just another task on the desktop of your development machine. The Android emulator is also based on QEMU. For more information about QEMU and details regarding its licenses, please visit `http://wiki.qemu.org/`.

The Tizen Emulator supports a variety of features, and the most important features are as follows:

> ▸ Full system emulation, including CPU, RAM, and peripheral devices such as the camera
>
> ▸ Event Injector for simulation of events
>
> ▸ Animation and OpenGL ES for hardware-accelerated 3D rendering support
>
> ▸ Telephony

Of course, the emulator has some limitations compared to a real Tizen device. The differences impact the behavior of features:

▶ **Input system**: The emulator provides a virtual touchscreen and its drivers are different from the ones for the physical devices.

▶ **Virtual sensor**: Values related to acceleration, light, gyroscope, proximity, motion, location, and battery are received through the Event Injector.

▶ **Telephony**: Voice calls, call waiting, outgoing call barring, and messaging are supported through the Event Injector. Video calls, call forwarding, incoming call barring, emulator-to-emulator calls, and SMS are not supported.

▶ **Power management**: The emulator offers internal implementation to turn on and off the display.

▶ **Supported media formats and codes**: Encoding of H.264 and decoding of AAC+, enhanced AAC+, and FLAC are not supported on the emulator.

Getting ready

Please ensure that you are running the Tizen Emulator on a computer with a minimum screen resolution of 1280 x 1024 pixels and the latest version of graphical drivers with OpenGL support. It is recommended to use an Intel CPU with **Virtualization Technology** (**VTx**). The performance of the emulator depends on the hardware of the computer and it might work slowly on low resource machines. Details about the requirements for the Tizen Emulator are available at `https://developer.tizen.org/downloads/sdk/installing-sdk/prerequisites-tizen-sdk`.

How to do it...

To create new instances of the Tizen Emulator, launch the Emulator Manager and click on the button with the label **Create New VM**.

Select the name of the emulator, display resolution, density, skin, and size of RAM. Then, enable or disable the GPU and the hardware visualization of the CPU. When all configurations are set, click on **Confirm**, as shown in the following screenshot:

The Tizen Emulator

The emulator will appear within the window of the Emulator Manager. Hit the play button to launch it. The loading of Tizen on the virtual machine may vary depending on the hardware of the development system. Wait until Tizen is completely loaded and then use it.

As an alternative, advanced users may launch the emulator from a terminal through a command with the following syntax:

```
/emulator-x86 --skin-args <skin options> --qemu-args <QEMU options>
```

Both skin options such as the height and width of the resolution as well as various QEMU options can be specified as arguments of the command. For details of the supported options, please check the user manual in the official Tizen SDK 2.2.1 development documentation:

```
https://developer.tizen.org/dev-guide/2.2.1/org.tizen.gettingstarted/
html/dev_env/emulator_startup_options.htm
```

See also

> ▶ You can communicate with the running Tizen emulator using Smart Development Bridge (SDB). For more information and details, please check the next recipe. Descriptions and examples of deploying and running applications on the emulator as well as simulating events with the Event Injector are available in *Chapter 11, Debugging Apps in Tizen*.

Getting started with Smart Development Bridge

Smart Development Bridge (SDB) is a command-line tool for communication with the Tizen emulator or connected Tizen devices. Its role in Tizen is the same as the role of **Android Debug Bridge** (**ADB**) in Android. SDB is an essential part of the Tizen SDK and it is installed with it. SDB manages multiple device connections and provides basic commands for application development and debugging. The main features of SDB are as follows:

- Manage connections to devices and/or the emulator
- File transfer between development systems and the connected Tizen Emulator/device
- Remote shell to execute commands on the Tizen Emulator/device
- Port forwarding from the host to the Tizen Emulator/device
- Debugging applications

SDB works as a typical client-server application and it consists of three main components:

- A client that runs on the development system and can be invoked from the command line using the SDB command.
- A server that manages the connection and the communication with the Tizen Emulator and devices. It runs as a background process on the development system.
- A daemon that runs on each Tizen Emulator or device.

Although not mandatory, it is convenient to add SDB to the environmental path. To do it, follow the steps given in this recipe, depending on the operating system of your development machine.

 SDB is also provided as a standard package for Linux distributions. If you are interested in installing only SDB, please download the appropriate package for your Linux distribution from `http://download.tizen.org/tools/`.

Getting ready

After successful installation of the Tizen SDK, SDB is located under `tizen_sdk/SDK/sdb`. To use the client, an SDB command must be executed within its directory unless the `sdb` location has been added to the environmental path variable.

How to do it...

To add SDB to the environmental path of Windows 7, perform the following steps:

1. Right-click on the **Computer** icon located on the desktop.
2. Select the **Advanced System** settings.
3. Click on the **Environmental Variables** button on the **Advanced** tab of **System Properties**.
4. Carefully append the location of SDB to the `Path` variable.

If you are using Windows XP, the following steps will be helpful if you want to add SDB to the environmental path:

1. Right-click on the **Computer** icon located on the desktop.
2. Click on **Properties**.
3. Select the **Advanced** tab of **System Properties**.
4. Click on the **Environmental Variables** button.
5. Carefully append the location of SDB to the `Path` variable.

 On Windows, the changes will take effect only after reboot.

To add SDB to the environmental path for all users on Ubuntu, append the SDB directory to the path that is defined at file `/etc/environment`. Log out and log in again or just reboot to apply the changes.

To add SDB to the environmental path for all users on Mac OS X Leopard and above, create a text file at the directory `/etc/paths.d/` and set the location of SDB within it using root privileges, for example, `sudo -s 'echo "<tizen_sdk>/sdb" > /etc/paths.d/sdb'`.

A quick and easy alternative approach to achieve a similar result on UNIX-like operating systems, such as Linux and Mac OS, without modifying `/etc/environment` or creating a file at `/etc/paths.d` is to create a symbolic link to SDB in the `bin` directory using root privileges, for example, `sudo ln -s <tizen_sdk>/sdb /bin/sdb`.

Please note that `<tizen_sdk>` in both examples must be replaced with the actual path, depending on the installation.

See also

▶   Please have a look at the next recipe to learn how to use the full capabilities of SDB.

Using Smart Development Bridge

SDB is a powerful tool with a lot of capabilities and features. Although you can successfully develop applications using the Tizen IDE without even knowing what SDB is, it is recommended to explore the options of the tool. SDB is a developer's best friend when it comes to management of a connected device, transferring files, and debugging applications.

How to do it...

Perform the following steps to enable and use SDB:

1. Make sure that the date and time on your devices is correct.
2. Enable the developer mode and USB debugging on a Tizen device by navigating to **Settings | Developer options | USB debugging**.
3. Connect the Tizen device to a computer.
4. Run the SDB command in a console using the following syntax:

    ```
    sdb [option] <command> [parameters]
    ```

According to the Tizen 2.2.1 official development guide, the values provided for option in the preceding command can be:

▶   -d: This stands for select device. This sends the specified command to a connected USB device. Please note that this option will fail if multiple Tizen devices are attached over USB.

▶   -e: This option is used to control an emulator. The error handling is similar to that of the option -d. If multiple emulators are running, this command will fail and an error will be returned. Direct the command to the only running emulator and return an error if more than one emulators are present.

▶   -s <serial number>: Tizen devices or emulators that are attached to a developer's computer are identified by their serial number. The -s option should be followed by the serial number of the device and SDB will take care to target the command only to the specified device.

The following is a list of all the supported SDB commands with some brief information about them:

Command	Details
`devices`	This provides a list of connected devices.
`connect <host>[:<port>]`	This connects to a device through TCP/IP.
`disconnect <host>[:<port>]`	This disconnects a device. The host and port parameters are optional. If they are not specified, all devices will be disconnected.
`push <local> <remote> [-with-utf8]`	This transfers a file from the development system to the connected Tizen device.
`pull <remote> [<local>]`	This transfers a file from the connected Tizen device to the development system.
`shell`	This accesses a remote shell of the connected Tizen device or emulator.
`shell <command>`	This remotely runs a single shell command to a connected Tizen device or emulator. Execution of the following commands is allowed: `ls`, `rm`, `mv`, `cd`, `mkdir`, `cp`, `touch`, `echo`, `tar`, `grep`, `cat`, `chmod`, `rpm`, `find`, `uname`, `netstat`, and `killall`.
`dlog [option] [<filter-spec>]`	This prints the current log out of the buffers of a connected device or emulator.
`install <path_to_tpk>`	This installs a `tpk` package.
`uninstall <appid>`	This uninstalls an application using its ID.
`forward <local> <remote>`	This specifies the `local` and `remote` socket to configure port forwarding.
`help`	This displays SDB help information and usage guides.
`version`	This prints the SDB version number.
`start-server`	This launches the SDB server if it is not already running.
`kill-server`	This terminates the SDB server if it is running.
`get-state`	This displays the status of the connection to devices.

Command	Details
`get-serialno`	This displays the serial number of a connected Tizen device.
`status-window`	This displays the status of a connected device until the developer manually terminates the command.
`root <on|off>`	This enables or disables the root account mode.

 If several Tizen Emulators and/or devices are running and connected at the same time, you have to specify the desired target at the SDB command. Otherwise, the execution of the command will fail.

Android developers will be happy to find out a lot of similarities between Tizen Smart Development Bridge and Android Debug Bridge. Similar names of both tools is not a coincidence. Both tools have common purposes. Most of the commands are executed using the same keywords on both platforms and have similar behavior.

The following are several use cases of SDB commands:

▶ List attached devices:

```
>sdb devices
```

▶ Running the shell of a specific device:

```
>sdb emulator-2610 shell
```

▶ Running a single shell command on a Tizen device:

```
>sdb emulator-2610 ls
```

See also

▶ The information provided by the log buffers of a device might be valuable during the debugging of Tizen applications. More details and advanced usage examples of `sdb dlog` are available in *Chapter 11, Debugging Apps in Tizen*.

▶ The full list of SDB supported commands as of Tizen SDK 2.2.1 is available at `https://developer.tizen.org/dev-guide/2.2.1/org.tizen.gettingstarted/html/dev_env/commands.htm`.

2

Introduction to the Tizen Ecosystem

In this chapter, we will cover:

- ▸ The Tizen app life cycle
- ▸ Tizen web app programming
- ▸ Tizen web APIs
- ▸ Localizing Tizen web apps
- ▸ Packaging Tizen web apps
- ▸ Tizen native app programming
- ▸ Packaging Tizen native apps
- ▸ Becoming a Tizen Store seller
- ▸ Publishing apps to Tizen Store

Introduction

The ecosystem and communities are essential for every open source project, and Tizen is no exception. Tizen is the OS of everything. It targets different devices, form factors, and CPU architectures, so it is a flexible software platform that can be used for multiple purposes.

Tizen can run on devices with ARM- or i586-compatible processors. The first commercially available Tizen device is the Samsung camera NX300. In 2014, Samsung also launched several smart watches with Tizen, and Intel manufactured the mini PC NUC. Please explore the last chapter of the book if you are interested in booting Tizen on various hardware devices or even building your own device.

Three types of installable applications are supported by Tizen:

- ▶ Web applications are developed using HTML5, JavaScript, and CSS. This is the recommended type, because these applications are supported by all Tizen profiles (IVI, mobile, wearable, and so on).

- ▶ Native applications are developed using C++ and Tizen native APIs. They are faster but more complex and difficult to port.

- ▶ Hybrid applications combine web and native applications. A hybrid application contains a single web application with a user interface and one or more native service applications that communicate with each other.

This chapter contains information about the life cycle of Tizen applications, an overview of the development tools, and technologies as well as guides to publishing and selling applications through Tizen Store. It is an excellent getting started guide to publishing your first Tizen application.

The Tizen app life cycle

The Tizen SDK provides tools to turn good ideas into excellent applications and to publish them to Tizen Store. The life cycle of Tizen applications is similar to the life cycle of mobile applications for Android and iOS, and it includes the steps described in the following section.

Getting ready

The life cycle of an application for Tizen can be divided into six major steps as shown in the following diagram:

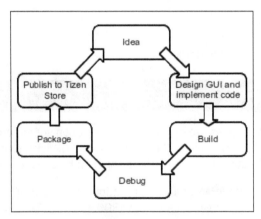

Tizen application life cycle

The development of an application is a continuous process. You have to provide regular updates with new features and enhancements. Arm yourself with patience. Some steps might require more time than expected. Sometimes, you may even need to go back to a previous step, for example, if the QA of Tizen Store rejects the application.

Before you start, make sure that you have successfully installed the Tizen developer environment. A Tizen device or emulator is required to debug applications. If you do not have a device, just create an emulator using Tizen **Emulator Manager**.

How to do it...

1. Come up with a good idea.

   A good idea lies behind each great mobile application. All you need is inspiration, but unfortunately, as far as I know, there are no strict rules, standards, or algorithms, so you have to think out of the box.

2. Design the application user interface (UI) and implement the backend.

   The user interface and the user experience are the key factors that convert a good idea into an exceptional application with a lot of downloads. Plan the development road map of the application carefully, and select the best approach for implementation. If your application communicates with a web service, wisely distribute the load between the mobile application and the server to achieve optimal performance. UML diagrams might help you to prepare well before you start coding. Always remember that a good plan can save you a lot of time during development.

3. Build a Tizen application.

   The Tizen IDE provides the tools required for easy building of a Tizen application with a single click. Before you start the build, you have to configure its settings. Navigate to **Project | Build Configuration** to manage the available build settings. After that, you can build the application at any appropriate time by hitting *F10* or navigating to **Project | Build Project**.

4. Debug the Tizen application.

   Try out the application on a Tizen device and emulator to verify that it is working as expected. Testing is very important, because even a minor bug can irritate users, and they might stop using your application.

5. Package the application.

   All files of the application have to be bundled into a package that can be installed on Tizen devices. The file extension of the package is `.tpk` for native applications and `.wgt` for web applications.

6. Certify the application and publish it to Tizen Store.

   The final step is to release your app to the market. The easiest way to reach millions of users from around the world is to distribute your application through application stores, such as the official Tizen Store.

Tizen is open, and so is its ecosystem. Tizen Store is the official store that is maintained by Samsung, but you can publish your applications to other stores too. If you wish, you can even create your own store.

See also

▶ Tutorials and examples about web applications for Tizen are available in the second part of this book. Check *Chapter 11, Debugging Apps in Tizen*, for details about debugging apps in Tizen. More information about packaging, certification, and publishing to Tizen Store is available in other recipes of this chapter.

Tizen web app programming

Web application development has been part of the Tizen project since its initial release. It is the recommended approach for application development on the platform. Millions of developers are already familiar with the basics of web development, so they can easily start developing applications for Tizen.

Tizen SDK provides all the tools necessary for development of Tizen web and hybrid applications. A web application contains HTML, CSS, and JavaScript files that are combined in a package with the extension `.wgt`. A hybrid application combines a web application with one or more native service applications.

Getting ready

Web applications are installed and executed as standalone applications on Tizen, thanks to the **Web Runtime** (**WRT**) engine. All standard HTML5 APIs are supported. There are certain features that are not covered by these APIs, so Tizen web runtime fills the gap by providing additional JavaScript functions.

This recipe demonstrates WRT in action by creating a simple Hello World web application and running it on a Tizen device or an emulator.

How to do it...

1. Launch the Tizen IDE, and if asked, choose a workspace.

2. Navigate to **File | New | Tizen Web Project**.

3. A wizard to create the project of the Tizen web application will appear. From **Template** select **Tizen Web UI Framework** and **Single Page Application**. Enter a project name, for example, `hello`. When you are ready, click on **Finish**.

4. Navigate to `config.xml` from **Project Explorer**, and open it using **Widget Configuration Editor**. By default, a double-click should open the file in **Widget Configuration Editor**. If not, place the mouse over the file, click on the right button, and select this option from **Open with**.

5. Open the **Overview** tab, and change the name to `HelloWorld`. This way, the name of the application will be different from the name of the project.

6. From **Project Explorer**, open `index.html`, replace its content with the following source code, and save the changes:

```
<!DOCTYPE html>
<html>
<head>
    <meta charset="utf-8"/>
    <meta name="description" content="Hello World!"/>
    <meta name="viewport" content="width=device-width,user-
scalable=no"/>
    <title>Hello World!</title>
    <link rel="stylesheet" href="tizen-web-ui-fw/latest/themes/
tizen-white/tizen-web-ui-fw-theme.css" name="tizen-theme"/>
    <script src="tizen-web-ui-fw/latest/js/jquery.js"></script>
    <script src="tizen-web-ui-fw/latest/js/tizen-web-ui-fw-libs.
js"></script>
    <script src="tizen-web-ui-fw/latest/js/tizen-web-ui-fw.js"
        data-framework-theme="tizen-white"></script>
    <script type="text/javascript" src="./js/main.js"></script>
    <link rel="stylesheet" type="text/css" href="./css/style.
css"/>
</head>
<body>
    <div data-role="page">
        <div data-role="header" data-position="fixed">
            <h1>Tizen Cookbook</h1>
        </div>

        <div data-role="content">
          <p>Hello World!</p>
        </div>
        <div data-role="footer" data-position="fixed">
```

```
            <h4>Packt Publishing</h4>
        </div>
    </div>
</body>
</html>
```

> **Downloading the example code**
>
> You can download the example code files for all Packt books you have purchased from your account at `http://www.packtpub.com`. If you purchased this book elsewhere, you can visit `http://www.packtpub.com/support` and register to have the files e-mailed directly to you.

7. Save all files.

8. Make sure that a Tizen device with the developer mode enabled is connected or Emulator is running. If you are unsure how to enable the developer mode, have a look at the recipe *Using Smart Development Bridge* from the previous chapter.

9. Select the project of the application from **Project View**, right-click on it, and from the menu that appears, navigate to **Run as | Tizen Web Application**. As an alternative, you can just hit the run button to deploy and launch the application.

How it works...

Upon creating a new project, the Tizen IDE automatically generates the directory structure and creates files if a template is selected.

All configurations and permissions of the application are set at the XML file `config.xml`. The Tizen IDE provides means to simplify the editing process of the file. The name, the identifier, the version, the icon file, as well as the entry file, which is `index.html` by default, are among the configurations stored in `config.xml`. Access to sensitive APIs should also be set by describing privileges at this file if the application uses such sensitive APIs.

Several JavaScripts and CSSes are included using the following HTML code to make sure that the application is compatible with Tizen WRT and use the standard Tizen look and feel:

```html
<link rel="stylesheet" href="tizen-web-ui-fw/latest/themes/tizen-white/tizen-web-ui-fw-theme.css" name="tizen-theme"/>
<script src="tizen-web-ui-fw/latest/js/jquery.js"></script>
<script src="tizen-web-ui-fw/latest/js/tizen-web-ui-fw-libs.js"></script>
<script src="tizen-web-ui-fw/latest/js/tizen-web-ui-fw.js" data-framework-theme="tizen-white"></script>
<script type="text/javascript" src="./js/main.js"></script>
```

The file `js/main.js` will be generated by the IDE, and it will contain the JavaScript source code for initialization of the application and for the handling of the back hardware button. Pay attention to the fact that jQuery is also included because the Tizen Web UI framework is based on jQuery Mobile.

If you have any trouble creating a Hello World application from scratch, use the example provided with the book.

See also

▶ More examples and advanced tutorials related to web applications for Tizen are available in the chapters from the second part of the book.

Tizen web APIs

Tizen provides a collection of APIs following the specification of W3C/HTML5 and the nonprofit industry consortium to create the open standards Khronos. A set of additional APIs that provide access to specific hardware and software capabilities of the devices are also provided. These APIs are based on JavaScript, and this programming language must be used to take advantage of the APIs.

This recipe provides just a brief overview of Tizen APIs. For more information and details, please check the documentation provided with the SDK Help at `https://developer.tizen.org/dev-guide/2.2.1/org.tizen.web.appprogramming/html/api_reference/api_reference.htm`.

Getting ready

The Tizen platform provides the following JavaScript-based APIs for development of web applications:

▶ **Alarm**: This API adds or removes date and time events through the methods provided by this API

▶ **Application**: This manages installed and running applications

▶ **Data Control**: This API helps in accessing and controlling the available shared data of other applications

▶ **Packages**: This API helps in installing and uninstalling packages or retrieving details about installed packages

- **Bluetooth**: This API provides control over the short distance communication protocol, Bluetooth

- **Messaging**: This API provides messaging capabilities through different popular communication channels: SMS, MMS, and e-mail

- **Network Bearer Selection**: This API controls and selects the network bearer

- **NFC**: This provides connection to other devices in close range using NFC

- **Push**: This API helps in receiving and handling push notifications from the izen remote server

- **Secure Element**: This API accesses data on the secure smart card chip

- **Content**: This API discovers and explores multimedia content, such as video or music

- **Download**: This API provides methods to download files over HTTP/HTTPS

- **Filesystem**: This API provides methods to access the filesystem, create, read, and write files

- **Message port**: This API provides capabilities for communication between different applications

- **Bookmark**: This API accesses and manages bookmarks

- **Calendar**: This API accesses and manages the calendar

- **Call History**: This API provides information about incoming and outgoing calls

- **Contact**: This API manages the address book

- **Data Synchronization**: This API provides interfaces for device data synchronization

- **Power**: This API is used for power management

- **System information**: This API provides information about the battery, CPU, storage, WiFi, cellular network, and so on

- **System setting**: This API provides access to various settings of the platform

- **Time**: This API retrieves information about date and time

- **Web setting**: This API control setting is specific to the web view of Tizen web applications

- **Notification**: This API notifies the user about events related to the application

How to do it...

Launch the Tizen IDE and create a new project for Tizen web application, and append the privileges required for the API that you plan to use for `config.xml`, for example, `http://tizen.org/privilege/alarm`.

Take, for instance, the following JavaScript code, which demonstrates the simple usage of the Alarm and Application APIs:

```
// Get the ID of the current application
var sAppId = tizen.application.getCurrentApplication().appInfo.id;

// Set an alarm which will occur after couple of hours
var myAlarm = new tizen.AlarmRelative(2 * tizen.alarm.PERIOD_HOUR);
if (null != myAlarm) {
  tizen.alarm.add(myAlarm, sAppId);
}
```

How it works...

All additional device APIs that are used in web applications for Tizen are accessed through the `tizen` JavaScript object. A set of generic functions, including error handling and filters, is also provided with the `tizen` object.

The Application API is used to retrieve the ID of the current application, and it is assigned to the JavaScript variable `sAppId`. After that, a relative alarm that will occur after a couple of hours is created and assigned to the variable `myAlarm` using the Alarm API. Finally, on the last line of the code snippet, the alarm is added to the alarm storage of the current application.

As you can see, both APIs used in the code snippet are accessed through the `tizen` JavaScript object.

See also

▸   This chapter contains only a brief overview of the available APIs. Tutorials and examples for most of them are available in the chapters from the second part of the book.

Localizing Tizen web apps

Internationalization and localization of your applications to different languages is a key factor for success. Localized content attracts the attention of a larger audience, which leads to more downloads, and, of course, better revenues.

Internationalization is the process of designing the application in such a way that various languages are supported. Localization is another process of adding specific local resources to the application, such as text translated to different languages.

In this recipe, you will learn how to a support multiple languages inside the Tizen web application using a folder-based technique for localization.

How to do it...

Perform the following steps to localize a Tizen application:

1. Open the application's project, and select its root folder at **Project View**.

2. From the main menu of the Tizen IDE, navigate to **Project | Localization | Localization Wizard...** as shown in the following screenshot:

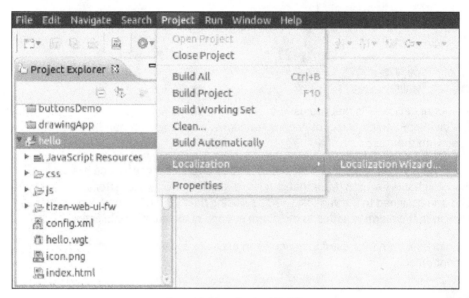

Launching Localization Wizard

3. On the first screen of **Localization Wizard**, choose the files that will be localized, and click on **Next**.

4. Select locales from the list of **Available locales**, and include them in the **Selected locales** list. After that, click on **Next**.

5. Select the files that have to be translated to the chosen locales by checking their filenames, and click on **Finish**.

 To change the global language on a Tizen device or Emulator during testing of application localization, navigate to **Settings | Language and keyboard | Display language**.

How it works...

Localization Wizard creates a folder called `locales` at the root level of the application package and creates separate folders in it for each selected locale. All files that have been chosen for localization of the selected locale will be included in its folder. For example, if we decide to create the French localization of `index.html`, then the folder `/locales/fr` will be created and the file will be copied in it.

If a file is not selected for localization, it will not appear in the `locales` folder, and its original version from the root level of the package will be automatically loaded.

When a web application is launched, Tizen will try to load the content using the current locale, which is configured by the user at the platform settings. If such a locale is not present, then the application will be loaded using its default localization.

There's more...

In Tizen web applications, dynamic string localization using JavaScript is also possible, thanks to the open source library, `Globalize`. Perform the following steps to enable and use this library:

1. Define translation tables for each supported language. For example, the following code snippet defines the default language (English) and French:

    ```
    Globalize.addCultureInfo("default", {
      messages: {
        "hello" : "Hello"
      }
    });

    Globalize.addCultureInfo("fr", {
      messages: {
        "hello" : "Bonjour"
      }
    });
    ```

2. Use a translation string with automatic or manual language selection as follows:

    ```
    console.log(Globalize.localize("hello"));
    console.log(Globalize.localize("hello", "fr"));
    ```

Pay attention to the fact that the messages are case sensitive. The output on the Tizen device or Emulator on which the display language has been set to English will be as follows:

```
Hello
Bonjour
```

For more information about the open source library, `Globalize`, visit `https://github.com/jquery/globalize`.

Packaging Tizen web apps

After the successful development and testing of a web application, all of its files must be bundled together into a single file called `package` that has the extension `.wgt`. The package contains all the HTML, CSS, JavaScript, and any other resource files of the application. The `.wgt` file is used to install web applications on Tizen devices and should be uploaded to Tizen Store when the application is published.

Getting ready

The tools to build Tizen applications are integrated with the Tizen IDE. The building process is simple and it is fully automated. Please ensure that the Tizen SDK and IDE are properly installed before you proceed.

 Make sure that an active secure profile has been set before you start the packaging of the web application. For more information, please read the recipe *Setting the Active Secure Profile* from *Chapter 1, The Tizen SDK*.

How to do it...

Perform the described actions to build a Tizen web application from the Tizen IDE:

1. Launch the Tizen IDE, and navigate to the **Project Explorer** view. Select the project of the application.

2. Right-click on the project, and navigate to **Project | Build Package**.

 Ensure that the package has been created successfully by checking the content of the project folder.

How it works...

The package produced by the Tizen IDE is created according to W3C recommendations for web applications. For more information, visit `http://www.w3.org/TR/widgets/`.

The content of the package is compressed using the ZIP archive algorithms and its file must have the extension `.wgt`. Its MIME type is `application/widget`.

Several files and folders with reserved names shown in the following table have to be included inside the package of the Tizen web application. After successful installation, a directory, whose name matches the package ID, is created at `/opt/usr/apps`. The directory hierarchy also includes folders `bin` (for the application's binary files), `data`, and `res`.

Name	Description
`config.xml`	Web widget's configurations.
`icon.gif`	Several file types for `icon` are supported.
`icon.ico`	
`icon.jpg`	
`icon.png`	
`icon.svg`	
`index.html`	Several file types are supported for main entry page. By default the name is `index`.
`index.htm`	
`index.svg`	
`index.xhtml`	
`index.htt`	
`locales`	Directory that contains localization data.

Reserve directory and filenames for web applications

Web applications can be installed through SDB through the Tizen IDE or the command-line interface if the developer mode is enabled. Users can download the application from **Tizen Store** or other stores once it is published.

The package manager of the operating system on the device is responsible for the installation and the management of installed applications. To see the list of all installed applications, launch **Settings** and select **Manage Applications**. Click on the application to remove it or to stop it if it is running.

See also

▸ Check the recipe *Tizen native app programming* to learn how to create multiproject applications and how to bundle hybrid applications.

Tizen native app programming

Since Tizen 2.0, it is possible to develop mobile applications using C/C++ programming languages. Although in most of the cases, web applications should be preferred and recommended, native programming is useful for faster performance, low-level access to device capabilities, compatibility with existing Bada applications, as well as third-party libraries and frameworks, such as Qt for Tizen. Native programming for Tizen supports both service applications and applications with GUI.

Getting ready

The native development framework for Tizen is quite complex. The most significant differences from the standard C++ are the exception handling mechanism and the two-phase constructors. Although Tizen does not use C++ exceptions, you can use try-catch statements for your own application's C++ exceptions.

Tizen native applications for mobile devices are based on the graphics stack of Bada, which is known as a native framework or **OSP** (Open Service Platform). During the port of existing Bada C++ applications, the OSP namespace should be renamed to Tizen. This porting process can easily be done through the Tizen IDE. The full list of available namespaces in the Tizen native framework is available at https://developer.tizen.org/dev-guide/2.2.1/org. tizen.native.apireference/namespaces.html.

Furthermore, Tizen native frameworks contain hidden gems, such as the specific life cycle of native applications and the macros used for logging.

Please explore in detail the native development documentation if you plan to develop sophisticated Tizen native mobile applications.

How to do it...

Follow these guidelines to create a simple Tizen native application:

1. Launch Tizen IDE and, if asked, choose a workspace. It is highly recommended to switch the IDE to native perspective.

2. Navigate to **File | New | Project...**.

3. A wizard to create a project will appear. From the list of different project types, select **Tizen | Native Tizen Project**, and after that, click on **Next**.

4. From **Template**, select **Tizen Form-based Application** and **Without SceneManager**. Enter a project name, for example, helloWorldNative. After that, click on **Finish**.

5. Select the project from the **Project View**, and right-click to open the context menu with additional options. Choose **Run Native UI Builder**.

6. Wait until Tizen **Native UI Builder** is completely loaded. Select Header of IDL_FORM from the **Outline** view.

7. Go to the **Properties** view of the **Native UI Builder**, and expand all properties. Change **Title Text** to Hello World.

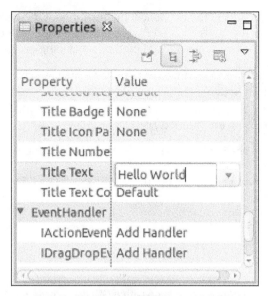

Changing Title Text from Tizen Native UI Builder

8. Save changes and close the Native UI Builder.

9. Open `manifest.xml` using the **Tizen Manifest Editor**, and select the **Features** tab.

10. Click on **Add**, select `http://tizen.org/feature/screen.size.all` to support all screen sizes, and confirm your choice.

11. Make sure that a Tizen device with enabled developer mode is connected or the emulator is running. Again, select the application's project in **Project View** of the Tizen IDE, and right-click to open the context menu. Navigate to **Run as | Tizen Native Application.** The alternative is just to hit the **Run** button to deploy and launch the application.

> Steps 9 and 10 are optional, but they are highly recommended, because Tizen Store may reject the application if the screen size feature is not specified, and a warning will be displayed during packaging.

How it works

Following this procedure, the Tizen IDE will automatically create the filesystem of the project as well as C++ and resource files.

The main class of a native Tizen mobile application must inherit the class `Tizen::App::UiApp` or the class `Tizen::App::ServiceApp`. Our example inherits `Tizen::App::UiApp` and overloads several methods including `OnAppInitializing()` and `OnAppInitialized()`.

After the launch of a native application, `OnAppInitializing()` is the first method that is called. After that method, `OnAppInitialized()` is also called, and it creates the frame of our example application using the method `AddFrame()`:

```
helloWorldFrame* phelloWorldFrame = new (std::nothrow)
helloWorldFrame;
TryReturn(phelloWorldFrame != null, false, "The memory is
insufficient.");
phelloWorldFrame->Construct();
phelloWorldFrame->SetName(L"helloWorldNative");
AddFrame(*phelloWorldFrame);
```

[Each Tizen native application with a GUI must have at least one frame.]

The `nothrow` statement is used as an argument of the new operator when `helloWorldFrame` is created to guarantee that an exception will not be thrown. Also note the `L` prefix of the hardcoded string of the name. It indicates that the text is a Unicode string.

While the application is running, each frame can be in one of the following three states: activated, deactivated, or minimized. Upon termination of the application, the method `OnAppTerminating()` gets called, and all resources must be released.

The modification of the header that had been done through Tizen Native UI Builder was saved as the XML file `IDL_FORM.xml`. The Native UI Builder simplifies the process, but the same effect will be achieved if the XML file is edited manually.

See also

► To find out details about native application development and C++ API references, please have a look at the sample native applications provided with the SDK, and visit the official Tizen documentation at `https://developer.tizen.org/documentation/dev-guide/2.2.1`.

Packaging Tizen native apps

After the successful development and testing of a native application, all of its files must be bundled together into a single installation file, whose extension is `.tpk`. This file is called `package`. It sounds similar to the **Android application package** file (**APK**), and it has the same purpose. The `.tpk` file is used to install native applications on Tizen devices and should be uploaded to Tizen Store when the application is published.

Getting ready

Native mobile applications that consist of several projects are also supported by Tizen. This type of application combines a GUI project with one or more projects of service applications that do not have a GUI.

 Make sure that an active secure profile has been set before you start the packaging of the native application. For details, please refer to the recipe *Setting Active Secure Profile* from *Chapter 1, The Tizen SDK*.

How to do it...

Perform the following steps to create a package of a Tizen native mobile application from a single project.

1. Locate the project of the application at the **Project Explorer** of Tizen IDE, and select it.

2. Click on the project, and from the context menu, choose **Project > Build Package > TPK**.

3. Finally, click on **OK**.

 Ensure that the package has been created successfully by checking the content of the project folder.

Perform the following steps to create a package of a Tizen native mobile application that consists of more than one project.

1. Open all projects that should be included in the package in the **Project Explorer** view of the Tizen IDE.

2. Select the project with GUI in **Project Explorer**, and right-click on it.

3. Go to **Properties | Project References**.

4. Check the project of the service applications related to the GUI project.

5. Click on **OK**, and proceed with the packaging of the GUI project.

 The package of an application created from multiple projects contains binaries, resources, and data files of all related projects. The application has a single `manifest.xml` file, and it merges the configurations of all projects.

How it works...

Both the packages, Tizen native mobile and Tizen web applications, are compressed with the ZIP algorithms. Unlike the web application, the extension of the native mobile application is `.tpk`. The MIME type of the package is `application/x-tizen.package-archive`. The content of the package is spread among the following directories, whose names are reserved:

Directory Name	Description
bin	Application's binaries
data	Private data
info	Metadata (including `manifest.xml`)
lib	Libraries
res	Resources
settings	Settings
shared	Shared resources

Reserved directories of a native mobile application

The Tizen package manager is responsible for installing, updating, and uninstalling the packages of both native and web applications. After successful installation, the package is extracted in a separate directory again at `/opt/usr/apps`, but the directory structure is slightly different from that of a web application.

To view all installed applications on a Tizen device or Emulator, launch **Settings**, and go to **Manage Applications**. To remove an application, select it from the list, click on **Uninstall**, and confirm the uninstallation. Applications can be also removed using **SDB** if the developer mode is enabled.

Becoming a Tizen Store seller

Tizen Store is the official and the first application marketplace for the Tizen platform. You can register and publish your applications at Tizen Store to reach users and increase your review.

 As an open source platform, Tizen allows installation of applications from other stores as well. Unlike iOS, there is place for more than one store in the Tizen ecosystem.

Getting ready

Registering with Tizen Store is free, and no special preparation is needed. Please prepare a scanned copy of your business registration certificate and your bank account details if you plan to request commercial status and publish paid applications.

How to do it...

To register as a Tizen Store seller, you should perform the following simple actions:

1. Launch your favorite web browser, and go to `http://seller.tizenstore.com`.
2. Click on **Sign Up Now**.
3. If you are an independent developer, select **Register as a Private Seller**. If you are representing a company, select **Register as a Corporate Seller**.
4. Follow the onscreen instructions (four steps), and provide the required information to complete the registration successfully.
5. To publish paid applications, you should obtain commercial status. Click on the **Request Commercial Seller Status** button on the last step of the registration, or log in and go to your profile page.

How it works...

Tizen Store is operated by Samsung. The registration is free. After registration, the seller must request commercial status to be able to offer paid applications.

The revenue from paid applications is split as 30 percent for Samsung and 70 percent for the seller. By the way, this is an industry-standard revenue split, because the same shares are reserved for the publishers at many application stores for other operating systems.

Payments to the sellers are made monthly if the due amount is at least $150. The supported options for payment to the publishers are via wire transfer to a registered bank account or through PayPal.

See also

▶ Refer to the next recipe to learn how to publish applications to Tizen Store. Check the Tizen Store terms and conditions for more details at `http://seller.tizenstore.com/help/termsAndConditions.as`.

Publishing apps to Tizen Store

After development, testing, and packaging of an application, it is time to launch it on the market. Register to Tizen Store, and publish your web or native application as free or paid content.

Getting ready

Before you start, it is highly recommended that you check the Tizen Store **Validation Guide**, which is available under the **Guides** section of the seller's website.

The application validation process is very strict. The quality assurance team of Tizen Store inspects each submission and ensures that it is properly working. Rejection of applications causes delays and losses for the developer, so it is better to get to know the validation criteria even before starting the development.

How to do it...

Upload and publish your Tizen application to Tizen Store in five simple steps:

1. Launch your favorite web browser, and go to `http://seller.tizenstore.com`.
2. Click on **Add New App**.
3. Fill in the basic information, upload the application's package, and after that, click on **Next** to proceed.
4. On the **Display Information** screen, fill the description, add tags, and so on. When you are ready, click on **Next**.
5. Verify the information that you have entered on the **Final Review** screen, and if everything is OK, click on **Confirm**.

If you have any questions, and you want to directly contact a representative of Tizen Store, navigate to **Support | My Q&A**, and click on **Write** to start a new discussion.

How it works...

The application uploaded is validated by the QA team, and if it is approved, it will become available for download from Tizen Store. The validation process takes approximately three days, and it is divided into two phases: **Initial Inspection** and **Dynamic Analysis**, and **Review and Final Confirmation**. The first phase checks for API privileges, security issues, malware, and so on. It is done automatically. The second phase is performed manually. If the application successfully passes both phases, its status will be changed to **Ready for Sale**. Otherwise, if the application fails to pass validation, a report with details will be provided to the seller.

See also

▶   For details regarding the application submission process, please log in to the website for Tizen Store sellers, and access the user's manuals by clicking on the **Guides** button.

Part 2

Creating Tizen Web Applications

Building a UI

Storing Data

Creating Multimedia Apps

Developing Social Networking Apps

Managing the Address Book and Calendar

Communication

Using Sensors

3
Building a UI

In this chapter, we will cover:

- ▸ An overview of widgets
- ▸ Creating buttons
- ▸ Creating list views
- ▸ Showing pop ups
- ▸ Using the Tizen Notification API
- ▸ Customizing the look and feel
- ▸ Drawing and writing text on a canvas
- ▸ Creating 3D objects with WebGL

Introduction

This chapter of the book is dedicated to graphical user interfaces. It includes tutorials for creating buttons, lists, pop ups, and notifications with Tizen Web UI Framework and jQuery Mobile. We'll also cover hints to make user-friendly mobile applications as well as easier customization of the application design are shared. Furthermore, reference guides for drawing 2D and 3D objects on an HTML5 canvas are also included.

An overview of widgets

Tizen Web UI Framework is based on several open source JavaScript libraries and frameworks: jQuery, jQuery Mobile, and Globalize.

Nowadays, jQuery Mobile is among the most popular frameworks to build web applications optimized for mobile devices, and it is not a surprise that Tizen relies on it. The framework is based on the popular JavaScript library, jQuery. jQuery Mobile is an open source project of jQuery foundation, and it is available under MIT license.

Getting ready

The page structure of a Tizen web application built with Tizen Web UI Framework is similar to jQuery Mobile. A typical page contains:

- A header
- Content
- A footer

Most of the widgets provided by Tizen UI Framework are based on jQuery Mobile. Several new widgets designed in a way that they match the Tizen native UI are also available.

The following table lists in alphabetical order all widgets provided by Tizen UI Framework as of the Tizen SDK 2.2.1:

Widget	Brief description
Autodividers	Automatically adds dividers between the items of a list. A similar option is available for jQuery Mobile lists.
Button	A basic push button inherited from jQuery Mobile.
Checkbox	Displays a standard checkbox. The user can choose whether to select it. Often, several checkboxes are grouped together, and the user can simultaneously select more than one option. This component also comes from jQuery Mobile.
Date, Time, or Date time picker	Widgets that simplify the input of date and/or time.
Extendable list	Provides a list view that can be extended.
Fast scroll	Simplifies scrolling and makes it faster.
Flip toggle	This is similar to a radio button as it displays a switch with two options. For example, on/off. The same widget exists in jQuery Mobile.
Footer	An essential widget inherited from jQuery Mobile. It is placed at the bottom of a page.
Gallery	A widget for displaying images.
Gallery 3D	A widget that allows 3D arrangement for the displayed images.
Handler	Scrollbar optimized for touchscreen devices.
Header	Another essential widget from jQuery Mobile. It is placed at the top of a page.

Widget	Brief description
HTML block	A widget that contains custom HTML code.
List	List view with multiple items, the appearance of which can be customized. This widget is the same as the one in jQuery Mobile.
List divider	A special item of a list that acts a separator. It is convenient for grouping items, and it also comes from jQuery Mobile.
Multimedia view	A widget that provides audio and video player.
Notification	An information widget that is displayed when events occur.
Pop up	A customizable widget to show information in a separate window. It has the same methods and events as the jQuery Mobile widget with the same name.
Progress	Indicates that there is an operation in progress.
Progress bar	Indicates the progress of an ongoing operation using percentages. This widget is taken from jQuery UI.
Search filter bar	A filter that simplifies searching in large text data. The same widgets exist in jQuery Mobile.
Slider	Another widget from jQuery Mobile. It collects a value picked by the user in a range defined by the developer.
Split view	Splits the content into several different views on the screen.
Swipe	An advanced list widget whose items can be swiped and buttons can appear in the place of each item.
Tab bar	Bundles buttons into a group. It is recommended to be located within the header or the footer of a page.
Token text area	A sophisticated widget that converts text entered by the user into a button.
Virtual grid	A widget optimized for loading and representing large data in a table.
Virtual list	A widget optimized to load and represent large data in a list.

How to do it...

Use the following HTML5 source code to create a page that contains a header with a title and a button, content with a list, and a footer:

```
<div data-role="page">
  <div data-role="header" data-position="fixed">
    <h1>Tizen</h1>
    <div data-role="button" data-icon="plus" class="naviframe-
      edit">Add</div>
    </div>
  <div data-role="content">
```

```
        <ul data-role="listview">
          <li data-role="list-divider">Chapter 3</li>
          <li>Building UI</li>
          <li>Creating Buttons</li>
          <li>Creating List Views</li>
        </ul>
        </div>
        <div data-role="footer" data-position="fixed">
        <h4>Packt Publishing</h4>
      </div>
    </div>
```

How it works...

The HTML5 code snippet demonstrates the usage of Tizen UI Web Framework based on jQuery Mobile.

A page is created using a `div` tag with the attribute `data-role` and value page. In HTML, tags with the `div` keyword are used to define a section of the document. The header and the footer are created in a similar way. The header contains a heading marked with `h1` and a button whose icon is set at the attribute `data-icon`. The value of `data-icon` should match an option from the available icon set provided by jQuery Mobile. The example uses `plus`.

The main components of the page are situated in a `div` element between the header and the footer, and this section is marked as `data-role="content"`. The examples in the previous section of this recipe show the usage of the list and list divider widgets.

See also

 ▸ Please refer to the recipe *Tizen web app programming* from *Chapter 2, Introduction to the Tizen Ecosystem*, to create a web application. Replace the body of `index.html` with the preceding example to try it out.

 ▸ More information about the widgets in Tizen UI Framework is available in the official documentation at `https://developer.tizen.org/dev-guide/ 2.2.1/org.tizen.web.uiwidget.apireference/html/widgets/ widget_reference.htm`.

Creating buttons

This recipe demonstrates how to create a Tizen web application with buttons and how to handle an event if the user clicks on any of these buttons.

Getting ready

Buttons in the Tizen UI Web Framework can be created using any of the following three options:

- Using HTML5 elements, such as `anchor` or `div`, with the attribute `data-role="button"`
- Using the `button` element of HTML5
- Using the `input` element of HTML5

> Tizen UI Web Framework is based on jQuery Mobile, and similar rules are applied for buttons. For details visit `https://developer.tizen.org/dev-guide/2.2.1/org.tizen.web.uiwidget.apireference/html/widgets/widget_button.htm`.

Feel free to create a button with the approach that suits you best depending on the situation.

Now we are ready to create buttons, so let's proceed with the development of a whole application.

How to do it...

1. Launch the Tizen IDE, and start a new Tizen web project.
2. Create a single-page application using Tizen Web UI Framework.
3. Open `index.html`, and replace the content of the `body` element with the following source code:

```
<div data-role="page">
  <div data-role="header" data-position="fixed">
    <h1>Buttons </h1>
  </div><!-- /header -->
  <div data-role="content">
    <p id="label">Please click a button.</p>
    <a id="btn1" href="#" data-role="button">Button 1</a>
    <button id="btn2">Button 2</button>
    <input type="button" id="btn3" value="Button 3" />
  </div>
  <div data-role="footer" data-position="fixed">
    <h4>Tizen Cookbook</h4>
  </div><!-- /footer -->
</div><!-- /page -->
```

4. Open `js/main.js`, and append the following source code to the JavaScript anonymous (lambda) function, which is assigned to the variable `init`:

```
$('#btn1').bind( "click", function(event, ui) {
  $('#label').text('Button 1 clicked.');
});

$('#btn2').bind( "click", function(event, ui) {
  $('#label').text('Button 2 clicked.');
});

$('#btn3').bind( "click", function(event, ui) {
  $('#label').text('Button 3 clicked.');
});
```

5. Save all changes and run the application on a real device, emulator, or simulator. If everything works correctly when you click a button, the text of the paragraph with the `id` label will be changed.

How it works...

The HTML5 source code that was inserted in `index.html` creates a page with header, footer, single paragraph with `id` label, and three buttons with the IDs `btn1`, `btn2`, and `bnt3`. Each button is created using one of these different options provided by the framework, but visually all of them look the same.

The source code inserted in the JavaScript file is based on the jQuery library. The first line binds the click event of the button with the ID `btn1` to a function that handles it. Have a look at the following line of code:

```
$('#btn1').bind( "click", function(event, ui) {
```

The dollar sign is an alias of `jQuery()`. This function returns a collection of elements from the DOM of the HTML based on the provided selector as an argument. The code snippet from this recipe uses ID selectors. jQuery is famous for its powerful tools to access DOM elements. The full list of supported selectors is available at `http://api.jquery.com/category/selectors/`.

The next line changes the text of the paragraph label using the method `text()`, which is provided by jQuery. Have a look at the following line of code:

```
$('#label').text('Button 1 clicked.');
```

It is important to note that according to the documentation of jQuery Mobile 1.3.2, which is included in Tizen SDK 2.2.1, `$(document).bind('pageinit')` must be used instead of `$(document).ready()`. Please note that the event `pageinit` has been replaced with `pagecreate` in jQuery Mobile 1.4.

If the handlers are not bound to the buttons at an appropriate place, most probably they will not work. Pay attention to the fact that they must be implemented as anonymous functions that are assigned to the variable `init`. After that, `init` is bound to the `pageinit` event, so the anonymous function is executed on page initialization. Have a look at the following line of code:

```
$(document).bind( 'pageinit', init );
```

Anonymous functions are first-class citizens of JavaScript. They are most commonly used as callbacks—functions that are executed asynchronously when an event occurs or at a later time. Although this usage of anonymous functions is often very convenient, you should pay attention to it; otherwise, you may end up at the so-called callback hell. Good suggestions on how to write and maintain easy-to-read JavaScript code with callbacks can be found at `http://callbackhell.com/`.

See also

▶ The project of the example application in this recipe is provided is present in the source code of the book. Please explore its source code if you have any trouble implementing the example on your own.

Creating list views

An old joke popular among developers says that there is no good mobile application without a list. This widget is very convenient for storing large amount of data, especially on devices with relatively small screens, such as smartphones or smart watches.

This recipe explains how to create a multipage application with a list view that includes several items, an item divider, and a search filter.

Although multipage application might sound fancy, in fact, it is just an application that contains two or more Tizen UI Web Framework pages, and it is very easy to create such an application.

Getting ready

Lists in Tizen UI Web Framework are created using HTML5 elements for ordered and unordered lists, `ol` and `ul`, combined with `data-role="listview"`.

How to do it...

1. Create a new project that uses the **Multi Page Application** template of **Tizen Web UI Framework**.

2. Create a new folder, `images`, from the **Project Explorer**.

3. Create a simple icon using your drawing application, and save it as `smile.png` inside the `images` folder.

4. Open `index.html` in the Tizen IDE, and replace the content of the `body` element with the following source code:

```
<div data-role="page" id="pageMain">
  <div data-role="header" data-position="fixed">
    <h1>List View</h1>
  </div><!-- /header -->

  <div data-role="content">
    <ul data-role="listview">
      <li data-role="list-divider">Samples</li>
      <li><a href="#pageInfo">Foo</a></li>
      <li><a href="#pageInfo">Bar <span data-role="button"
        data-inline="true" data-icon="arrow-
        r"></span></a></li>
        <li class="ui-li-has-multiline"><a
          href="#pageInfo"><img
          src="images/smile.png"
class="ui-li-bigicon" />
Foo
<span class="ui-li-text-sub">Bar</span><span data-
  role="button" data-inline="true" data-icon="info"
data-style="circle"></span></a></li>
    </ul>
  </div><!-- /content -->
  <div data-role="footer" data-position="fixed">
    <h4>Tizen Cookbook</h4>
  </div><!-- /footer -->
</div><!-- /pageMain -->
<div data-role="page" id="pageInfo" data-add-back-btn="true">
  <div data-role="header" data-position="fixed">
    <h1>Read-only List</h1>
  </div><!-- /header -->
  <div data-role="content">
    <ul data-role="listview">
      <li>baz</li>
      <li>qux</li>
```

```
      </ul>
    </div><!-- /content -->
    <div data-role="footer" data-position="fixed">
      <h4>Tizen Cookbook</h4>
    </div><!-- /footer -->
  </div><!-- /pageInfo -->
```

5. Save all changes, and run the application on an emulator or a device. The application should look like the following:

List views

How it works...

The source code of the body element in the preceding example application contains only HTML5 and CSS.

Two pages are created in two different `div` elements, and each of them contains `data-role="page"`. Both pages contain a header, footer, and list.

The `id` label of the first page is `pageMain`. Each item of the list is created using the `li` element. The list contains the following items:

- A list divider created with the value `list-divider` of the attribute `data-role`. Have a look at the following line of code:

  ```
  <li data-role="list-divider">Samples</li>
  ```

▶ A simple item. Have a look at the following line of code:

```
<li><a href="#pageInfo">Foo</a></li>
```

▶ An item with a button on the right-hand side of the text. The button is created using a span element. It has a default style and a right arrow for an icon set through the attribute data-icon. Have a look at the following code snippet:

```
<li><a href="#pageInfo">Bar <span data-role="button" data-
inline="true" data-icon="arrow-r"></span></a></li>
```

▶ A two-line item with an image (img) on the left-hand side and a button on the right-hand side. The style of the button is circle, and its icon is info. The CSS class ui-li-as-multiline is used to enable multiple lines, and the class ui-li-text-sub marks its second line:

```
<li class="ui-li-has-multiline"><a href="#pageInfo"><img
src="images/smile.png"
class="ui-li-bigicon" />
Foo
<span class="ui-li-text-sub">Bar</span><span data-role="button"
data-inline="true" data-icon="info"
data-style="circle"></span></a></li>
```

The second page displays a simple read-only list. It has id pageInfo. The back button that is displayed at the footer is actually set at the div element of the page using data-add-back-btn="true":

```
<div data-role="page" id="pageInfo" data-add-back-btn="true">
```

See also

▶ Please check the Tizen documentation to see the full list of supported styles for list widgets at https://developer.tizen.org/dev-guide/2.2.1/org.tizen.web.uiwidget.apireference/html/widgets/widget_list.htm.

Showing pop ups

Do you remember the ugly JavaScript built-in functions alert() and confirm()? Both are useful, but their design is stuck in the 1990s, and alternatives are needed for modern mobile applications.

Tizen Web UI Framework offers pop ups with a much better look and a customizable design that can fit the needs of your application. In this recipe, we will create a single-page application with a button that opens a pop up.

How to do it...

1. Launch the Tizen IDE, and create a new Tizen Web Project.

2. Create a single-page application using Tizen Web UI Framework.

3. Open `index.html`, and replace the content of the `body` element with the following source code:

```
<div id="popupConfirm" data-role="popup" class="center_
title_2btn">
  <div class="ui-popup-title">
    <h1>Mathematical Joke</h1>
  </div>
  <div class="ui-popup-text">There are only 10 types of people in
    the world: those who understand binary, and those who
    don&#39;t. Right?</div>
  <div class="ui-popup-button-bg">
  <a id="btnConfirmYes" href="#" data-rel="back" data-
    role="button" data-inline="true">Yes</a>
  <a id="btnConfirmNo" href="#" data-rel="back" data-role="button"
data-inline="true">No</a>
  </div>
</div>
<div data-role="page">
  <div data-role="header" data-position="fixed">
    <h1>Showing Pop-ups</h1>
  </div><!-- /header -->
  <div data-role="content">
    <p id="label">Click the button below to open a pop-
      up.</p>
    <a href="#popupConfirm" id="btnConfirm" data-
      role="button">Push Me!</a>
  </div><!-- /content -->
  <div data-role="footer" data-position="fixed">
    <h4>Tizen Cookbook</h4>
  </div><!-- /footer -->
</div><!-- /page
```

4. Open `js/main.js`, and insert the following source code into the anonymous JavaScript function, which is assigned to variable `init`. Have a look at the following code:

```
$('#btnConfirmYes').bind( "click", function(event, ui) {
  $('#label').text('Absolutely!');
});
$('#btnConfirmNo').bind( "click", function(event, ui) {
  $('#label').text('Sorry! It seems that you didn\'t get
    the binary joke.');
});
```

5. Run the application, and have fun with the old but gold binary joke.

How it works...

The HTML5 that was appended in the third step to the `body` element of `index.html` contains a page and a pop up with two buttons. The pop up is represented by a `div` element with `id popupConfirm` and `data-role="popup"`. The CSS class `center_title_2btn` defines its type. The other available types are as follows:

- `center_info`
- `center_title`
- `center_basic_1btn`
- `center_title_1btn`
- `center_title_2btn`
- `center_title_3btn`
- `center_button_vertical`
- `center_checkbox`
- `center_liststyle_1btn`
- `center_liststyle_2btn`
- `center_liststyle_3btn`

 The buttons are arranged horizontally next to each other for all types with more than one button, except for `center_button_vertical`.

The JavaScript appended to `main.js` binds handlers to the buttons of the pop up. The text content of the paragraph with the `id` label is changed depending on the user's choice.

Tizen Web UI Framework and jQuery Mobile do not support the chaining of pop ups. This means that it is not possible to invoke a pop up from another pop up. From a designer's point of view, it is also not recommended to use the chaining of pop ups, as it has negative impact on the user experience. Anyway, if you insist on it, a workaround is available; open a pop up with a minimal timeout after closing the first pop up by implementing `setTimeout()` after the `popupafterclose` event.

See also

- Please refer to the Tizen Web UI and jQuery Mobile documentation for a full list of all events and methods as well as details about the pop up types at `https://developer.tizen.org/dev-guide/2.2.1/org.tizen.web.uiwidget.apireference/html/widgets/widget_popup.htm`.

Using the Tizen Notification API

The Notification API allows developers to display messages to users outside their applications. Notifications are useful when the user has to be informed about events or the status of an ongoing process. They are displayed in one place, which is shared between notifications from each application and the system.

Follow the tutorial in this recipe to learn how to use the Tizen Notification API to display `SIMPLE` and `PROGRESS` notifications in Tizen.

Getting ready

Several different types of notifications exist in Tizen:

- `SIMPLE`: This is a `basic text` notification

- `THUMBNAIL`: This notification includes both text and thumbnails

- `ONGOING`: This is a notification that informs the user whether the application is running

- `PROGRESS`: This provides information about the current status of a job and its progress

The first two types of notifications can be removed by the user. The other types cannot be removed by the user, and the application should take care of their removal. The notification API is quite flexible, and as a developer, you can choose the types that exactly match the needs of your application.

How to do it...

1. Launch Tizen IDE, and start a new Tizen Web Project.
2. Create a single-page application using Tizen Web UI Framework.
3. Insert the following HTML code that creates two buttons inside the body of `index.html`:

```
<div data-role="page">
  <div data-role="header" data-position="fixed">
    <h1>Using Tizen Notification API</h1>
  </div><!-- /header -->

  <div data-role="content">
    <button id="btnSimpleNotification">Simple Notification</
button>
```

```
        <button id="btnProgressNotification">Progress Notification</
button>
    </div><!-- /content -->


    <div data-role="footer" data-position="fixed">
        <h4>Tizen Cookbook</h4>
    </div><!-- /footer -->
</div><!-- /page -->
```

4. Paste the following JavaScript function inside `main.js`:

```javascript
function postSimpleNotification()
  {
    try {
      var notificationDict = {
        content: "Hello World."
      };
        simpleNotification = new
          tizen.StatusNotification("SIMPLE",
          "Notification", notificationDict);
          tizen.notification.post(simpleNotification);
    } catch (err) {
      console.log("Unable to post simple notification.");
    }
  }


function postProgressNotification()
  {
    try {
      var notificationDict = {
        content: "Please wait..."
        };
        progressNotification = new
          tizen.StatusNotification("PROGRESS",
          "Progess", notificationDict);
          tizen.notification.post(progressNotification);
    } catch (err) {
      console.log("Unable to post progress notification.");
    }
  }


function updateProgressNotification()
 {
```

This function as well as the other functions in this recipe use the try-catch block to handle exceptions, such as `WebAPIException`. They are thrown by the methods of the Notification API if an error occurs.

The `try` statement defines a block in which the source code should be tested for any errors. The keyword `throw` must be used to raise an exception. The exception terminates the execution of the source code at the `try` block, and the control is passed to the `catch` block. Rules and commands for handling intercepted exceptions are defined in it:

```
try {
    progressNotification.content = "Almost done!";
    tizen.notification.update(progressNotification);
} catch (err) {
    console.log("Unable to update progress notification.");

}
}
```

```
function removeProgressNotification()
{
  try {
    tizen.notification.remove(progressNotification.id);
  } catch (err) {
    console.log("unable to remove progress notification.");
  }
}
```

```
function runProgressDemo()
{
  postProgressNotification();
```

The second argument of the function `setTimeout()` is the delay in milliseconds. Six thousand (6,000) milliseconds is equal to 6 seconds and 10,000 milliseconds is equal to 10 seconds. Have a look at the following code:

```
setTimeout(updateProgressNotification,6000);
setTimeout(removeProgressNotification,10000);
}
```

5. Bind the click events of both buttons to the JavaScript functions from the previous step by inserting the following code snippet into the anonymous JavaScript function that is assigned to variable `init`:

```
$('#btnSimpleNotification').bind( "click", function(event, ui) {
  postSimpleNotification();
});
```

```
$('#btnProgressNotification').bind( "click", function(event, ui) {
  runProgressDemo();
});
```

6. Add notification privileges to `config.xml`:

   ```
   <tizen:privilege name="http://tizen.org/privilege/notification"/>
   ```

7. Save all modified files, and run the application.

How it works...

The application contains a single application and two buttons. The click event of the button with ID `btnSimpleNotification` is bound to JavaScript function `postSimpleNotification()`. When this function is executed, a simple notification with the title **Notification** and text **Hello World** is displayed on the screen as follows:

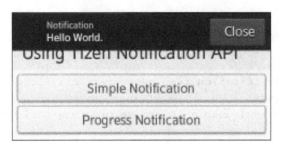

Simple notification

A click on the button with the ID `btnProgressNotification` leads to the execution of the function `runProgressDemo()`. A progress notification with the title **Progress** and text **Please wait...** is posted. After 6 seconds, it is updated, and the text is changed to **Almost done!** The notification is removed 10 seconds after its occurrence. The function `updateProgressNotification()` is responsible for the update, and the function `removeProgressNotification()` removes the notification. The delay of the execution of both functions is achieved using the JavaScript built-in function `setTimeout()`. You can explore the implementation of all functions added to `main.js` to understand how the Notification API is used. Have a look at the following screenshot:

The Progress notification before and after the update

Optionally, an icon and/or a sound can be added by specifying the path to the image and/or a sound file in the JavaScript object that is created for the notification.

It is mandatory to add privileges as described in step 6; otherwise, the application will not work properly, because it will not be able to post any notifications. Use a device or Emulator to test and debug applications which post notifications.

See also

▶ If you are interested in posting push notifications to the Tizen device from a server, please take a look at the recipe *Receiving push notifications* in *Chapter 8, Communication*.

▶ To explore the full capabilities of the Notification API, please visit `https://developer.tizen.org/dev-guide/2.2.1/org.tizen.web.device.apireference/tizen/notification.html`.

Customizing the look and feel

Have you ever been in a situation when the customer changes the requirements in the middle of a project, and you have to modify the whole design of the application? Or have you been in a situation when you have to deliver the same application to different customers with different themes and images?

CSS is the language used to describe the look and format of web applications. Every web developer should be familiar with it. Unfortunately the maintenance and the modification of complex CSS files might be difficult. You can always use CSS in Tizen web applications, but in the case described, the most painless solution is to rely on a CSS preprocessor, such as **LESS** or **Sass**.

This recipe demonstrates the basic usage of LESS for a Tizen web application. I hope that based on the experienced gained here, you should be able to generate complex CSS through LESS.

Getting ready

LESS is an open source dynamic language, which brings variables, mixins, operations, and functions to CSS. LESS can be executed on the client side through JavaScript or on a server.

 Valid CSS code is valid LESS code as well.

How to do it...

Perform the following steps to generate CSS from LESS online. This simple example changes the fonts and the colors of text headings:

1. Load the website `http://less2css.org/` using your favorite web browser.

2. Insert the LESS source code that customizes the colors and the fonts of the headings:

```
@color1: #c0c0c0;
@color2: #880000;
@font: Arial, Helvetica, sans-serif;
h1, h2, h3 {
   font-family: @font;
}
h1 {
   color: @color1;
   background-color: @color2;
}
h2 {
   color: @color2;
   background-color: @color2;
}
h3 {
   color: @color2;
}
```

 Please feel free to change the colors by modifying the values of the LESS variables.

3. Copy the generated CSS to the clipboard. The CSS should be similar to the following example:

```
h1, h2, h3 {
   font-family: Arial, Helvetica, sans-serif;
}
h1 {
   color: #c0c0c0;
   background-color: #880000;
}
h2 {
   color: #880000;
   background-color: #880000;
}
```

```
h3 {
    color: #880000;
}
```

4. Select a project in the **Project Explorer** view of the Tizen IDE, right-click on it, and navigate to **New | CSS File**. Follow the onscreen instructions to complete the creation of the file with the name `myHeadings.css`.

5. Paste the copied content into the newly created CSS file, and save it.

6. Add the following HTML line to `index.html` to load the CSS file as an external style sheet into the application:

```
<link rel="stylesheet" type="text/css" href="myHeadings.css">
```

 The advantage in this example is that only the value of the variable should be modified to change the color of all headings. The real power of LESS can be seen in large projects that consist of a large number of style sheets.

How it works...

LESS is compiled to CSS through an online tool powered by the open source project less-preview. The source code of the project is available at GitHub under MIT license, and its maintainer is Brian Frichette. For details, please visit `https://github.com/brian-frichette/less-preview/`.

The LESS code snippet in the preceding example is very simple. On the first three lines are declared and initialized LESS variables. According to the rules, a variable starts with the prefix @ followed by its name. A colon is used to initialize its value.

The font family is set at the LESS variable `@font`, and its value is set at the CSS grouping for h1, h2, and h3:

```
h1, h2, h3 {
    font-family: @font;
}
```

The other LESS variables `@color1` and `@color2` are used to set the font and the background colors of the headings.

The output of the successful execution of the LESS source code is valid CSS. When the CSS is ready, it must be loaded in the Tizen web application as described in steps 3 through 6.

▶ If you are curious to learn more about CSS preprocessors, you can extend your knowledge with a couple of books written by Alex Libby: *Instant SASS CSS How-to* and *Instant LESS CSS Preprocessor How-to*.

Drawing and writing text on a canvas

One of the main advantages of HTML5 is that it can be used as a replacement of Adobe Flash for drawing. The HTML5 canvas element opens new horizons to create cutting-edge animations inside web and mobile applications or games.

This recipe demonstrates drawing and writing text on the HTML5 canvas with JavaScript in a Tizen web application. Follow the steps given in this recipe to create a single page Tizen web application with two buttons. The first button writes the text **Hello Tizen** and draws a blue square and an orange circle. The second button clears the screen.

Drawing on a canvas in the Tizen web application

Getting ready

Canvas is a new element that was introduced in HTML5. The attributes `id`, `width`, and `height` of the canvas can be specified. By default, the canvas is empty and JavaScript should be used to create and control its content.

How to do it...

1. Launch the Tizen IDE, and start a new **Tizen Web Project**.
2. Create a **Single Page Application** using Tizen Web UI Framework.
3. Right-click on the project in the Project Explorer view, and select **New | Other | JavaScript | JavaScript Source File** to create the file `draw.js`.
4. Save the following JavaScript code to draw on a canvas to `draw.js`:

```
function draw()
{
  var drawer = $('#pic')[0].getContext("2d");
  //write text
  drawer.fillStyle= '#000000';
  var nTextHeight = 20;
```

The `font` property in the HTML5 canvas supports the same syntax as the CSS fonts. Tizen offers a dedicated font family, which is called TizenSans, but in this application, the popular Arial font is used. For more information about the typography guidelines in Tizen, please visit `https://developer.tizen.org/documentation/ux-guide/visual-style/typography`.

```
  drawer.font= nTextHeight + "px Arial";
  drawer.fillText('Hello Tizen',0 , nTextHeight);
  //draw a blue square
  drawer.fillStyle= '#3366CC';
  var nSquareSide = 50;
  drawer.fillRect(0, nTextHeight+10, nSquareSide, nSquareSide);
  //draw an orange circle
  drawer.fillStyle='#FF6600';
  drawer.beginPath();
  var nRadius = 25;
  var nCenterX = nSquareSide + nRadius + 10;
  var nCenterY = nTextHeight + 10 + nRadius;
  drawer.arc(nCenterX, nCenterY, nRadius, 0, 2*Math.PI);
  drawer.fill();
}
```

```
function clear()
{
  var canvas = $('#pic')[0];
  var drawer = canvas.getContext("2d");
  drawer.clearRect(0, 0, canvas.width, canvas.height );
}
```

5. Include the new JavaScript file before loading `main.js` in `index.html`. Have a look at the following code:

```
<script type="text/javascript" src="./js/draw.js"></script>
```

6. Insert the following HTML inside the body of `index.html` to create a canvas and a couple of buttons:

```
<div data-role="page">
  <div data-role="header" data-position="fixed">
    <h1>Drawing Demo</h1>
  </div><!-- /header -->

  <div data-role="content">
    <canvas id="pic" width="200" height="200"></canvas>
    <button id="btnDraw">Draw</button>
    <button id="btnClear">Clear</button>
  </div><!-- /content -->

  <div data-role="footer" data-position="fixed">
    <h4>Tizen Cookbook</h4>
  </div><!-- /footer -->
</div><!-- /page -->
```

7. Handle button clicks by adding the following source code to the anonymous JavaScript function, which is assigned to the variable `init` in `main.js`:

```
$('#btnDraw').bind( "click", function(event, ui) {
  draw();
});
$('#btnClear').bind( "click", function(event, ui) {
  clear();
});
```

8. Save all files, and run the application on a device or Emulator.

How it works...

A canvas with the ID `pic` and width and height equal to 200 px is created in `index.html` as follows:

```
<canvas id="pic" width="200" height="200"></canvas>
```

The click events of buttons with IDs `btnDraw` and `bntClear` invoke the JavaScript functions `draw()` and `clear()`. Both functions are implemented in the file `draw.js`.

 At the `head` of the `index.html` file, `draw.js` must be loaded before the file `main.js`; otherwise, the application will not work properly.

The JavaScript function `draw()` writes text on the screen using `fillText()` on the canvas object. After that, it invokes the canvas object's function `fillRect()` and draws a blue square whose sides are 25 px. Finally, the functions `arc()` and `fill()` are executed to draw an orange circle with radius 25 px.

 The coordinates (0, 0) correspond to the upper-left corner of the drawing area.

See also

▸ All tricks to draw on the HTML5 canvas should be valid for a Tizen web application. More HTML5 examples about drawings and animations can be found in Eric Rowell's book *HTML5 Canvas Cookbook*.

Creating 3D objects with WebGL

Twenty years ago, 3D graphics and OpenGL were restricted primarily to CAD software and games. Back then, websites were very, very simple. The times have changed and Web technologies have evolved dramatically. Nowadays, thanks to WebGL, it is possible to create sophisticated 3D cross-platform animations and games directly inside the HTML5 canvas through JavaScript APIs.

The story of WebGL started in 2006, but it was officially released for the first time in 2011. Today, a nonprofit organization called Khronos Group takes care of the standard. WebGL is based on OpenGL ES. OpenGL is a high-performance 2D and 3D graphics API, and ES is its flavor for embedded devices. WebGL is maintained by a working group started by Khronos Group. Employees of Apple, Google, Mozilla, and other leading vendors are among its members.

This advanced recipe demonstrates how to create a 3D animation by drawing a cube that swivels clockwise inside a Tizen web application. After launching the application, the user must press the **Play** button to start the animation as displayed in the following screenshot:

WebGL demo on Tizen

Getting ready

This application is based on the spinning WebGL box example that is available on the public GitHub repository of Khronos Group. Several external JavaScript files that are copyrighted by Apple, Google, and Khronos Group are used in this example according to their copyright notices. For details regarding their licenses and the terms of use, please read the comments at the beginning of each file.

How to do it...

1. Launch the Tizen IDE, and start a new Tizen Web Project.
2. Create a single-page application using the Tizen Web UI Framework.

3. Visit the GitHub repository of WebGL by Khronos Group at `https://github.com/KhronosGroup/WebGL` to locate, download, and save the following files to the `js` directory of the project:

   ❑ `webgl-utils.js`

   ❑ `webgl-debug.js`

   ❑ `J3DI.js`

   ❑ `J3DIMath.js`

4. Right-click on the project in the **Project Explorer** view, navigate to **New | Other | JavaScript | JavaScript Source File**, and create the file `draw.js`.

5. Insert the following JavaScript source code into the newly created file `draw.js`. Have a look at the following code:

```
var g_nCurrentRotation = 360;
var g_nRotationAngle = 1.0;
var global = {};
var g_nRequestId = 0;

function setupColors(webGL)
{
  var colors = new Uint8Array(
        [  0, 1, 0, 1,    0, 1, 0, 1,    0, 1, 0, 1,    0, 1, 0, 1,
//main - green
           0, 0, 1, 1,    0, 0, 1, 1,    0, 0, 1, 1,    0, 0, 1, 1,
// right - blue
           1, 0, 0, 1,    1, 0, 0, 1,    1, 0, 0, 1,    1, 0, 0, 1,
//top - red
           1, 1, 0, 1,    1, 1, 0, 1,    1, 1, 0, 1,    1, 1, 0, 1,
//left - yellow
           0, 0, 0, 1,    0, 0, 0, 1,    0, 0, 0, 1,    0, 0, 0, 1,
// bottom - black
           0, 0, 0, 1,    0, 0, 0, 1,    0, 0, 0, 1,    0, 0, 0, 1
]// back - black
                                          );
    // Set up the vertex buffer for the colors
    global.box.colorObject = webGL.createBuffer();
    webGL.bindBuffer(webGL.ARRAY_BUFFER,
      global.box.colorObject);
    webGL.bufferData(webGL.ARRAY_BUFFER, colors,
      webGL.STATIC_DRAW);
}
```

The preceding code snippet declares several global variables and initializes them with default values. It also includes a function `setupColors()`, which sets the colors of each side of the cube. The following source code implements the function `init()`, which prepares the drawing area, and it has to be inserted in the same file:

```
function init()
{
    var canvas = document.getElementById('screen');
    var webGL = WebGLUtils.setupWebGL(canvas);
    if (!webGL) {
      return;
    }
    global.program = simpleSetup(
        webGL, "vshader", "fshader",
        [ "vNormal", "vColor", "vPosition"], [ 1, 1, 1, 1 ],
10000);
```

The following line sets a uniform variable for the shaders, who take the shape data and transform it into pixels on the screen:

```
    webGL.uniform3f(webGL.getUniformLocation(global.program,
"lightDir"), 0, 0, 1);


    global.box = makeBox(webGL);


    setupColors(webGL);
```

Several 4 x 4 matrices will be created from the class `J3DIMatrix4`. They will be used for vector transformations at the function `draw()`:

```
    global.mvMatrix = new J3DIMatrix4();
    global.u_normalMatrixLoc =
      webGL.getUniformLocation(global.program, "u_normalMatrix");
    global.normalMatrix = new J3DIMatrix4();
    global.u_modelViewProjMatrixLoc =
      webGL.getUniformLocation(global.program,
      "u_modelViewProjMatrix");
    global.mvpMatrix = new J3DIMatrix4();


    webGL.enableVertexAttribArray(0);
    webGL.enableVertexAttribArray(1);
    webGL.enableVertexAttribArray(2);


    webGL.bindBuffer(webGL.ARRAY_BUFFER, global.box.vertexObject);
    webGL.vertexAttribPointer(2, 3, webGL.FLOAT, false, 0, 0);


    webGL.bindBuffer(webGL.ARRAY_BUFFER, global.box.normalObject);
    webGL.vertexAttribPointer(0, 3, webGL.FLOAT, false, 0, 0);
```

```
    webGL.bindBuffer(webGL.ARRAY_BUFFER, global.box.colorObject);
    webGL.vertexAttribPointer(1, 4, webGL.UNSIGNED_BYTE, false, 0,
0);

    webGL.bindBuffer(webGL.ELEMENT_ARRAY_BUFFER, global.box.
indexObject);

    return webGL;
}
```

The next function sets the viewport. Initially, the object is represented with modeling coordinates, which, after that, are transformed to world, view and finally to viewport coordinates. As a result, the 3D scene is transformed into a 2D projection, which is displayed on the screen of the device:

```
function setupView(webGL)
{
    var canvas = document.getElementById('screen');
    webGL.viewport(0, 0, canvas.width, canvas.height);
    global.perspectiveMatrix = new J3DIMatrix4();
    global.perspectiveMatrix.perspective(30, 1, 1, 10000);
    global.perspectiveMatrix.lookat(0, 0, 7, 0, 0, 0, 0, 1, 0);
}
```

Now is the time to implement the most important function of these examples, `draw()`. It is responsible for drawing each frame of the animation. Please append the following source code inside the file `draw.js` too:

```
function draw(webGL)
{
    setupView(webGL);
```

Make sure that the canvas is clean before drawing anything. Have a look at the following code snippet:

```
    webGL.clear(webGL.COLOR_BUFFER_BIT | webGL.DEPTH_BUFFER_BIT);

    global.mvMatrix.makeIdentity();
    global.mvMatrix.rotate(20, 1,0,0);
    global.mvMatrix.rotate(g_nCurrentRotation, 0,1,0);

    global.normalMatrix.load(global.mvMatrix);
    global.normalMatrix.invert();
    global.normalMatrix.transpose();
    global.normalMatrix.setUniform(webGL, global.u_
normalMatrixLoc, false);

    global.mvpMatrix.load(global.perspectiveMatrix);
```

```
    global.mvpMatrix.multiply(global.mvMatrix);
    global.mvpMatrix.setUniform(webGL, global.u_
modelViewProjMatrixLoc, false);

    webGL.drawElements(webGL.TRIANGLES, global.box.numIndices,
webGL.UNSIGNED_BYTE, 0);

    //Enable clockwise rotation
    g_nCurrentRotation -= g_nRotationAngle;
    if (0 > g_nCurrentRotation) {
        g_nCurrentRotation = 360;
    }
}

function pause(event) {
  event.preventDefault();
    if (undefined !== g_nRequestId) {
        window.cancelAnimFrame(g_nRequestId);
        g_nRequestId = undefined;
    }
}

function resume() {
    init();
    animate();
}

function run() {
    var canvas = document.getElementById('screen');
    canvas.addEventListener('webglcontextlost', pause, false);
    canvas.addEventListener('webglcontextrestored', resume,
false);

    var webGL = init();
    if (!webGL) {
      return;
    }

    var animate = function() {
        draw(webGL);
        g_nRequestId = window.requestAnimFrame(animate, canvas);
    };
    animate();
}
```

6. Open `index.html`, and replace its code with the following:

```html
<!DOCTYPE html>
<html>

<head>
    <meta charset="utf-8"/>
    <meta name="description" content="WebGL 3D demonstration app
for Tizen"/>
    <meta name="viewport" content="width=device-width,user-
scalable=no"/>

    <link rel="stylesheet" href="tizen-web-ui-fw/latest/themes/
tizen-white/tizen-web-ui-fw-theme.css" name="tizen-theme"/>
    <title>WebGL 3D</title>
    <script src="tizen-web-ui-fw/latest/js/jquery.js"></script>
    <script src="tizen-web-ui-fw/latest/js/tizen-web-ui-fw-libs.
js"></script>
    <script src="tizen-web-ui-fw/latest/js/tizen-web-ui-fw.js"
        data-framework-theme="tizen-white"></script>
    <script type="text/javascript" src="./js/webgl-utils.js"></
script>
    <script type="text/javascript" src="./js/webgl-debug.js"></
script>

    <script type="text/javascript" src="./js/J3DI.js"></script>
    <script type="text/javascript" src="./js/J3DIMath.js"></
script>

    <script type="text/javascript" src="./js/main.js"></script>
    <link rel="stylesheet" type="text/css" href="./css/style.
css"/>
```

Insert the following couple of scripts inside the HTML `head` to implement a vertex shader that takes care of each corner of each rendered triangle:

```
<script id="vshader" type="x-shader/x-vertex">
uniform mat4 u_modelViewProjMatrix;
uniform mat4 u_normalMatrix;
uniform vec3 lightDir;

attribute vec3 vNormal;
attribute vec4 vColor;
attribute vec4 vPosition;

varying float v_Dot;
varying vec4 v_Color;

void main()
```

```
    {
        gl_Position = u_modelViewProjMatrix * vPosition;
        v_Color = vColor;
        vec4 transNormal = u_normalMatrix * vec4(vNormal, 1);
        v_Dot = max(dot(transNormal.xyz, lightDir), 0.0);
    }
</script>
```

The following source code implements a fragment shader. It applies the texture and the lighting on each pixel of each transformed triangle:

```
<script id="fshader" type="x-shader/x-fragment">
precision mediump float;

varying float v_Dot;
varying vec4 v_Color;

void main()
{
    gl_FragColor = vec4(v_Color.xyz * v_Dot, v_Color.a);
}

</script>

<script type="text/javascript" src="./js/draw.js"></script>

</head>
```

Continue by appending the source code of the HTML body as follows. This creates a user interface with a couple of buttons through which the user controls the animation:

```
<body>
    <div data-role="page">
        <div data-role="header" data-position="fixed">
            <h1>WebGL 3D</h1>
        </div><!-- /header -->

        <div data-role="content" style="background-color:
#FFFFFF;">
            <button id="btnPlay">Play</button>
            <canvas id="screen" width="200" height="200"></canvas>
        </div><!-- /content -->

        <div data-role="footer" data-position="fixed">
            <h4>Tizen Cookbook</h4>
        </div><!-- /footer -->
    </div><!-- /page -->
</body>
</html>
```

7. Open `main.js` and register the function `run()` as a handler of the button **Play** as follows:

```
$('#btnPlay').bind( "click", function(event, ui) {
    run();
    $('#btnPlay').button( "disable" );
});
```

8. Save all changes, and run the application on a Tizen device or Emulator.

 The full source code of this project is provided with the book. The application has been successfully tested on a device with Tizen 2.2.1.

How it works...

All external JavaScript files are loaded at the head of `index.html`. The files downloaded in step 3 of the preceding tutorial provide basic functions to simplify the common usage of WebGL. Scripts for the vertex and fragment shaders are also included in `index.html` with IDs `vshareds` and `fshaders`.

A button with the ID `btnPlay` and a canvas with the ID `screen` are situated on the `div` element with the main content of the page. The canvas is used as a drawing area, and both its width and height are 200 px.

The animation starts on the click event of the button `btnPlay`, and the button becomes disabled. The entry point of the animation is the JavaScript function `run()`, which is implemented in the file `draw.js`. It initializes the WebGL context through the function `init()`, which is also implemented in the same file. Furthermore, the functions `pause()` and `resume()` are bound to the canvas events `webglcontextlost` and `webglcontextrestored`.

The current state of the rotation is stored in the global JavaScript variable, `g_nCurrentRotation`, and its initial value is 360. The rotation per single step of the animation is defined in another global JavaScript variable with the name `g_nRotationAngle`.

 Increase the value of `g_nRotationAngle` to speed up the rotation and decrease the value to slow it down.

The cube is created via the function `makeBox()`, and it is drawn on the screen using the JavaScript function `draw()`. It rotates clockwise, so on each execution of `draw()`, the angle is subtracted from the current state. When `g_nCurrentRotation` reaches a value below 0, it is set back to 360, and the animation starts all over again. The canvas is cleared at the beginning of `draw()` through the function `clear()`, and the cube is displayed via the function `drawElements()`.

The colors of the cube's sides are set at the function `setupColors()`. Edit the values of the array `colors` if you want to change the colors. The preceding example uses solid colors, but if you want, you can also set a different gradient for each side. The background color is white. It is set as a style of the page content's HTML `div` element and as an argument to the function `simpleSetup()`, which is called by the function `init()`.

See also

> ► The demo repository of Khronos Group's contains a long list of different WebGL applications. Feel free to try them with Tizen at `http://www.khronos.org/webgl/wiki/Demo_Repository`.

4

Storing Data

In this chapter, we will cover:

- ▶ Writing files
- ▶ Reading files
- ▶ Creating a simple text editor
- ▶ Downloading files
- ▶ Using web storage
- ▶ Creating Web SQL Database
- ▶ Executing queries in Web SQL Database
- ▶ Retrieving data from Web SQL Database
- ▶ Using IndexedDB

Introduction

Data management is becoming more and more important in the modern world. Billions of Internet-connected mobile and wearable devices already exist on the market. Now, the next big challenge is to improve communication and data synchronization between these devices as well as to provide better user experience. Each new mobile device model has a larger internal memory, and at the same time, the popularity of cloud services is constantly increasing. Nowadays, storing and managing information is more important than ever.

This chapter offers technical details about storing and accessing data on Tizen devices. It contains articles about file management, web storage, and Web SQL Database APIs as well as a tutorial about downloading files over the Internet.

Writing files

Files on a Tizen device can be accessed through the **Filesystem API**. The filesystem of the platform is divided into several virtual roots:

- ► `documents`
- ► `images`
- ► `videos`
- ► `music`
- ► `ringtones`
- ► `wgt-package`
- ► `wgt-private`
- ► `wgt-private-tmp`

Files located outside of any of the virtual paths from the preceding list can still be accessed from the actual root through their URI. For example, the URI of the directory `/etc/` is `file:///etc`.

The API supports four modes to open a file:

- ► `r`: This mode opens a file only for reading.
- ► `rw`: This mode opens a file for both reading and writing.
- ► `w`: This mode opens a file only for writing.
- ► `a`: This mode opens a file for writing and places the cursor at its end. The new data will be appended to the existing content of the file.

The code snippets in this recipe demonstrate how to create a text file and save data to it. Since the content of the file will not be read in these particular cases, only modes `w` and `a` are appropriate.

Getting ready

A privilege is required to save data to a file using the Filesystem API. Before you start, make sure that the following privilege has been added to the `config.xml` file of the project:

```
http://tizen.org/privilege/filesystem.write
```

How to do it...

Follow these instructions to save text to a file using the Tizen Filesystem API:

1. Use the following code snippet to prepare for file operations by obtaining an object associated with the virtual path for `documents`:

```
var documentsDir;

function onError(e) {
  console.log('error: ' + e.message);
}

function onResolveSuccess(dir) {
  documentsDir = dir;
}

tizen.filesystem.resolve('documents', onResolveSuccess,
  onError, 'w');
```

2. Execute the function `createFile()` to make an empty file. The name of the file must be passed as an argument to the function, for example, `foo.txt`:

```
try {
  documentsDir.createFile('foo.txt');
}
catch (err) {
  console.log('Unable to create file: '+err);
}
```

3. Implement a callback function that will write the text `bar` to a stream associated with the file:

```
function write(fileStream) {
  try {
    fileStream.write('bar');
    fileStream.close();
  } catch (err) {
    console.log('Unable to save file: ' + err.message);
  }
}
```

4. Open the file created in the second step to write and save data in it using the callback function implemented in the previous step, as follows:

```
try {
  file = documentsDir.resolve('foo.txt');
  file.openStream('w', write, onError);
```

```
    } catch (errWrite) {
      console.log('Unable to open file for writing: ' +
        errWrite.message);
    }
```

How it works...

The Tizen Filesystem API works asynchronously, and because of this, a lot of functions are executed through callbacks. The successful cases as well as the error cases are processed using callbacks. Do not assume that everything will work as expected, and carefully handle errors.

A global JavaScript object, `documentsDir`, is initialized at the callback function `onResolveSuccess()`. After that, the rest of the file operations are done by calling functions associated with this object. The functions `createFile()`, `resolve()`, and `openStream()` throw exceptions if any error occurs during their execution. It is important to add try-catch blocks and to handle potential exceptions properly. Please note that in this recipe, any exceptions that might occur are logged in the console. In real applications, you should integrate the error reporting with the user interface and make it user friendly.

The function `write()` saves data to a file stream and then closes it. The function works asynchronously, and it is invoked as a callback upon the successful execution of `openStream()`.

Reading files

The Tizen Filesystem API provides a couple of different ways to read a file. The primary option is using a file stream, and the alternative is to get the whole content of the file as a string through the function `readAsText()`. Both approaches work asynchronously and require a callback function for successful completion and another function for handling potential errors.

Please keep in mind that the Filesystem API is specific to Tizen, and its features must be accessed through the JavaScript object `tizen.filesystem`.

Getting ready

Before you start coding, make sure that a privilege to read files has been added to the `config.xml` file of your project as follows:

```
http://tizen.org/privilege/filesystem.read
```

How to do it...

Follow these two steps to read text from a file using a stream:

1. Prepare an object that represents the `documents` directory:

```
var documentsDir;

function onError(e) {
  console.log('error: ' + e.message);
}

function onResolveSuccess(dir) {
  documentsDir = dir;
}
tizen.filesystem.resolve('documents', onResolveSuccess,
  onError, 'w');
```

2. Use the following code snippet to read the content of a file using a stream. This approach allows us to read the file chunk by chunk, and it consumes less memory than reading the whole file at once:

```
function read(fileStream) {
  try {
    var sFileContent =
      fileStream.read(fileStream.bytesAvailable);
    console.log('file content: ' + sFileContent);
    fileStream.close();
  } catch (err) {
    console.log('Unable to read file: ' + err.message);
  }
}

function readFile()
{
  try {
    file = documentsDir.resolve('foo.txt');
  }
  catch (exc) {
    return;
  }

  try {
    file.openStream('r', read, onError);
  } catch (err) {
    console.log('Unable to open file for reading: ' +
      err.message);
  }
}
```

If you prefer to read the whole content of a text file without a stream, you should use the function `readAsText()` as shown in the following example:

```
function showFileContent(data) {
  console.log(data);
}

function readFileWithoutStream() {

  var file;
  try {
    file = documentsDir.resolve('foo.txt');
  }
  catch (err) {
    return;
  }

  try {
    file.readAsText(showFileContent, onError);
  } catch (err) {
    console.log('Error reading file without a stream:' +
      err.message);
  }
}
```

How it works...

You may have already noted that the first step for both operations, writing and reading files, is to create an object that represents the working directory. In this example, the virtual root of the used directory is `documents`.

The first approach to reading files relies on streams. Tizen provides an interface called `FileStream` that is used for both reading and writing operations.

The most important function is `openStream()`. A couple of callback functions have to be passed as its arguments. The first function will be invoked if the file content has been read successfully. In the previous example, the name of this function was `readFile()`. The second argument is a function that is invoked on an error.

The function `readFile()` receives the file stream as an argument, tries to understand the size of the available data, and then tries to read it using the function `read()` of the `FileStream` interface.

The alternative approach does not rely on streams, but it still uses callback functions that are passed as arguments to `readAsText()`. Upon successful execution, the whole data is passed to a callback function, which, in our example, is called `showFileContent()`.

Feel free to implement anonymous JavaScript functions for the callbacks if you prefer to do so.

Both the code snippets to read files with and without a stream call the same function `onError()` upon failure. In this recipe, the implementation of this callback function is very simple, as it just prints the error message to the web console.

No matter which approach to reading files you prefer, it is mandatory to include privileges to read files.

See also

▶ The next recipe contains a tutorial on how to create a simple text editor, and it will guide you step by step in the implementation of both reading and writing text files with streams in an application.

Creating a simple text editor

This recipe offers a tutorial on how to create a simple text editor based on the knowledge of writing and reading files from the previous recipes. The source code of the example application is simple and easy to understand.

The content of a text file is loaded inside `textarea` at the application's startup. The user can modify the text and, after that, save it to the same file by clicking on the **Save** button at the top of the screen.

How to do it...

Follow these steps to create a simple text editor for Tizen:

1. Launch the Tizen IDE and start a new Tizen Web Project.
2. Create a single-page application using **Tizen Web UI Framework**.
3. Open the file `config.xml` using Widget Configuration Editor and select the tab **Privileges**. Click on the **Add** button and select the following internal privileges:

   `http://tizen.org/privilege/filesystem.read`

   `http://tizen.org/privilege/filesystem.write`

4. Update the content of `index.html` to match the following code:

   ```
   <!DOCTYPE html>
   <html>

   <head>
   ```

```html
    <meta charset="utf-8"/>
    <meta name="description" content="Simple text editor for
      Tizen."/>
    <meta name="viewport" content="width=device-width,user-
      scalable=no"/>

    <link rel="stylesheet" href="tizen-web-ui-
      fw/latest/themes/tizen-white/tizen-web-ui-fw-theme.css"
      name="tizen-theme"/>
    <title>Simple Text Editor</title>
    <script src="tizen-web-ui-fw/latest/js/jquery.js"></script>
    <script src="tizen-web-ui-fw/latest/js/tizen-web-ui-fw-
      libs.js"></script>
    <script src="tizen-web-ui-fw/latest/js/tizen-web-ui-
      fw.js"
  data-framework-theme="tizen-white"></script>
  <script type="text/javascript"
      src="./js/file.js"></script>
  <script type="text/javascript"
      src="./js/main.js"></script>
    <link rel="stylesheet" type="text/css"
      href="./css/style.css"/>
</head>

<body>
  <div data-role="page">
    <div data-role="header" data-position="fixed">
      <h1>Simple Text Editor</h1>
    </div><!-- /header -->

    <div data-role="content">
      <a href="#" id="btnSave" data-role="button" data-
        icon="check">Save</a>
      <textarea id="textbox"></textarea>
    </div><!-- /content -->

    <div data-role="footer" data-position="fixed">
     <h4>Tizen Cookbook</h4>
    </div><!-- /footer -->
  </div><!-- /page -->
</body>
</html>
```

5. Right-click on the project in the **Project Explorer** view, navigate to **New** | **Other** | **JavaScript** | **JavaScript Source File**, and create the file `file.js`.

6. Open `file.js` and insert the following source code:

```
var documentsDir;

var sTxtFile = 'simpleTextFile.txt';

function onError(e) {
   console.log('error: ' + e.message);
}
```

7. Implement JavaScript functions to read and write data using file streams in the same source file. Have a look at the following code:

```
function read(fileStream) {
   try {
   $('#textbox').val(fileStream.read(fileStream.bytesAvailable
   ));
      fileStream.close();
   } catch (err) {
      console.log('Unable to read file: ' + err.message);
   }
}

function write(fileStream) {
   try {
      fileStream.write($('#textbox').val());
      fileStream.close();
   } catch (err) {
      console.log('Unable to save file: ' + err.message);
   }
}
```

8. Declare a function, `loadFile()`, that loads the content of the file inside a text area if the file exists, as follows:

```
function loadFile()
   {
   try {
      file = documentsDir.resolve(sTxtFile);
   }
   catch (exc) {
      return;
   }

   try {
```

```
      file.openStream('r', read, onError);
    } catch (err) {
      console.log('Unable to open file for reading: ' + err.
message);
    }
  }

  function onResolveSuccess(dir) {
    documentsDir = dir;
    loadFile();
  }
```

9. Append the JavaScript functions, `createFile()` and `saveFile()`, through which content is saved into the text file, as follows:

```
function createFile()
  {
    try {
      documentsDir.createFile(sTxtFile);
      file = documentsDir.resolve(sTxtFile);
  }
    catch (err) {
      console.log('Unable to create file: '+err.message);
      return false;
    }
    return true;
  }

function saveFile()
  {
    var bFileExists = true;
    try {
      file = documentsDir.resolve(sTxtFile);
    }
    catch (errFile) {
      if (false == createFile()) {
        return;
      }
    }

    try {
      file.openStream('w', write, onError);
    } catch (errWrite) {
      console.log('Unable to open file for writing: ' +
        errWrite.message);
    }
  }
```

10. Append the following code snippet to the initialization function in the file `main.js`:

```
tizen.filesystem.resolve('documents', onResolveSuccess,
    onError, 'rw');

$('#btnSave').bind( "click", function(event, ui) {
    saveFile();
});
```

11. Save all changes, build the application, and run it on the Tizen Emulator or device.

> This example uses `console.log()` to print errors that may occur during the
> execution of the application. These messages are outputted on the console
> only to simplify debugging. Please note that it is not recommended to leave
> `console.log()` in production code. It is used as a simple error handling
> technique only for this example. You can display error messages in pop ups or
> notifications instead.

How it works...

The example relies on the Tizen Filesystem API to create, read, and write a file. The privileges set in the third step are mandatory. Without them, the exception `WebAPIException` with the error type `SecurityError` will be thrown, and the application will not work as expected.

The user interface of the simple text editor has a single button and an input field. The function `loadFile()` is called at the launch of the application if the documents directory is successfully resolved. It opens `simpleTextFile.txt` as read only, asynchronously gets its content, and loads it into the text area.

The function `saveFile()` is called each time the **Save** button is clicked. It opens `simpleTextFile.txt` to write and replaces its data with the content of the HTML5 `textarea` with ID `textbox`. If the file does not exist, then `saveFile()` tries to create it by executing the function `createFile()`.

Both reading and writing of the file are achieved asynchronously through file streams and callback functions. After successful completion of the operations, the file streams are closed.

The name of the text file is stored in the global variable `sTxtFile`, which is used by all functions. The file is located in the virtual root for documents. Have a look at the following screenshot:

A simple text editor for Tizen

See also

▸ Please refer to the official documentation to find more detailed information about the Tizen Filesystem API at `https://developer.tizen.org/dev-guide/2.2.1/org.tizen.web.device.apireference/tizen/filesystem.html`.

Downloading files

Tizen provides a **Download API**, which is dedicated only to asynchronous transfer of data from the URL of a remote server to the storage of the device. This API is very flexible, but it is still easy to use. For example, the developer has the option to specify explicitly whether a cellular or a Wi-Fi connection should be used for a specific download. During the download process, the file has one of the following states: QUEUED, DOWNLOADING, PAUSED, CANCELED, COMPLETED, and FAILED.

The usage of this API will be demonstrated with an example application that downloads PNG and JPEG images and saves them to the filesystem location defined for images.

Getting ready

The privilege `http://tizen.org/privilege/download` must be granted in Tizen applications in order to use the Download API. An exception will be thrown when the function `start()` of the interface `DownloadManager` is executed if an application does not have the required privilege.

How to do it...

Create a Tizen web application to download images by performing the following steps:

1. Launch the Tizen IDE and create a new Tizen Web Project.

2. Select **Tizen Web UI Framework** and **Single Page Application** from the available options of the wizard.

3. Open the file `config.xml` using the Widget Configuration Editor, select the tab **Privileges**, and click on the **Add** button. Insert the following internal privilege:

   `http://tizen.org/privilege/download`

4. Replace the content of `index.html` with the following source code:

```
<!DOCTYPE html>
<html>

<head>
    <meta charset="utf-8"/>
    <meta name="description" content="Tizen application for
downloading PNG and JPEG images."/>
    <meta name="viewport" content="width=device-width,user-
scalable=no"/>

    <link rel="stylesheet" href="tizen-web-ui-fw/latest/themes/
tizen-white/tizen-web-ui-fw-theme.css" name="tizen-theme"/>
    <title>Image Download</title>

    <script src="tizen-web-ui-fw/latest/js/jquery.js"></script>
    <script src="tizen-web-ui-fw/latest/js/tizen-web-ui-fw-libs.
js"></script>
    <script src="tizen-web-ui-fw/latest/js/tizen-web-ui-fw.js"
        data-framework-theme="tizen-white"></script>

    <script type="text/javascript" src="./js/download.js"></
script>
    <script type="text/javascript" src="./js/main.js"></script>
    <link rel="stylesheet" type="text/css" href="./css/style.
css"/>
```

```
        </head>

        <body>
            <div data-role="page">
                <div data-role="header" data-position="fixed">
                    <h1>Image Download</h1>
                </div><!-- /header -->

                <div data-role="content">
                <label for="inputImageURL">Image URL:</label>
                <input type="text" name="inputImageURL"
                    id="inputImageURL" value="" />
            <a href="#" id="btnDownload" data-
                role="button">Download</a>
            <p id="label"></p>
                </div><!-- /content -->

                <div data-role="footer" data-position="fixed">
                    <h4>Tizen Cookbook</h4>
                </div><!-- /footer -->
            </div><!-- /page -->
        </body>
        </html>
```

5. Open the context menu of the **Project Explorer** view by right-clicking on it, navigate to **New | Other | JavaScript | JavaScript Source File**, and create the file download.js.

6. Open download.js and append the following code to it:

```
var nDownloadImageId = 0;
var bIsPause = false;

function checkFileExtension(sFilename) {
  sFileExtension =
    sFilename.split('.').pop().toLowerCase();
  var extensions = ['png', 'jpg', 'jpeg'];
  if ( -1 == extensions.indexOf(sFileExtension) )
  {
    return false;
  }
  return true;
}

function reset() {
  bIsPause = false;
  nDownloadImageId = 0;
  $('#btnDownload').text('Download');
}
```

7. Implement a listener to handle download events:

```
var listener =
{
  onprogress: function(id, receivedSize, totalSize)
  {
    var nDownloadProgress = Math.round( (receivedSize /
      totalSize) * 100);
    $('#label').text(nDownloadProgress+'% completed');
  },

  onpaused: function(id)
  {
    bIsPause = true;
    $('#btnDownload').text('Resume');
  },

  oncanceled: function(id)
  {
  },

  oncompleted: function(id, sFullPath)
  {
    $('#label').text('Image saved as: ' + sFullPath);
    nDownloadImageId = 0;
    $('#btnDownload').text('Download');
  },

  onfailed: function(id, error)
  {
    $('#label').text('Download failed: ' + error.name);
    reset();
  }
};

function handleButton() {
  if (0 == nDownloadImageId) {
    var sURL = $('#inputImageURL').val();
    if (false == checkFileExtension(sURL)) {
      throw "PNG and JPG files allowed only.";
    }
    var downloadRequest = new tizen.DownloadRequest(sURL,
      "images");
    nDownloadImageId = tizen.download.start(downloadRequest,
listener);

    $('#btnDownload').text('Pause');
```

```
    }
    else if (true == bIsPause) {
      tizen.download.resume(nDownloadImageId);
      bIsPause = false;
      $('#btnDownload').text('Resume');
    }
    else {
      tizen.download.pause(nDownloadImageId);
      $('#btnDownload').text('Pause');
    }
  }
```

8. Append the following code snippet to the initialization function in the file `main.js`:

```
$('#btnDownload').on( "click", function(event, ui) {
  try {
    handleButton();
  }
  catch(err){
    $('#label').text(err);
    reset();
  }
});
```

9. Save all changes. Build and run the application on the Tizen Emulator or device.

How it works...

When the application is launched, the user must enter the URL to an image and click on the **Download** button. The file extensions allowed are `png`, `jpg`, and `jpeg`. Other extensions are not allowed to start the download. The user can pause and resume the download by clicking on the **Download** button during the download process.

Successfully downloaded images are stored at the images virtual root, and they can be accessed directly from the Tizen default **Gallery** application.

The ID of the only button in this simple example is `btnDownload`. In the file `main.js`, its click event is associated with an anonymous function that calls `handleButton()`. The called function is implemented in the file `download.js`, and it has a different behavior depending on the state of the application.

The global variable `nDownloadImageId` stores the ID of the ongoing download. If there is no download in progress, its value is zero. The global Boolean variable `bIsPause` indicates whether the current download has been paused.

The download starts with the following two lines of code in the function `handleButton()`, and its identifier is stored as nDownloadImageId:

```
var downloadRequest = new tizen.DownloadRequest(sURL, "images");
nDownloadImageId = tizen.download.start(downloadRequest, listener);
```

The `start()` function accepts arguments as an object with details regarding the download request as well as the download callback, which is optional. The only mandatory argument of the constructor of the interface `DownloadRequest` is the URL; optionally, other parameters, such as the destination, the name of the saved file, and the type of the network connection, can be set. The download callback handles events for `onprogress()`, `onpaused()`, `oncanceled()`, `oncompleted()`, and `onfailed()`. For more details, please refer to the documentation of the interface `DownloadCallback` at `https://developer.tizen.org/dev-guide/2.2.1/org.tizen.web.device.apireference/tizen/download.html#::Download::DownloadCallback`.

See also

- ▶ Please look at the documentation of the Filesystem API to find out the most appropriate virtual paths to store the downloaded files. Storing files in suitable locations enhances the user experience, because the files will be easily located and accessed through system applications too. For example, applications for photo sharing or editing graphics look for files at the directory for images.

- ▶ More information and details about the Download API in Tizen SDK 2.2.1 are available at `https://developer.tizen.org/dev-guide/2.2.1/org.tizen.web.device.apireference/tizen/download.html`.

Using web storage

Tizen web applications can take full advantage of HTML5 web storage. The data saved in `localStorage` is stored permanently in the memory of the device, while the data stored in `sessionStorage` is kept temporarily as long as the application is running. On Tizen, the size of the session storage is unlimited, and you may store up to 5 MB of data at the local storage. Both storage types implement the interface storage, so the same methods for data manipulations are available, which are as follows:

- ▶ `key(n)`: This returns the name of the element with a position in the list of stored data that matches the number provided as an argument.

- ▶ `getItem(key)`: This returns the value that corresponds to the key passed as an argument.

- ▶ `setItem(key, value)`: This saves a key-value pair into the storage.

- ► `removeItem(key)`: This finds and removes an element from the storage with the key provided as an argument.

- ► `clear()`:This removes all key-value pairs from the storage object.

 Please note that web storage is a standard API in HTML5, so no privileges are required to use it in a Tizen application.

This recipe shows you how to create an application that stores a text note permanently using `localStorage` and how to provide an undo option using `sessionStorage`.

How to do it...

Follow this guide to create a Tizen web application that uses web storage:

1. Launch the Tizen IDE and start a new Tizen Web Project.

2. From the wizard of the new project, first choose **Tizen Web UI Framework** and then choose **Single Page Application.**

3. Open `index.html` and replace its source code with the following HTML5 code:

```
<!DOCTYPE html>
<html>

<head>
    <meta charset="utf-8"/>
    <meta name="description" content="Web storage demo app."/>
    <meta name="viewport" content="width=device-width,user-
scalable=no"/>

    <link rel="stylesheet" href="tizen-web-ui-fw/latest/themes/
tizen-white/tizen-web-ui-fw-theme.css" name="tizen-theme"/>
    <title>NoteApp</title>
    <script src="tizen-web-ui-fw/latest/js/jquery.js"></script>
    <script src="tizen-web-ui-fw/latest/js/tizen-web-ui-fw-libs.
js"></script>
    <script src="tizen-web-ui-fw/latest/js/tizen-web-ui-fw.js"
        data-framework-theme="tizen-white"></script>
    <script type="text/javascript" src="./js/storage.js"></script>
    <script type="text/javascript" src="./js/main.js"></script>
    <link rel="stylesheet" type="text/css" href="./css/style.
css"/>
</head>

<body>
```

```
    <div data-role="page">
        <div data-role="header" data-position="fixed">
            <h1>NoteApp</h1>
        </div><!-- /header -->

        <div data-role="content">
        <textarea id="textbox"></textarea>
        <a href="#" id="btnUndo" data-role="button" data-
           icon="refresh">Undo</a>
        </div><!-- /content -->

        <div data-role="footer" data-position="fixed">
            <h4>Tizen Cookbook</h4>
        </div><!-- /footer -->
    </div><!-- /page -->
</body>
</html>
```

4. Add a new JavaScript file with the name `storage.js` by right-clicking on the **Project Explorer** view, and navigate to **New | Other | JavaScript | JavaScript Source File** from the menu that appears.

5. Insert the following JavaScript functions into `storage.js`:

```
function load() {
  var content = localStorage.getItem('note');
  if (null != content) {
    $('#textbox').val(content);
  }
  $('#btnUndo').hide();
}

function save() {
  var sContent = $('#textbox').val();
  var previousVersion = localStorage.getItem('note');
  if (sContent != previousVersion) {
    sessionStorage.setItem('undo', previousVersion);
    $('#btnUndo').show();
  }
  localStorage.setItem('note', sContent);
}

function undo() {
```

```
      var content = sessionStorage.getItem('undo');
      if (null != content) {
        $('#textbox').val(content);
        localStorage.setItem('note', content);
        $('#btnUndo').hide();
      }
    }
```

6. Open `main.js` and append the following code to the initialization function:

```
load();
$('#textbox').bind('input propertychange', function() {
  save();
});
$('#btnUndo').on( "click", function(event, ui) {
  undo();
});
```

7. Save all modified files, build the application, and run it.

How it works...

The application stores data for a single note using `localStorage`. At startup of the application function, `load()` retrieves data for the key note from the persistent web storage and sets it as content of `textarea` with the ID `textbox`.

The function `save()` is executed each time the user changes the content of `textarea`. It saves the previous version of the text in `sessionStorage` with the key `undo` and the current version to `localStorage`.

When the user clicks on the button **Undo**, the value corresponding to the key `undo` at `sessionStorage` is loaded by the function `undo()`. The application supports only a single previous state, so the **Undo** button can be clicked just once. This button is hidden at application startup, and it is shown only when the option to go back is available. Have a look at the following screenshot:

A Tizen web application to save notes using web storage

Creating Web SQL Database

So far in this chapter, we have discussed storing data in text files and web storage. Now it is time to focus on relational databases. Tizen web applications support **Web SQL Database**. The underlying implementation of the Web SQL Database API in HTML5 relies on the **SQLite** database.

SQLite is written in C, and its source code is in the public domain. According to its creators, SQLite is probably the most popular SQL database in the world, as it is shipped with the majority of modern smartphones and web browsers, and it is also built in PHP.

It should be mentioned that development of the Web SQL Database API by W3C working groups stopped in 2010, because all parties involved were using SQLite and the underlying engine of the API. Since then, W3C working groups have focused on the standardization of alternative APIs, such as web storage and **Indexed Database**. In my opinion, this should not worry you too much because Tizen supports the Web SQL Database API, and, as a matter of fact, it is very convenient.

Getting ready

The Web SQL Database API supports both asynchronous and synchronous operations. Please note that all examples in this recipe, and the subsequent two recipes, are related to the same API and contain asynchronous operations only.

How to do it...

The following code snippet establishes the connection with the database `simpleTextEditor`:

```
var db = null;
var dbVersion = 1.0;
var dbName = "simpleTextEditor";
var dbDesc = "Database for a simple text editor";
var dbSize = 1024 * 1024; //1MB
try {
  db = openDatabase(dbName, dbVersion, dbDesc, dbSize);
}
catch(err) {
  console.log(err.message);
}
```

 The function `openDatabaseSync()` should be used to create a new database or open an existing database synchronously. It expects the same arguments as those for `openDatabase()`.

How it works...

The preceding code snippet tries to open a database asynchronously using the function `openDatabase()`. If the database does not exist, the function tries to create it. The mandatory arguments for `openDatabase()` are name, version, full display name (description), as well as the estimated database's size in bytes. An empty string can be passed as an argument for the version, and, in this case, the database will be opened no matter what its version is.

A callback function can be specified as an optional last argument. It will be invoked if the database is opened successfully. In the preceding example, an anonymous function that logs a message to the console has been implemented.

An exception might be thrown in the event of an error, such as a database version mismatch or security issue.

See also

▶ Please find tutorials and examples of how to execute SQL statements and how to handle the data retrieved using the Web SQL Database API in the subsequent two recipes. If you are interested in more information about the W3C specification, please visit `http://www.w3.org/TR/webdatabase/`.

Executing queries in Web SQL Database

The most important operations related to any database, including Web SQL Database, are executing SQL queries. The most frequently used SQL statements are CREATE TABLE, INSERT, UPDATE, and SELECT. Of course, SQLite, the engine behind Web SQL Database, supports a variety of other SQL statements. It should be possible to use each one of them in Tizen web applications. The full list of supported statements and syntax details about each of them can be found in the documentation available at `http://sqlite.org/lang.html`.

This recipe explains how to execute SQL queries using the Web SQL Database API in HTML5.

How to do it...

The following examples demonstrate how to execute SQL statements to create a new table and how to insert data into it:

1. Use the source code in the following sample to execute a single SQL statement:

```
function createTable() {
  db.transaction(function (transaction) {
    transaction.executeSql("CREATE TABLE IF NOT EXISTS
      tizenSimpleTextEditor (id INTEGER PRIMARY KEY,
      content TEXT)");
  });
}
```

2. Use the following source code to execute a sequence of several SQL statements with dynamically passed values:

```
function insertData() {
  db.transaction(function (transaction) {
    transaction.executeSql("INSERT INTO
      tizenSimpleTextEditor(id, content) VALUES (?, ?)",
      [1, 'foo']);
    transaction.executeSql("INSERT INTO
      tizenSimpleTextEditor(id, content) VALUES (?, ?)",
      [2,   'bar']);
  });
}
```

How it works...

Queries can be executed using a database object and the functions `transaction()`, `readTransaction()`, and `changeVersion()`. All of them invoke a callback function in which database operations are performed through the function `executeSql()`. The function accepts up to four arguments, but only the first with the SQL statement is mandatory. The optional arguments are an array with values for the SQL statement, a callback function to handle the result of the query, and a callback function to handle errors.

Pay attention to the question marks in the SQL statements, such as in the following example:

```
transaction.executeSql("INSERT INTO tizenSimpleTextEditor(id,
    content) VALUES (?, ?)", [1, 'foo']);
```

They will be automatically replaced by the values passed as an array. The special symbols at each value will also be automatically escaped. This is a convenient and safe approach that can prevent SQL errors and injections.

Exceptions are thrown in the event of database errors, which means that the functions `createTable()` and `insertData()` from the previous examples must be called within try-catch blocks.

See also

▸   Instructions on how to create an application that creates a Web SQL Database API and how to execute SQL queries is included in the next recipe.

Retrieving data from Web SQL Database

Let's develop an application that puts together everything related to the Web SQL Database API from the previous recipe and additionally demonstrates how to retrieve data.

The application is based on the simple text editor explored in a previous recipe. It has the same user interfaces, but instead of reading and writing files, its backend uses Web SQL Database.

How to do it...

Follow this tutorial to create a Tizen web application powered by Web SQL Database:

1.   Launch the Tizen IDE and start a new Tizen Web Project.

2.   From the wizard meant to create a new project, select **Tizen Web UI Framework** and **Single Page Application**.

3. Update the content of `index.html` to match the following code:

```html
<!DOCTYPE html>
<html>

<head>
  <meta charset="utf-8"/>
  <meta name="description" content="Simple text editor for Tizen
powered by Web SQL database."/>
  <meta name="viewport" content="width=device-width,user-
scalable=no"/>

  <link rel="stylesheet" href="tizen-web-ui-
    fw/latest/themes/tizen-white/tizen-web-ui-fw-theme.css"
    name="tizen-theme"/>
  <title>Web SQL Database Demo</title>
  <script src="tizen-web-ui-
    fw/latest/js/jquery.js"></script>
  <script src="tizen-web-ui-fw/latest/js/tizen-web-ui-fw-
    libs.js"></script>
  <script src="tizen-web-ui-fw/latest/js/tizen-web-ui-
    fw.js"
 data-framework-theme="tizen-white"></script>
  <script type="text/javascript" src="./js/db.js"></script>
  <script type="text/javascript" src="./js/main.js"></script>
  <link rel="stylesheet" type="text/css"
    href="./css/style.css"/>
</head>

<body>
  <div data-role="page">
    <div data-role="header" data-position="fixed">
      <h1>Web SQL Database Demo</h1>
    </div><!-- /header -->

    <div data-role="content">
      <a href="#" id="btnSave" data-role="button" data-
      icon="check">Save</a>
      <textarea id="textbox"></textarea>
    </div><!-- /content -->

    <div data-role="footer" data-position="fixed">
      <h4>Tizen Cookbook</h4>
    </div><!-- /footer -->
  </div><!-- /page -->
</body>
</html>
```

4. Go to the **Project Explorer** view, select the project, and right-click on it to open a context menu. Navigate to **New | Other | JavaScript | JavaScript Source File** to add a new file db.js to the project.

5. After that, open the file db.js and insert the following JavaScript code:

```
var db = null;
var dbTable = 'tizenSimpleTextEditor';

function openDb() {
  var dbVersion = 1.0;
  var dbName = "simpleTextEditor";
  var dbDesc = "Database for a simple text editor";
  var dbSize = 1024 * 1024; //1MB
  db = openDatabase(dbName, dbVersion, dbDesc, dbSize);
}

function retrieveData() {
  db.transaction(function (transaction) {
    transaction.executeSql("CREATE TABLE IF NOT EXISTS
      "+dbTable+" (id INTEGER PRIMARY KEY, content TEXT)");
    transaction.executeSql("SELECT content FROM "+dbTable+"
      WHERE id = ?", [1],
    function (sqlTransaction, sqlResult) {
      if (0 < sqlResult.rows.length) {
        $('#textbox').val(sqlResult.rows.item(0).content);
      }
    });
  });
}
```

The implementation of the functions load() and save() should also be placed in the same file as follows:

```
function load() {
  try {
    openDb();
    retrieveData();
  }
  catch(err) {
    alert('Unable to load data!');
    console.log('Unable to load data: '+err.message);
  }
}

function save() {
  try {
    if (null == db) {
      throw {message:"Database has not been opened."};
```

```
        }
        db.transaction(function (transaction) {
          var sTxt = $('#textbox').val();
          transaction.executeSql("REPLACE INTO "+dbTable+"(id,
            content) VALUES (?, ?)", [1, sTxt]);
        });
      }
      catch(err) {
        alert('Unable to save data!');
        console.log('Unable to save data: '+err.message);
      }
    }
```

6. Insert the following source code into the initialization function in the file `main.js`:

```
load();

$('#btnSave').bind( "click", function(event, ui) {
  save();
});
```

7. Save all changes, build the application, and run it on the Tizen Emulator or device.

How it works...

The application has exactly the same user interface and user experience as the application developed in the recipe *Creating a simple text editor*. The only difference is that the text is loaded and saved in the table `tizenSimpleTextEditor` of Web SQL Database's `simpleTextEditor`.

The database table has two columns: `id` and `content`. The type of column `id` is `INT`, and it is the primary key. The type of the other column is `TEXT`. Please note that the full list of data types in SQLite is available at `http://www.sqlite.org/datatype3.html`.

The function `load()` is called immediately after the application's launch by the initialization function at the file `main.js`. It tries to open a database and to retrieve the value of the saved text by executing the functions `openDb()` and `retrieveData()`. If the database does not exist, it will be created by the function `openDb()`.

The function `retrieveData()` creates a table `tizenSimpleTextEditor` if it does not exist, retrieves data by executing a `SELECT` statement, and handles its result in an anonymous callback function as follows:

```
function (sqlTransaction, sqlResult) {
  if (0 < sqlResult.rows.length) {
    $('#textbox').val(sqlResult.rows.item(0).content);
  }
}
```

The variable `sqlResult` is an object that contains information about the last inserted row (if any) in the property `insertId`, the number of affected rows in the property `rowsAffected`, and an array of `rows` of all returned rows. In this case, there are no inserted or affected rows because an SQL `SELECT` statement was executed. The structure of the table `tizenSimpleTextEditor` allows only a single row or no rows to be returned. If the result contains a single row, the value of its property content is shown at the HTML5 `textarea` with the ID `textbox`. A loop should be used to iterate over the returned array in other cases where the `SELECT` statement may return more than one row.

The function `save()` performs a transaction that executes a SQL `REPLACE` query to store the value of `textbox` into the database table `simpleTextEditor` with the ID 1. Please note that this table has a single row, because this is just a sample application. In real applications, you should use a database only if you have numerous records in its tables.

See also

▸ Refer to the documentation of SQLite about the syntax of the supported SQL commands at `http://sqlite.org/docs.html`.

▸ Details regarding the Web SQL Database API can be found in the latest versions of the specifications for the standard by the W3C working group from November 18, 2010 at `http://www.w3.org/TR/webdatabase/`.

Using IndexedDB

The last recipe of the chapter is dedicated to IndexedDB. These databases are integrated naturally in JavaScript, and their specifications are standardized by W3C. This implies that source code for IndexedDB will work on other web browsers and platforms with HTML5 support.

How to do it...

The following code snippets demonstrate how to store and manipulate the top goal scorers from the 2014 FIFA World Cup in an indexed database using JavaScript:

1. Create and open a database:

```
window.indexedDB = window.indexedDB || window.webkitIndexedDB;

window.IDBTransaction = window.IDBTransaction || window.
webkitIDBTransaction;
window.IDBKeyRange = window.IDBKeyRange || window.
webkitIDBKeyRange;

var db;
var request = window.indexedDB.open("FIFA2014", 1);

request.onerror = function(event) {
  console.log("error");
};

request.onsuccess = function(event) {
  db = request.result;
};
```

2. Insert initial data into the database:

```
request.onupgradeneeded = function(event) {
  var db = event.target.result;
  var objectStore = db.createObjectStore("goalscorers",
    {keyPath: "id"});
  objectStore.add({id: "1", name: "James Rodriguez",
    country: "Columbia", goals: 6});
  objectStore.add({id: "2", name: "Thomas Muller", country:
    "Germany", goals: 5});
}
```

Create a function that inserts an object into the database:

```
function addGoalscorer(nId, sName, sCountry, nGoals) {
  var req = db.transaction(["goalscorers"],
    "readwrite").objectStore("goalscorers").add({ id: nId,
    name: sName, country: sCountry, score: nGoals});
  req.onsuccess = function(event) {
    console.log("Goalscorer added.");
  };

  req.onerror = function(event) {
```

```
      alert("Unable to add a goalscorer.");
    }
  }
```

Create a function that removes an object from the database:

```
function removeGoalscorer(key) {
  var req = db.transaction(["goalscorers"],
  "readwrite").objectStore("goalscorers").delete(key);

  req.onsuccess = function(event) {
    console.log("The selected goalscorer has been
    removed.");
  };

  req.onerror = function(event){
    console.log("Unable to remove the selected
    goalscorer.");
  };
}
```

3. Create a function that reads all objects stored in an indexed database:

```
function readGoalscorers() {
  var objectStore =
    db.transaction("goalscorers").objectStore
    ("goalscorers");

  objectStore.openCursor().onsuccess = function(event) {
    var cursor = event.target.result;
    if (cursor) {
      console.log("id:" + cursor.key + " Name: " +
      cursor.value.name + "(" + cursor.value.country + "),
      goals: " + cursor.value.goals);
      cursor.continue();
    }
  };
}
```

How it works...

IndexedDB stores objects. The code snippets in this recipe insert, delete, and read objects that represent the top goal scorers from the 2014 FIFA World Cup.

The data is manipulated through the JavaScript object `db`. The database is opened using `window.indexedDB.open()`. This function will create the database if it does not exist before opening it. The first argument is the name of the database. The second argument is optional. If provided, it must be an integer value that matches the version of the database. For example, in the code snippet from the first step, the database version is set to `1`.

The event `onupgradeneeded` is triggered if a database is created or updated. According to the code snippet implemented in the second step, the first two top goal scorers will be inserted in the database immediately after its creation.

The functions `addGoalscorer()` and `removeGoalScorer()` perform transactions in the `readwrite` mode to modify the stored data. The mode of the transaction in the function `readGoalscorers()` is not explicitly specified, and the default value `readonly` is assigned to it. This function only retrieves data without making any modifications to the database, so the default mode is sufficient for it.

The code snippets in this recipe print all retrieved data of eventual errors that might occur in the console. Please note that this is a simple example to demonstrate the usage of IndexedDB. In real applications, this source code should be integrated with the GUI.

Also note that any of the functions implemented in the last three steps must be executed only after successful initialization of the `db` object.

See also

> ▸ Explore the W3C specification to learn more about the full features of IndexedDB at `http://www.w3.org/TR/IndexedDB/`.

5
Creating Multimedia Apps

In this chapter, we will cover the following recipes:

- ▸ Playing local audio files
- ▸ Playing local video files
- ▸ Launching video in an external player
- ▸ Taking a photo
- ▸ Generating linear barcodes
- ▸ Scanning linear barcodes
- ▸ Generating QR codes
- ▸ Scanning QR codes

Introduction

Multimedia capabilities are always among the most important and easily distinguishable features of smart devices. No matter what the form factor or the purpose of a Tizen device is, it will run multimedia applications if it has a graphical user interface.

This chapter will cover the most common multimedia tasks: playing audio and video files, online video streaming, working with cameras, and processing barcodes.

Playing local audio files

Several years ago, it was a real challenge to play a sound or a video on different browsers and platforms. Today, HTML5 offers us standard means for playing both audio and video files and makes the life of developers so much better.

In the first recipe of this chapter, a Tizen web application that plays an audio file will be developed using only HTML5.

Getting ready

Before you start, ensure that MP3 files are present on the Tizen device and emulator. Use the `sdb push` command to transfer a MP3 file from your development computer to the Tizen device or emulator, for example:

```
sdb push happy.mp3 /opt/usr/media/Sounds/
```

How to do it...

Perform the following steps to create a Tizen web application that plays the file that has been copied to the Tizen device or emulator:

1. Launch the Tizen IDE and create the Tizen Web project.
2. Select **Tizen Web UI Framework** and then **Single Page Application** from the wizard to create the project.
3. Replace the content of `index.html` with the following source code:

```
<!DOCTYPE html>
<html>

<head>
    <meta charset="utf-8"/>
    <meta name="description" content="Simple audio player for
Tizen"/>
    <meta name="viewport" content="width=device-width,user-
scalable=no"/>

    <link rel="stylesheet" href="tizen-web-ui-fw/latest/themes/
tizen-white/tizen-web-ui-fw-theme.css" name="tizen-theme"/>
    <title>Simple Audio Player</title>
    <script src="tizen-web-ui-fw/latest/js/jquery.js"></script>
    <script src="tizen-web-ui-fw/latest/js/tizen-web-ui-fw-libs.
js"></script>
```

```
        <script src="tizen-web-ui-fw/latest/js/tizen-web-ui-fw.js"
            data-framework-theme="tizen-white"></script>
        <script type="text/javascript" src="./js/main.js"></script>
        <link rel="stylesheet" type="text/css" href="./css/style.
css"/>
    </head>

    <body>
        <div data-role="page">
            <div data-role="header" data-position="fixed">
                <h1>Simple Audio Player</h1>
            </div><!-- /header -->
```

Please note that the URI of the audio file should be changed to match the sound file on your Tizen device or emulator.

```
            <div data-role="content">
            <audio src="file:///opt/usr/media/Sounds/happy.mp3" controls
autoplay></audio>
            </div><!-- /content -->

            <div data-role="footer" data-position="fixed">
                <h4>Tizen Cookbook</h4>
            </div><!-- /footer -->
        </div><!-- /page -->
    </body>
</html>
```

4. Save all changes.
5. Build the application and after that run it on a Tizen emulator or device.

How it works

The standard W3C HTML5 `audio` element is responsible for playing the MP3 file. A URI according to the Tizen file system rules is set as a value of the `src` attribute. The attribute `controls` adds buttons for controlling the process of sound reproduction. The last attribute `autoplay` is used to play the sound with the launch of the application.

The other available attributes that can be used with the `audio` tag are `loop`, `muted`, and `preload`. The supported audio formats are MP3, Ogg Vorbis, and WAV.

The Tizen web application used to play a local audio file

See also

▶ Details regarding the standard HTML5 audio element are available at `http://www.w3.org/TR/html5/embedded-content-0.html#the-audio-element`.

▶ It is also possible to launch audio files in an external player from the Tizen web application. Have a look at the *Launching video in an external player* recipe and try to load an audio instead of video file.

Playing local video files

Tizen provides an API for retrieving multimedia files on the local storage of the device. In this example, an application that retrieves video files using the Content API and playing them with the HTML5 element `video` will be created.

The `Content` API is responsible for the discovery of media files such as videos, audio files, photos, and other images. The following video formats are supported in Tizen web applications: 3GP, AVI, ASF, OGV, MP4, MKV, and WMV.

Getting ready

Before you start, ensure that video files are present on the device. The easiest way is to copy several videos from your computer to the Tizen device or emulator using SDB and its command `push`.

For example, the following command transfers the file `happy.mp4` from the current directory of the computer to the directory `/opt/usr/media/Videos/` of the attached Tizen device or emulator:

```
sdb push happy.mp4 /opt/usr/media/Videos/
```

Please note that new videos uploaded to the device with SDB may not appear in the content database unless you reboot the device or use the Content API to create them.

How to do it...

Perform the following steps to create a Tizen web application that retrieves and plays video files:

1. Launch the Tizen IDE.

2. Create a new Tizen Web project for **Multi Page Application** using **Tizen Web UI Framework**.

3. Open the `config.xml` file using the Widget Configuration Editor and go to the **Privileges** tab. Click on the **Add** button and select **http://tizen.org/privilege/content.read** to use this privilege.

4. Replace the content of `index.html` with the following source code:

```
<!DOCTYPE html>
<html>
<head>
    <meta charset="utf-8"/>
    <meta name="description" content="Simple video player
      for Tizen"/>
    <meta name="viewport" content="width=device-width,user-
      scalable=no"/>
    <link rel="stylesheet" href="tizen-web-ui-
      fw/latest/themes/tizen-white/tizen-web-ui-fw-
      theme.css" name="tizen-theme"/>
    <title>Simple Video Player</title>
    <script src="tizen-web-ui-
      fw/latest/js/jquery.js"></script>
    <script src="tizen-web-ui-fw/latest/js/tizen-web-ui-fw-
      libs.js"></script>
    <script src="tizen-web-ui-fw/latest/js/tizen-web-ui-
      fw.js"
```

```
                        data-framework-theme="tizen-white"></script>
        <script type="text/javascript"
          src="./js/videoManager.js"></script>
        <script type="text/javascript"
          src="./js/main.js"></script>
        <link rel="stylesheet" type="text/css"
          href="./css/style.css"/>
  </head>
  <body>
```

5. Continue by appending the following source code for the first page:

```
    <div data-role="page" id="videoManager">
        <div data-role="header" data-position="fixed">
            <h1>Simple Video Player</h1>
        </div><!-- /header -->
        <div data-role="content">
            <h2>Videos</h2>
            <ul id="listVideos" data-role="listview"></ul>
        </div><!-- /content -->
        <div data-role="footer" data-position="fixed">
            <h4>Tizen Cookbook</h4>
        </div><!-- /footer -->
    </div><!-- /page one -->
```

6. Insert the second page in the same file, as shown in the following code:

```
    <div data-role="page" id="videoPlayer">
        <div data-role="header" data-position="fixed">
            <h1>Simple Video Player</h1>
        </div><!-- /header -->
        <div data-role="content">
            <h2>Video Player</h2>
            <video id="player" width="320" height="240" src=""
controls></video>
            <p><a href="#videoManager" data-role="button">Back</
a></p>
        </div><!-- /content -->
        <div data-role="footer" data-position="fixed">
            <h4>Tizen Cookbook</h4>
        </div><!-- /footer -->
    </div><!-- /page two -->
  </body>
  </html>
```

7. Add a new JavaScript file `videoManager.js` in the `js` directory and place the following source code below it:

```javascript
function onError(response) {
  console.log( "Error: " + response.name);
}

function selectVideo(sContentURI) {
  $("#player").attr("src",sContentURI);
  $.mobile.changePage("#videoPlayer");
}

function bindClick(item, sContentURI) {
  item.bind("click", function(event) {
    selectVideo(sContentURI);
  });
}

function createListItem(sText) {
  return $('<li>').append($('<a/>', {
    'href': '#',
    'text': sText
  }));
}

function mediaItems (media) {
  if (0 == media.length) {
    $('#listVideos').append(createListItem('No data'));
  }
  else {
    for(var nVideoIter in media) {
      var listItem =
        createListItem(media[nVideoIter].title);
      bindClick(listItem, media[nVideoIter].contentURI);
      $('#listVideos').append(listItem);
    }
  }
  $('#listVideos').listview('refresh');
}

function loadVideos() {
  var filter = new tizen.AttributeFilter("type", "EXACTLY",
    "VIDEO");
  tizen.content.find(mediaItems, onError, null, filter);
}
```

8. Open `main.js` and replace the automatically generated code for handling the hardware back button in the initialization function with the following code:

```
loadVideos();

var backEvent = function(e) {
  if ( e.keyName == "back" ) {
    unregister();
  }
};
```

9. Save all changes, build, and run the application on a Tizen emulator or device.

How it works

The application contains two pages. A list of all video files available on the local storage is shown on the first page. The user can click on each video and be transferred to the second page where the video is loaded and can be played. If no videos are found, the message **No data** is displayed on the first page.

The `find()` function from the Tizen Content API is used by the `loadVideos()` function to discover the available video files. On success, the `mediaItems()` function creates a list and loads the titles of all retrieved videos. When an item of the list is clicked, the `selectVideo()` function transfers the user to the second page and loads the video.

Please pay attention to the handling of the hardware back button in the penultimate step of this recipe. A menu and back hardware buttons should be present on each Tizen mobile device. The strings `back` and `menu` have to be used to identify which hardware button has been clicked.

See also

▶ The same approach can be used to retrieve audio files. The HTML5 audio element should be used as explained in the previous recipe if an audio file should be played. Please explore the next recipe if you are interested in programmatically launching an external application for playing videos.

▶ Details regarding the standard HTML5 video tag can be found at `http://www.w3.org/TR/html5/embedded-content-0.html#the-video-element`.

▶ More information about Tizen Content API is available at `https://developer.tizen.org/dev-guide/2.2.1/org.tizen.web.device.apireference/tizen/content.html`.

Launching video in an external player

In this recipe, you will learn another approach for playing video files. This time instead of playing the video inside the current application, it will be loaded in an external player, which will be launched using the Tizen Application API.

Getting ready

As in the previous recipes, a video file has to be present on the Tizen device or emulator used for testing. Ensure that a file exists by copying a video using SDB. For example, the following command transfers the `happy.mp4` file from the computer to the targeted Tizen device:

```
sdb push happy.mp4 /opt/usr/media/Videos/
```

How to do it...

Perform the following steps to create an application that plays a video file in an external application:

1. Launch the Tizen IDE and start a new Tizen Web project.

2. From the wizard to create a new project, select **Tizen Web UI Framework** and then **Single Page Application**.

3. Open the `config.xml` file using the Widget Configuration Editor and go to the tab **Privileges**. Click on the **Add** button and select **http://tizen.org/privilege/application.launch** to use this privilege.

4. Replace the content of `index.html` with the following source code:

```
<!DOCTYPE html>
<html>

<head>
    <meta charset="utf-8"/>
    <meta name="description" content="Play video file in
      external player"/>
    <meta name="viewport" content="width=device-width,user-
      scalable=no"/>

    <link rel="stylesheet" href="tizen-web-ui-
      fw/latest/themes/tizen-white/tizen-web-ui-fw-
      theme.css" name="tizen-theme"/>
    <title>Play Video in External Player</title>
    <script src="tizen-web-ui-
      fw/latest/js/jquery.js"></script>
```

```
            <script src="tizen-web-ui-fw/latest/js/tizen-web-ui-fw-
               libs.js"></script>
            <script src="tizen-web-ui-fw/latest/js/tizen-web-ui-
               fw.js"
                data-framework-theme="tizen-white"></script>
        <script type="text/javascript"
          src="./js/videoManager.js"></script>
            <script type="text/javascript"
              src="./js/main.js"></script>
            <link rel="stylesheet" type="text/css"
               href="./css/style.css"/>
        </head>

        <body>
            <div data-role="page">
                <div data-role="header" data-position="fixed">
                    <h1>Launch External Video Player</h1>
                </div><!-- /header -->

                <div data-role="content">
              <a href="#" id="btnPlay" data-role="button">Play
              Video</a>
                </div><!-- /content -->

                <div data-role="footer" data-position="fixed">
                    <h4>Tizen Cookbook</h4>
                </div><!-- /footer -->
            </div><!-- /page -->
        </body>
        </html>
```

5. Click the right mouse button over **Project Explorer** and select **New**, then select **Other**, then **JavaScript**, and then **JavaScript Source File** to add a new JavaScript file with the name `videoManager.js`.

6. Insert the following JavaScript functions into `videoManager.js`:

```
function onSuccess() {
}

function onError(err) {
  console.log("Error: " + err.name);
}

function launchVideoPlayer() {
  var appControl = new
    tizen.ApplicationControl
    ("http://tizen.org/appcontrol/operation/view",
    "file:///opt/usr/media/Videos/happy.mp4");
```

```
tizen.application.launchAppControl(appControl, null,
    onSuccess, onError);
}
```

7. Append the following source code to the initialization function at `main.js`:

```
$('#btnPlay').on( "click", function(event, ui) {
  launchVideoPlayer();
});
```

8. Save all changes. Build the application and after that, launch the application on a Tizen emulator or device.

How it works

The previous example uses the Application API. The `launchVideoPlayer()` function launches an external application to play a video file specified by URI. Please note that the filename should match the name of a video file present on your device or emulator.

There's more...

The example in this recipe opens a video player using the operation ID `http://tizen.org/appcontrol/operation/view`. The other available options for operation ID are as follows:

▶ The `http://tizen.org/appcontrol/operation/call` operation makes a phone call to a number specified with the `tel` scheme

▶ The `http://tizen.org/appcontrol/operation/dial` operation launches the dial pad with the entered phone number specified with the `tel` scheme

▶ The `http://tizen.org/appcontrol/operation/create_content` operation creates content as a photo

▶ The `http://tizen.org/appcontrol/operation/compose` operation composes a message, for example, SMS or e-mail

▶ The `http://tizen.org/appcontrol/operation/pick` displays a list of items that return the item selected by the user

▶ The `http://tizen.org/appcontrol/operation/share` operation shares data with other applications

▶ The `http://tizen.org/appcontrol/operation/multi_share` operation shares multiple items with other applications

See also

▶ Please refer to the official documentation of the Tizen Application API for more details at `https://developer.tizen.org/dev-guide/2.2.1/org.tizen.web.device.apireference/tizen/application.html`

Taking a photo

All modern mobile devices are equipped with high-quality cameras with great capabilities for recording videos and capturing photos. In this recipe, you will learn how to create a Tizen web application for capturing and displaying images using the device's camera.

How to do it...

Perform the following steps to create a new project and to build a Tizen Web application capable of taking photos:

1. Launch the Tizen IDE and create a new Tizen Web project for **Single Page Application** using **Tizen Web UI Framework**.

2. Open the `config.xml` file with the Widget Configuration editor and select the **Privileges** tab. Click on the **Add** button and insert the **http://tizen.org/privilege/ content.read** privilege.

3. Edit `index.html` by replacing its content with the following HTML5:

```
<!DOCTYPE html>
<html>
<head>
  <meta charset="utf-8"/>
  <meta name="description" content="Simple Tizen web application
for taking photos."/>
  <meta name="viewport" content="width=device-width,user-
scalable=no"/>

  <link rel="stylesheet" href="tizen-web-ui-fw/latest/themes/
tizen-white/tizen-web-ui-fw-theme.css" name="tizen-theme"/>
  <title>Photographer</title>
  <script src="tizen-web-ui-fw/latest/js/jquery.js"></script>
  <script src="tizen-web-ui-fw/latest/js/tizen-web-ui-fw-libs.
js"></script>
  <script src="tizen-web-ui-fw/latest/js/tizen-web-ui-fw.js" data-
framework-theme="tizen-white"></script>
  <script type="text/javascript" src="./js/photographer.js"></
script>
  <script type="text/javascript" src="./js/main.js"></script>
  <link rel="stylesheet" type="text/css" href="./css/style.css"/>
</head>

<body>
```

The following HTML creates a single page with an element for capturing a photo and an image placeholder for displaying it:

```html
<div data-role="page">
  <div data-role="header" data-position="fixed">
  <h1>Photographer</h1>
</div><!-- /header -->

  <div data-role="content">
      <p><label id="labelPhoto" for="photo">Take a photo</label>
      <input id="photo" type="file" accept="image/*"
capture="camera" name="file" style="display:none;">
      </p>
      <p><img id="photoFrame" src="" width="200" /></p>
  </div><!-- /content -->

  <div data-role="footer" data-position="fixed">
      <h4>Footer content</h4>
      </div><!-- /footer -->
  </div><!-- /page -->
</body>
</html>
```

4. Go to **Project Explorer**, click the right button of the mouse and select **New,** then **Other**, then **JavaScript**, and then **JavaScript Source File**. Create a new file with the name `photographer.js`.

5. Insert the following JavaScript source code into `photographer.js`:

```javascript
function onError(response) {
  console.log( "Error: " + response.name);
}

function loadImage(media) {
  if (0 < media.length) {
    $("#photoFrame").attr("src",media[0].contentURI);
    $('#photoFrame').show();
  }
}

function findImages() {
  var filterBy = new tizen.AttributeFilter("type", "EXACTLY",
"IMAGE");
  var orderBy = new tizen.SortMode("modifiedDate", "DESC");
  tizen.content.find(loadImage, onError, null, filterBy,
   orderBy);
}
```

Modify main.js by inserting the source code below into the
initialization function:

```
$('#photoFrame').hide();

$('#photo').change(function() {
  console.log( "images saved." );
  findImages();
});
```

6. Save all files, build, and run the application on a Tizen emulator or device.

 The Tizen emulator will try to capture images using a web camera on the development computer, if one is available.

How it works

The camera is activated when the user clicks on the **Take a photo** label. After that, if the user decides to click on the back button without taking a photo, nothing will happen, but if he shoots a photo, the content of the hidden input field will be changed and the `findImages()` function will be triggered. The purpose of this function is to retrieve all images and to sort them by their modification date in descending order. The first image in the provided result set is the latest photo taken by the user. The `loadImage()` function processes the result and loads these images in the HTML5 image element with the `photoFrame` ID.

The JavaScript in the `photographer.js` file uses a Tizen Content API to retrieve the latest image, and the privilege `content.read` must be set or `WebAPIException` with the type `SecurityError` will be thrown.

There's more...

Video and audio files can be recorded in a Tizen web application in a similar way. The attribute `accept` of the HTML5 input element should be set to `video/*` to record videos. For capturing sounds, its value should be `audio/*`.

The value of the attribute `capture` in the `<input>` tag should match one of the following options: `camera`, `camcorder`, `microphone`, and `filesystem`. Please note that its default value is `filesystem` and in this mode, the user is asked to select a file from the local storage.

See also

▶ Explore the `SelfCamera` sample application shipped with the Tizen SDK to learn how to create more advanced web applications capable of displaying video stream from the front camera and capturing a photo.

Generating linear barcodes

The rest of the recipes in this chapter are dedicated to barcodes. There are two major groups of barcodes; they are as follows:

▶ **One-dimensional** (**1D**) barcodes, which contain only lines with the same height and a different width. The common 1D barcode types are Code 39, Code 128, Code 25 Interleaved 2 of 5, UPS, EAN-8, and EAN-13.

▶ **Two-dimensional** (**2D**) barcodes, which depending on their type can contain different geometric figures and patterns. The most popular 2D barcode types are QR Code, DataMatrix, and Aztec Code.

Generation and scanning are complex and specific operations depending on the type of barcode. The recommended and easiest way for implementation is to use proven third-party open source libraries.

In this recipe, you will learn how to generate one-dimensional Code 39 and Code 25 Interleaved 2 of 5 barcodes using JavaScript in Tizen web applications. The open source project, jquery-barcode, will be used because it can be easily integrated in applications created with the Tizen UI framework, which is based on jQuery Mobile and jQuery. The project is available under MIT license and can be downloaded from `https://code.google.com/p/jquery-barcode/`.

How to do it...

Perform the following steps to create a Tizen web application capable of generating linear barcodes:

1. Launch the Tizen IDE and start a new Tizen Web project for **Single Page Application** using **Tizen Web UI Framework**.

2. Append the following CSS class to the `styles.css` file, which is located in the `css` directory:

```
.barcodeImg {
  display: none;
  width:200px;
  height:50px;
  border:1px solid #003366;
}
```

3. Download the `jquery-barcode` library and save it at the `js` directory.

4. Replace the content of `index.html` with the following source code:

```
<!DOCTYPE html>
<html>
<head>
```

```
            <meta charset="utf-8"/>
            <meta name="description" content="Generate one-
                dimensional Code 39 and Code 25 Interleaved 2of 5
                barcodes"/>
            <meta name="viewport" content="width=device-width,user-
                scalable=no"/>

            <link rel="stylesheet" href="tizen-web-ui-
                fw/latest/themes/tizen-white/tizen-web-ui-fw-
                theme.css" name="tizen-theme"/>
            <title>Linear Barcode Generator</title>
            <script src="tizen-web-ui-
                fw/latest/js/jquery.js"></script>
            <script src="tizen-web-ui-fw/latest/js/tizen-web-ui-fw-
                libs.js"></script>
            <script src="tizen-web-ui-fw/latest/js/tizen-web-ui-
                fw.js"
                data-framework-theme="tizen-white"></script>
          <script src="./js/jquery.barcode.0.3.js"></script>
            <script type="text/javascript"
                src="./js/main.js"></script>
            <link rel="stylesheet" type="text/css"
                href="./css/style.css"/>
    </head>
    <body>
        <div data-role="page">
            <div data-role="header" data-position="fixed">
                <h1>Linear Barcode Generator</h1>
            </div><!-- /header -->
            <div data-role="content">
        <a href="#" id="btnCode39" data-role="button" data-
        icon="check">Code39</a>
        <div id="barcode39" class="barcodeImg">1234</div>
        <br />
        <a href="#" id="btnI25" data-role="button" data-
        icon="check">Code 25 Interleaved 2of 5</a>
        <div id="barcodeI25" class="barcodeImg">1234</div>
            </div><!-- /content -->
            <div data-role="footer" data-position="fixed">
                <h4>Tizen Cookbook</h4>
            </div><!-- /footer -->
        </div><!-- /page -->
    </body>
    </html>
Insert the source code below into to initialization
    function at main.js:
```

```
$('#btnCode39').bind( "click", function(event, ui) {
  $('#barcode39').barcode({code:'code39'});
  $('#barcode39').show();
  $('#btnCode39').hide();
});

$('#btnI25').bind( "click", function(event, ui) {
  $('#barcodeI25').barcode({code:'I25'});
  $('#barcodeI25').show();
  $('#btnI25').hide();
});
```

5. Save all changes and run the application on a Tizen emulator or device.

How it works

The application contains two buttons. Barcodes are generated upon click and the clicked button disappears. The height, the width, and the border of the barcodes are set in the `barcodeImg` CSS class.

The library jquery-barcode takes the HTML content of an element, creates a barcode based on it, and replaces it with the generated image of the barcode. Both buttons of the sample application developed in this recipe generate barcodes from the `1234` input data. In real-world applications, it is recommended to display a loading label while the barcode is being generated.

There's more...

Another useful open source JavaScript library for generation of Code 39 barcodes is called `barcode-39.js`. It is available under MIT license and it is developed by Erik Zettersten. The source code is available on GitHub at `https://github.com/erik5388/barcode-39.js`.

See also

► Check out the next recipe to learn how to read linear barcodes and retrieve data from them

Scanning linear barcodes

This recipe will show you how to read linear Code 39 barcodes in Tizen web applications. The most popular open source JavaScript library available at GitHub (at the time of the writing of this book) called `BarcodeReader` will be used. It was developed by Eddie Larsson and it supports recognition of Code 39 as well as Code 128, Code 93, and EAN-13 barcodes.

Getting ready

Insert an image with appropriate barcode at the root directory of the project. For example, the image can be generated using the examples in the previous recipe.

Download `BarcodeReader` from GitHub and insert its files into the `js` directory of your projects. For more information about BarcodeReader, refer to `https://github.com/EddieLa/BarcodeReader`.

How to do it...

Perform the following three easy steps to implement a linear barcode scanning feature based on BarcodeReader in a Tizen web application that uses the Tizen Web UI framework:

1. Insert the HTML for a barcode image (for example, with the name `code39.png`) as well as a paragraph and a button, as shown in the following code:

```
<img id="imgBarcode" src="code39.png">
<p id="labelResult"></p>
<a href="#" id="btnScan" data-role="button">Scan</a>
```

2. Place the following code before the `initialization` function of the application:

```
barcodeScanner = new Worker("js/DecoderWorker.js");
barcodeScanner.onmessage = function(e) {
  if (false == e.data.success) {
    $('#labelResult').html("Error");
    return;
  }
  var tempArray = e.data.result;
  for (var nIter = 0; nIter < tempArray.length; nIter++) {
    if(-1 == resultArray.indexOf(tempArray[nIter])) {
      console.log(tempArray[nIter]);
      resultArray.push(tempArray[nIter]);
    }
  }
  $('#labelResult').html(resultArray.join("<br />"));
};

function scanBarcode() {
  $('#labelResult').html('Please wait...');
  ctx.drawImage(document.querySelector('#imgBarcode'),
  0,0,Canvas.width,Canvas.height);
  resultArray = [];
  barcodeScanner.postMessage({pixels: ctx.getImageData(0,0,Canvas.
width,Canvas.height).data, width: Canvas.width, height: Canvas.
height, cmd: "normal"});
}
```

3. Append the following source code to the initialization function:

```
Canvas = document.createElement("canvas");
Canvas.width=320;
Canvas.height=240;
ctx = Canvas.getContext("2d");
var resultArray = [];

$('#btnScan').bind( "click", function(event, ui) {
  scanBarcode();
});
```

How it works

The barcode is read from image with the ID `imgBarcode` when the user clicks on the button with the ID `btnScan`. The image processing is started by the `scanBarcode` function and the result of the job is done by the JavaScript object, `barcodeScanner` and the `BarcodeReader` library. A web worker is used to run the script `js/DecoderWorker.js` in the background without affecting the overall performance of the application. The final result is shown in the HTML p tag with the ID `labelResult`. If the barcode cannot be recognized, the displayed value with `labelResult` will be **Error**.

A sample Tizen web application for scanning linear barcodes

> ▶ For more details, please explore the source code of the application, which is provided with other example applications of this book

Generating QR codes

Quick Response (**QR**) is the most popular type of barcode nowadays and is classified as a 2D barcode.

QR codes were invented by the Japanese corporation **DENSO**, which is part of the Toyota Group. They were first used for tracking parts in automotive manufacturing. The usage of QR codes quickly expanded to other industries because of the excellent capabilities for storing data of the format. The popularity of QR codes increased even more with the rise of smartphones with high resolution cameras.

In the next recipe, we'll discuss QR code generation in Tizen web applications using third party open source JavaScript libraries.

Getting ready

A third-party open source JavaScript library that is part of the project qrcode-generator will be used in this recipe. The source code is available on GitHub.

Add the `qrcode.js` file to the `js` directory of your Tizen web application's project. This file is available at `https://github.com/kazuhikoarase/qrcode-generator/tree/master/js`.

How to do it...

Perform the following steps to generate QR codes in your Tizen web application with JavaScript:

1. Include the JavaScript file at the head of the HTML file, as shown in the following code:

   ```
   <script type="text/javascript"
     src="./js/qrcode.js"></script>
   ```

2. Create a user interface with HTML:

   ```
   <label for="basic">Text:</label>
   <input type="text" name="name" id="inputText" value=""  />
   <a href="#" id="btnGenerateQR" data-role="button">Generate
     QR Code</a>
   <div id="barcode"></div>
   ```

3. Implement a JavaScript function that generates QR code from the text entered by the user:

```
function generateQrCode() {
  var sInput =
    $('#inputText').val().replace
    (/^[\s\u3000]+|[\s\u3000]+$/g, '');
  try {
    var barcodeQR = qrcode(4, 'M');
    barcodeQR.addData(sInput);
    barcodeQR.make();
    $('#barcode').html(barcodeQR.createImgTag(8));
  }
  catch (err){
    $('#barcode').html(err.name + ": " + err.message);
  }
}
```

4. Create a button handler that executes the JavaScript function. The recommended location of this code is inside the initialization function at main.js:

```
$('#btnGenerateQR').bind( "click", function(event, ui) {
  generateQrCode();
});
```

How it works

The generateQrCode() function takes the user input from inputText, creates a QR code, and places it at div with the barcode ID. Please note that a regular expression has been used to remove invalid characters. According to the documentation of the third party library, the type of the QR code may vary between 1 and 10. The mask pattern and the BCH code (class of cyclic redundancy check) depends on the specified type. The permitted values for the error correction level are:

▸ Low (L): Up to 7 percent of the encoded data can be restored

▸ Medium (M): Up to 15 percent of the encoded data can be restored

▸ Quartile (Q): Up to 25 percent of the encoded data can be restored

▸ High (H): Up to 30 percent of the encoded data can be restored

The purpose of the error correction level is to define how much backup data should be added to the barcode. Medium error correction has been used for the previous example.

The barcode image is created and displayed using the `createImgTag()` function. Optionally, the size of the cell and the margin can be passed as its arguments. The default value of the size is two and the default margin is four times bigger.

A Tizen Web application showing the generation QR codes

There's more...

The format of the data encoded as a QR code depends on its purpose. The previous example encodes just plain text. If you want to serialize a website, the prefix `URL` should be added. For storing a phone number inside a barcode, add the prefix `TEL`. If you want to create a QR code that stores contact information, it is highly recommended to stick to the `vcard` format.

See also

▶ A sample Tizen web application for QR code creation based on the previous tutorial is provided with this book. Please use this as a reference if you have any issues with the implementation.

Scanning QR codes

The library ZXing (pronounced *Zebra Crossing*) is so popular for Android applications that it has become a de facto standard for scanning barcodes. It is created using Java and it has been ported to several other languages and platforms. A JavaScript port of ZXing by Lazar Laszlo has been published at GitHub under the name jsqrcode. The source code of both the main project and the JavaScript port are available under Apache License Version 2.0.

Getting ready

Obtain the source code of jsqrcode and copy all JavaScript files into the js directory of your project. Download jsqrcode from `https://github.com/LazarSoft/jsqrcode`.

The next example decodes the QR code from the image with the filename qr.png. Either ensure that this image is bundled at the root directory of the project or set another location at HTML attribute src of the image.

How to do it...

Perform the following steps to integrate QR code scanning in a Tizen web application:

1. Include the JavaScript files of jsqrcode in the following order:

```
<script type="text/javascript" src="js/grid.js"></script>
<script type="text/javascript" src="js/version.js"></script>
<script type="text/javascript" src="js/detector.js"></script>
<script type="text/javascript" src="js/formatinf.js"></script>
<script type="text/javascript" src="js/errorlevel.js"></script>
<script type="text/javascript" src="js/bitmat.js"></script>
<script type="text/javascript" src="js/datablock.js"></script>
<script type="text/javascript" src="js/bmparser.js"></script>
<script type="text/javascript" src="js/datamask.js"></script>
<script type="text/javascript" src="js/rsdecoder.js"></script>
<script type="text/javascript" src="js/gf256poly.js"></script>
<script type="text/javascript" src="js/gf256.js"></script>
<script type="text/javascript" src="js/decoder.js"></script>
<script type="text/javascript" src="js/qrcode.js"></script>
<script type="text/javascript" src="js/findpat.js"></script>
<script type="text/javascript" src="js/alignpat.js"></script>
<script type="text/javascript" src="js/databr.js"></script>
```

2. Create a simple user interface using HTML, for example, the following code:

```
<img id="imgBarcode" src="qr.png">
<p id="labelResult"></p>
<a href="#" id="btnScan" data-role="button">Scan</a>
```

3. Create a button handler in the initialization function. By default this function is situated in the `main.js` file:

```
qrcode.callback = function(data) {
   $('#labelResult').html('Result: '+data); };

$('#btnScan').bind( "click", function(event, ui) {
   var sImgSrc = $('#imgBarcode').attr("src");
   qrcode.decode(sImgSrc);
});
```

> Please note that while writing this recipe, the latest version of `jsqrcode` had several minor JavaScript errors. The same errors appear when the example application for scanning QR codes provided with the book was built. Despite the issues, proceed with the packaging and testing the application because the errors do not affect QR code scanning.

How it works

The usage of `jsqrcode` for scanning QR codes from images is very simple. The user interface of the tutorial in this recipe contains three components as follows:

- ▸ An image in which the barcode that will be scanned is loaded
- ▸ A label where the data read from the QR code will be displayed
- ▸ A button that starts the scanning procedure

An anonymous function for processing the read data is set as a callback to the JavaScript object `qrcode`. The `decode()` method of the same object is called to scan the image. The file path and name of the barcode are taken from the `src` attribute of image with the ID `imgBarcode` and are provided as an argument to `decode()`.

A Tizen web application for scanning QR code from an image

See also

▶ You can create a Tizen web application that scans QR codes captured from the camera by combining the source code from this recipe with a feature for taking photos

6
Developing Social Networking Apps

In this chapter, we will cover the following recipes:

- ▸ Developing Facebook apps in Tizen
- ▸ Fetching a Facebook news feed
- ▸ Obtaining Facebook friends list
- ▸ Accessing Facebook profile information
- ▸ Reading Facebook messages
- ▸ Retrieving Facebook notifications
- ▸ Updating a Facebook status
- ▸ Filtering a Tizen news feed from Twitter
- ▸ Developing a LinkedIn app in Tizen
- ▸ Retrieving LinkedIn updates

Introduction

In less than a decade, social networks have become an essential part of modern life. Most people love social networks although it must be said that there are people who hate them. Nowadays, social networks are so popular that whether you like them or not, sooner or later, you will have to develop a social Tizen application.

New social networks evolve every day but this chapter will focus only on the most popular ones: Facebook, Twitter, and LinkedIn. At the same time, although we will not discuss it in detail, it is worth mentioning the open source social engine, `pump.io`, which powers `Identi.ca`.

While you are developing a Tizen application, please remember that different parts of the world are dominated by different social networks. A lot of networks with regional impact such as the **Russian VK (Вконтакте)** exist and integration with them should be carefully considered for applications targeting the population of specific countries. It is also important to keep in mind that some social networks are not available in certain regions. For example, in China, Facebook has not been available since 2008 and access to Twitter was blocked a year later.

The recipes in this chapter are based on the public APIs provided directly by the social networks. If you are interested in a simpler solution for authentication, you may try out third-party services such as `https://oauth.io/`.

Developing Facebook apps in Tizen

Facebook provides a powerful API for browsing and managing data. The authorization is based on OAuth 2.0. The developer must create a Facebook application and obtain an access token from the user before they can access and use their sensitive information. Each API function requires specific permissions; the Facebook user must grant privileges to the application when they start using it. Otherwise, the API will not work.

In this recipe, you will learn how to create a Facebook application and to obtain an access token using the easiest authorization grant with JavaScript.

Getting ready

The Facebook developers' portal requires you to log in with existing Facebook user credentials. It is not possible to develop a Facebook application without being registered to the social network. Before you proceed, please ensure that you have a Facebook account.

How to do it...

Perform the following steps to create a new Facebook application:

1. Visit `https://developers.facebook.com/` and log in using your Facebook credentials.

2. Select **Apps** and then select **Create a new app**, as shown in the following screenshot:

Create a new Facebook application

3. Enter **Display Name** and **Namespace**. After that, select a category and click on **Create App**, as shown in the following screenshot:

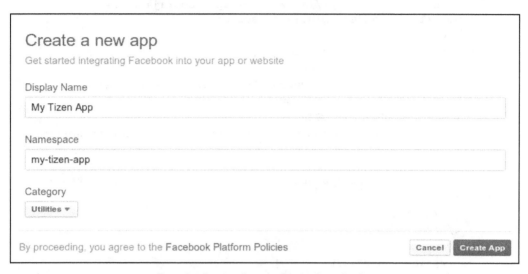

Enter details regarding your Facebook application

4. Go to **Settings** and to set **App Domains**, select a contact e-mail and select a platform.

5. When you are ready to publish your Facebook application to the general public, go to **Status & Review**, select the **On** button and confirm your choice, as shown in the following screenshot:

Releasing Facebook application to everyone

The next step is to obtain an access token from the user, which will be used in the Tizen web application. The simplest way to obtain an access token through JavaScript placed on the domain configured at the Facebook application settings requires only three steps, as follows:

1. Create an HTML file with the following source code:

```
<!DOCTYPE html>
<html lang="en">
    <head>
```

```
        <meta charset="utf-8">
        <title>Facebook Authentication</title>
        <script src="http://ajax.googleapis.com/ajax/libs/
jquery/1.11.0/jquery.min.js"></script>
        <script>
$( document ).ready(function() {
  var sDelimiter = '#access_token=';
  var nDelimiterPos = document.URL.indexOf(sDelimiter);
  var sAccessToken = 'unknown';
  if (-1 != nDelimiterPos) {
     sAccessToken = document.URL.substring(nDelimiterPos+sDelimit
er.length);
  }
  $('#token').text('Facebook access token: ' + sAccessToken);
});
        </script>
    </head>
    <body>
      <p id="token"></p>
    </body>
</html>
```

2. Provide the `https://graph.facebook.com/oauth/authorize?type=user_agent&client_id=<Facebook app ID>&redirect_uri=<Web site>&scope=<Facebook application permissions>` URL to a Facebook user, which will redirect them to your web page.

3. Replace `<Facebook app ID>`, `<Web site>`, and `<Facebook application permissions>` with appropriate values depending on the settings and the needs of your application. All permissions required by the APIs used by the application should be listed as a value of the `scope` parameter. For example, `scope=read_stream, read_mailbox`.

How it works

OAuth 2.0 is an leading industry standard authorization framework. After years of hard work and a lot of discussions, the final version of the specifications was published in October 2012 at `http://tools.ietf.org/html/rfc6749`.

OAuth enables third-party applications such as Tizen web applications to access limited resources on behalf of their owners through a web service. The Facebook Graph API implements the OAuth 2.0 standard and using it, for example, a Tizen web application can post a status update on behalf of a Facebook user. However, to do this, the Tizen web application must be registered as a Facebook application and it must have an access token, with adequate permissions, granted by the user.

Facebook still does not provide an SDK, especially for Tizen. So, the login flow demonstrated in this recipe has been built manually. Strictly following OAuth 2.0, the Facebook Graph API provides a couple of different ways to create authorization grants appropriate for Tizen web applications as follows:

- **Authorization code**: In this scenario, the Facebook application receives a code and after that, exchanges it for an access token. Details regarding this type of authorization grant are available in section 1.3.1 of OAuth 2.0 specifications and example implementations using the Facebook Graph API, provided at `https://developers.facebook.com/docs/facebook-login/manually-build-a-login-flow/`.

- **Implicit**: The implicit authorization flow is simpler but it is also less secure. An access token is directly issued and provided to the Facebook application through an HTTP redirection. This approach is specially designed for JavaScript and similar scripting languages because the Facebook application does not have to share its secret. For more information, please refer to section 1.3.2 of the OAuth 2.0 specifications.

The example in this recipe relies on the implicit authorization grant as it is implemented with JavaScript. Only the client ID, the redirect URL, and a list of required permissions are provided to the Facebook Graph API. Upon success, the API redirects the user agent back to the configured destination and the JavaScript parses the granted access token from the URL. Upon success, the access token is printed on the screen. If an error occurs, the **Facebook access token: unknown** message is displayed.

The example in this recipe assumes that the JavaScript will be placed on a website. However, it is worth mentioning that Facebook offers an alternative. Desktop applications are allowed to set the `https://www.facebook.com/connect/login_success.html` redirect URL so that it is possible to implement a solution for obtaining access tokens directly in a Tizen application.

See also

- After obtaining an access token, please refer to the subsequent recipes to learn how to use the most common features of the Graph API in the Tizen web application

- If you need more information about the Facebook login flow, please do not hesitate to read the documents on the developers' portal at `https://developers.facebook.com/docs/facebook-login`

- The list of available scopes and details regarding Facebook permissions are available at `https://developers.facebook.com/docs/facebook-login/permissions/`

Fetching a Facebook news feed

The most famous and easily recognizable feature of Facebook is its news feeds. Every user of the social network is familiar with the Facebook news feed as it contains up-to-date information from their friends, pages, and groups.

In this recipe, you will learn how to retrieve and display the news feed in a Tizen web application using the Graph API.

Getting ready

Before you start, make sure that you have a valid Facebook access token. The user must have granted the `read_stream` permission to the application in this example.

How to do it...

Perform the following steps to integrate a Facebook news feed into a Tizen web application:

1. Allow the application to access websites by adding the following line to `config.xml`:

    ```
    <access origin="*" subdomains="true"></access>
    ```

2. Initialize the JavaScript variable, `sAccessToken`, with the Facebook access token, which should be obtained as explained in the previous recipe.

3. Insert an unordered list with the ID `listFb` in the HTML of the application:

    ```
    <ul id="listFb" data-role="listview"></ul>
    ```

    Implement the following JavaScript function that executes an AJAX request to the Facebook Graph API:

    ```
    function getFacebookNewsFeed(){
      $.ajax({
        type : "GET",
        url  :'https://graph.facebook.com/me/home?access_token='
    +sAccessToken,
        success : function(data) {
          for (var nIter in data.data) {
            var sMessage = data.data[nIter].message;
            if (undefined !== sMessage) {
                var sImgSrc = 'http://graph.facebook.com/' + data.
    data[nIter].from.id + '/picture?type=square';
                var img = $( '<img>', {'src' : sImgSrc,
    'style':'float: left; padding-right: 4px;' } );
                var title = $( '<h2>' ).html(data.data[nIter].from.
    name);
                var text = $('<span>').html(sMessage);
                var listItem = $('<li>').append($( '<p>' ).append(img,
    ```

```
title, text));
        $('#listFb').append(listItem);
      }
    }
    $('#listFb').listview('refresh');
  },
  error : function() {
    var listItem = $('<li>').html("Access denied");
    $('#listFb').append(listItem);
    $('#listFb').listview('refresh');
  }
});
}
```

How it works

The application obtains the Facebook feed using the Graph API and shows only the news with text messages. The profile image and the name of the user, page, or the group is displayed next to their status.

A Tizen application retrieving a Facebook news feed

If there is an issue with the access token text, **Access denied** will be displayed on the screen.

The URL request is sent to the Facebook servers asynchronously using the jQuery function `$.ajax()`. If the news feed is retrieved successfully, a JSON is received and it is handled by the function associated with `success`. An item of the unordered list, `listFb`, is created for each page with a text message. Image, title marked with tag `h2` as well as the plain text of the messages are added as a paragraph to the list item. The Facebook profile image of the author of the status is retrieved based on their unique ID.

See also

▸ Explore the Facebook Graph API documentation to learn more about all the data provided with the news feed per user at `https://developers.facebook.com/docs/graph-api/reference/user/home/`

Obtaining Facebook friends list

Friendship is the greatest treasure, especially on Facebook. In this recipe, you will learn how to obtain a user's list of friends using an asynchronous HTTP request to Facebook Graph API. The total number of friends, the profile image, and the full name of each user will be displayed in the frontend of the sample Tizen application.

Getting ready

Obtain a valid Facebook access token before proceeding to the next example. The permission `user_friends` is required to perform a request to the Graph API regarding the user's friends.

How to do it...

Perform the following steps to integrate the algorithm for obtaining a list of Facebook friends in a Tizen web application:

1. Enable access to websites by appending the following line to `config.xml`:

   ```
   <access origin="*" subdomains="true"></access>
   ```

2. Declare the JavaScript variable `sAccessToken` and initialize it with the Facebook access token granted to the application by the user.

3. Create an HTML5 document using a Tizen Web UI Framework that includes the following code:

   ```
   <div data-role="page">
     <div data-role="header" data-position="fixed">
       <h1>Facebook Friends <span id="labelFbFriendsCount"></span></h1>
     </div><!-- /header -->
   ```

```
    <div data-role="content">
      <ul id="listFbFriends" data-role="listview"></ul>
    </div><!-- /content -->

    <div data-role="footer" data-position="fixed">
      <h4>Tizen Cookbook</h4>
    </div><!-- /footer -->
  </div><!-- /page
```

4. Create the following JavaScript functions to obtain and sort all friends of the current user:

```
function compareName(objA, objB) {
  var textA = objA.name.toLowerCase();
  var textB = objB.name.toLowerCase();
  return ((textA < textB) ? -1 : ((textA > textB) ? 1 :
    0));
}


function getFacebookFriends(){
  $.ajax({
    type : "GET",
    dataType : 'json',
    url : 'https://graph.facebook.com/me/
friends?fields=name,picture&
    access_token='+sAccessToken,
      success : function(data) {
        var friends = data.data.sort(compareName);
        for (var nIter in friends) {
          var sImg = friends[nIter].picture.data.url;
          var img = $( '<img>', {'src' : sImg,
            'style':'float: left; padding-right: 4px;' } );
          var name = $( '<h2>' ).html(friends[nIter].name);
          var listItem = $('<li>').append($( '<p>'
            ).append(img, name));
          $('#listFbFriends').append(listItem);
        }
        $('#labelFbFriendsCount').text(' ('+friends.length+')');
        $('#listFbFriends').listview('refresh');
      },
      error : function() {
          var listItem = $('<li>').html("Error");
        $('#listFbFriends').append(listItem);
        $('#listFbFriends').listview('refresh');
      }
    });
}
```

5. Execute `getFacebookFriends()` to request the list of friends.

How it works

The application retrieves a person's friends and shows them in an alphabetical order. The `getFacebookFriends()` function performs an AJAX request using jQuery to `/me/friends` of the Facebook Graph API. Only the `name` and `picture` fields per user are requested.

If the AJAX request is completed without any issues, the result is handled at the method `success`. Friends are sorted alphabetically by the JavaScript function `sort()` and the function `compareName()` that acts as comparator. A row with the profile image and the name of each user is added to the HTML5 list with the ID `listFbFriends`. Finally, the total number of friends are added to a span with the ID `labelFbFriendsCount` at the header of the page.

Please note that if the asynchronous request to Facebook Graph API fails, the **Error** message will be displayed on the screen. The request may fail due to different issues, for example, invalid access token or lack of `user_friends` permissions.

See also

▶ For details regarding the API for obtaining Facebook friends, please have a look at the Graph API documentation at `https://developers.facebook.com/docs/graph-api/reference/user/friends/`

▶ Visit `https://developers.facebook.com/docs/graph-api/reference/user/friends/` to see the full list of fields available per user.

Accessing Facebook profile information

In this recipe, we will create an example application that reads the public information of the Linux Foundation from their pages. The information is retrieved using the Facebook Graph API.

How to do it...

Perform the following steps to retrieve profile information using the Facebook Graph API and to display it in a Tizen web application:

1. Allow the application to access websites by adding the following line to `config.xml`:

```
<access origin="*" subdomains="true"></access>
```

2. Create a HTML `div` element with the ID `info`.

3. Create a JavaScript function that executes the request to Facebook:

```
function getFacebookInfo(sId)

{
  $.ajax({
```

```
        type : "GET",
        dataType : 'json',
        url :
          'https://graph.facebook.com/'+sId+'?fields=name,
          about,picture',
        success : function(data) {
          var img = $('<img>',{ 'src': data.picture.data.url,
            'style':'float: left; padding: 5px;' });
          var header = $('<h1>').text(data.name);
          var about = $('<p>').text(data.about);
          $('#info').append(img, header, about);
        },
        error : function() {
          $('#info').html('Error');
        }
      });
    }
```

4. Call the function at an appropriate place inside your source code with the ID of a page or Facebook user. For example:

```
getFacebookInfo('41911143546');
```

How it works

The application performs an asynchronous request using the Facebook user ID. The request retrieves only the name, basic information, and the photo of the selected user. These fields are public and they do not require any permission. If a problem occurs, a label with the **Error** text is shown on the screen.

The previous example source code retrieves information about the Facebook page of the Linux Foundation through its ID `41911143546`. To find the ID of another page or profile, extract its name from its URL, append it to the end of `http://graph.facebook.com/`, and retrieve the ID from the returned JSON. For example, the Facebook page of the Linux Foundation is `https://www.facebook.com/TheLinuxFoundation`; so, its name is `TheLinuxFoundation` and in this case, the URL to the Graph API should be `http://graph.facebook.com/TheLinuxFoundation`.

If you prefer to retrieve information about the current user, use `me` instead of the user ID in the URL and provide an access token. For example, the `https://graph.facebook.com/me?fields=name&access_token=` URL finds the full name of the user identified by an access token, which should be appended to its end.

Information about the Facebook page of the Linux Foundation

See also

▸ Please read the documentation provided by Facebook to learn details about the permissions and the other available fields for profiles at `https://developers.facebook.com/docs/graph-api/reference/user/`

Reading Facebook messages

Messages are another key Facebook feature that quickly become popular to all users around the world. In this recipe, we will create a sample Tizen application for browsing conversations using the Facebook Graph API.

Getting ready

Before you start with the development of the following example, please make sure that you have a valid access token granted by a Facebook user. The permission `read_mailbox` is required to perform the actions in this recipe.

How to do it...

Perform the following instructions to create a simple Tizen web application to browse Facebook messages:

1. Launch the Tizen IDE and start a new Tizen Web Project.

2. Select **Tizen Web UI Framework** and **Single Page Application** from the available options of the wizard.

3. Append the following line to `config.xml` in order to allow access to Internet sites:

```
<access origin="*" subdomains="true"></access>
```

4. Replace the content of `index.html` with the following source:

```
<!DOCTYPE html>
<html>

<head>
    <meta charset="utf-8"/>
    <meta name="description" content="Sample application
      for browsing facebook inbox."/>
    <meta name="viewport" content="width=device-width,user-
      scalable=no"/>

    <link rel="stylesheet" href="tizen-web-ui-
      fw/latest/themes/tizen-white/tizen-web-ui-fw-
      theme.css" name="tizen-theme"/>
    <title>Facebook Messages</title>

    <script src="tizen-web-ui-
      fw/latest/js/jquery.js"></script>
    <script src="tizen-web-ui-fw/latest/js/tizen-web-ui-fw-
      libs.js"></script>
    <script src="tizen-web-ui-fw/latest/js/tizen-web-ui-
      fw.js"
        data-framework-theme="tizen-white"></script>
```

5. Include an external JavaScript file with functions related to the Facebook Graph API:

```
<script type="text/javascript" src="./js/facebook.js"></script>
<script type="text/javascript"
  src="./js/main.js"></script>
<link rel="stylesheet" type="text/css"
  href="./css/style.css"/>
</head>

<body>
    <div data-role="page">
```

```
            <div data-role="header" data-position="fixed">
                <h1>Facebook Messages</h1>
            </div><!-- /header -->

            <div data-role="content">
```

6. Insert a list view and a button inside the content of the page:

```
            <ul id="listFbMessages" data-role="listview"></ul>
            <a href="#" id="btnBack" data-role="button"
            style="display: none">Back</a>
            </div><!-- /content -->

            <div data-role="footer" data-position="fixed">
                <h4>Tizen Cookbook</h4>
            </div><!-- /footer -->
        </div><!-- /page -->
</body>
</html>
```

7. Create a new file with the name `facebook.js` in the `js` directory and save the following code into it:

```
var sAccessToken = '';
```

8. Replace the value of the `sAccessToken` variable with an access token granted by a Facebook user:

```
var messages = null;

function bindListItem(obj, nIndex) {
  obj.bind("click", function(event) {
    showFacebookThread(nIndex);
  });
}

function showFacebookThread(nThreadIndex) {
  var thread = messages[nThreadIndex].comments.data;
  $('#listFbMessages').empty();
  for (var nIter in thread) {
    var name = $( '<h2>' ).html(thread[nIter].from.name);
    var message = $('<p>').html(thread[nIter].message);
    var listItem = $('<li>').append($( '<div>' ).append(name,
message));
    $('#listFbMessages').append(listItem);
  }
  $('#listFbMessages').listview('refresh');
  $('#btnBack').show();
}
```

```
function showMessages() {
  $('#btnBack').hide();
  $('#listFbMessages').empty();
  for (var nIter in messages) {
    var listItem = $('<li>').append($( '<p>'
      ).append(messages[nIter].to.data[1].name));
    bindListItem(listItem, nIter);
    $('#listFbMessages').append(listItem);
  }
  $('#listFbMessages').listview('refresh');
}
```

9. Proceed with the implementation of a JavaScript function, which makes an asynchronous request to Facebook servers:

```
function getFacebookMessages() {
  $.ajax({
    type : "GET",
    url :'https://graph.facebook.com/me/inbox?access_token='
      +sAccessToken,
    success : function(data) {
      messages = data.data;
      showMessages();
    },
    error : function() {
      var listItem = $('<li>').html("Error");
      $('#listFbMessages').append(listItem);
      $('#listFbMessages').listview('refresh');
    }
  });
}
```

10. Append the following code snippet to an initialization function in the `main.js` file:

```
getFacebookMessages();

$('#btnBack').bind("click", function(event) {
  showMessages();
});
```

11. Save all changes and run the application on a Tizen emulator or device.

How it works

The application executes an asynchronous HTTP request to Facebook servers using `jQuery.ajax()`. Because of this, a rule for accessing website should be added to the configuration file of the application as shown in step 3.

The user interface of the application consists of a list and a back button, which are created using HTML5 in `index.html`. Initially, the list is empty and the back button is hidden.

The `getFacebookMessages()` function is executed with the launch of the application. It performs the HTTP request to the Facebook servers and on success, stores the received data in variable messages. After that, it calls the `showMessages()` function, which displays the list of people with whom the user has communicated. The `bindListItem()` function associates a click with any of these people with the `showThread()` function. Facebook conversations are organized into threads; so, the purpose of the `showThread()` function is to display all messages for the selected thread in the list.

The back button has the ID `btnBack` and it is displayed after the last message. Please note that the button is shown only if the user has selected a message thread. Upon clicking on it, the function `showMessages()` is called to hide the back button and to show again the list of contacted people.

See also

▶ Have a look at the official documentation for details regarding accessing a person's inbox using the Facebook Graph API at `https://developers.facebook.com/docs/graph-api/reference/user/inbox/`

▶ If you are interested in the integration of chat capabilities inside your application, please refer to the documentation of Facebook Chat API at `https://developers.facebook.com/docs/chat/`

Retrieving Facebook notifications

The Facebook Graph API also provides an interface for managing notifications through HTTP requests. In this recipe, you will learn how to retrieve and handle Facebook notifications.

Getting ready

The source code in this recipe requires the `manage_notifications` permission. Please obtain an access token from the Facebook user, which grants this permission to your application.

How to do it...

Perform the following steps to integrate the Graph API for notifications in a Tizen web application:

1. Make sure that access to websites is permitted by adding the following line to `config.xml`:

   ```
   <access origin="*" subdomains="true"></access>
   ```

2. Initialize the JavaScript variable `sAccessToken` with a valid Facebook access token.

3. Create an unordered HTML5 list with the ID `listNotifications`:

   ```
   <ul id="listNotifications" data-role="listview"></ul>
   ```

4. Create a JavaScript function that sends an asynchronous HTTP request to Facebook servers to retrieve notifications:

   ```javascript
   function getFacebookNotifications()
   {
     $.ajax({
       type: "GET",
       url:
         'https://graph.facebook.com/me/
         notifications?access_token='+sAccessToken,
       success: function(data) {
         for(var nIter in data.data) {
           var sImgSrc = 'http://graph.facebook.com/' +
           data.data[nIter].from.id + '/picture?type=square';
           var img = $( '<img>', {'src' : sImgSrc, 'style':'float:
   left; padding-right: 4px;' } );
           var name = $( '<h2>'
             ).html(data.data[nIter].from.name);
           var text =
             $('<span>').html(data.data[nIter].title);
           var listItem = $('<li>').append($( '<p>'
             ).append(img, name, text));
           $('#listNotifications').append(listItem);
         }
         $('#listNotifications').listview('refresh');
       },
       error: function() {
         $('#listNotifications').append($('<li>').
           html("Error"));
         $('#listNotifications').listview('refresh');
       }
     });
   }
   ```

5. Call the `getFacebookNotifications()` function when you want to retrieve notifications and load them into the list.

How it works

The HTTP request for retrieving notifications and the response of the Facebook Graph API is similar to the API for the news feed. You will notice that the source code in this recipe is almost the same as for the *Fetching Facebook news feed* recipe.

The `getFacebookNotifications()` function makes an asynchronous HTTP request using `jQuery.ajax()`. On success, the result is loaded into an HTML list with ID. If an error occurs, the **Error** text is displayed in the same list.

See also

▸ Explore the Facebook Graph API documentation for more details related to notifications at `https://developers.facebook.com/docs/graph-api/reference/user/notifications/`

Updating a Facebook status

So far in this chapter, we have discussed how to get a news feed, list of friends, profile information, messages, and notifications. Now, it is time to do something more interesting. Let's post a Facebook status.

Getting ready

A valid access token is required to publish content on behalf of the user through the Facebook Graph API. According to the Facebook developer's documentation, the permission `publish_stream` has to be used when posting a message to a Facebook page. To post on the timeline of a user, the permission `publish_actions` must be used.

How to do it...

Perform the following steps to create a JavaScript function to update a Facebook status in the Tizen web application:

1. Enable access to websites by inserting the following line into `config.xml`:

   ```
   <access origin="*" subdomains="true"></access>
   ```

2. Declare a JavaScript variable, `sAccessToken`, with global scope and initialize it with a valid access token.

3. Create a JavaScript function that executes the request to Facebook:

   ```
   function updateFacebookStatus(sMessage) {
     $.ajax( {
   ```

```
    url : "https://graph.facebook.com/me/feed",
    type : "POST",
    crossDomain: true,
    data: { access_token: sAccessToken, message: sMessage },
    cache : false,
    success : function(data) {
      if ( (undefined == data) || (undefined !=
        data.error)) {
        console.log('Unable to update status');
      } else {
        console.log("Status updated");
      }
    },
    error : function(error, sStatus, exception) {
      console.log('Error: ' + error.responseText);
    }
  });
}
```

This is just a sample. If you plan to use the `updateFacebookStatus()` function in production code, please replace all `console.log()` executions with appropriate handlers.

How it works

The `updateFacebookStatus()` function performs an asynchronous HTTP POST request to publish a Facebook status on behalf of the user through the Graph API. The text of the status is provided as an argument to the function. For example, the following line will try to post the message Tizen to the timeline of the user:

```
updateFacebookStatus('Tizen');
```

The sample implementation in this recipe is connected to a GUI; so, operation statuses are printed directly onto the console. On success, the **Status updated** message will appear in the log.

See also

▸ For more information about publishing using the Facebook Graph API, please visit https://developers.facebook.com/docs/graph-api/using-graph-api/#publishing

Filtering a Tizen news feed from Twitter

In this recipe, we will conquer another popular social network. Twitter was launched in 2006 as a microblogging platform and it is famous for the limitation of 140 characters per message. The restriction of the message length has been set for compatibility with SMS.

Due to security issues, the usage of the Twitter API of custom web and mobile applications has recently become a bit harder. In this recipe, we will authenticate the user from a server-side script and the retrieved data will be passed to a Tizen web application, which will process the data using JavaScript.

Getting ready

You need a Twitter account to create an application. Please make sure that you are signed up to Twitter before you proceed.

How to do it...

Perform the following steps to create a Twitter application in less than five minutes:

1. Visit the website `https://dev.twitter.com/apps/` and log in with your Twitter credentials.

2. Click on **Create New App**.

3. Enter **Application details**, agree the developer rules, and click on **Create your Twitter application**.

 Please note that the callback URL can be left blank in our case.

4. Click on the **API Keys** tab of your application and click on **Create my access token**.

After you have successfully created a Twitter application, you can proceed with the development of a server-side application that will transfer Twitter data to a Tizen application on a mobile device. Perform the following steps to create a very simple PHP script that filters the 10 most recent tweets about #tizen:

1. Download the open source library `TwitterOAuth` from GitHub and place it on the server at `https://github.com/abraham/twitteroauth`.

2. Create a PHP script and insert the following source code into it:

```php
<?php
$sApiKey = '';
$sApiSecret = '';
```

```
$sAccessToken = '';
$sAccessTokenSecret = '';

session_start();
```

Include TwitterOAuth using the PHP built-in function `require_once()`. Please change the path if you have installed the library on a different location.

```
require_once("twitteroauth/twitteroauth/twitteroauth.php");

$twitter = new TwitterOAuth($sApiKey, $sApiSecret, $sAccessToken,
$sAccessTokenSecret);
$result = $twitter->get('https://api.twitter.com/1.1/search/
tweets.json?q=%23tizen&count=10&result_type=recent');
print json_encode($result);
?>
```

3. Assign the API key and secret key, as well as the access token and its secret key to the PHP variable on the first lines of the script.

Finally, it is time to develop a Tizen application that will read Twitter data from the PHP script and will display it to the user. Launch the Tizen IDE and create or update a new or new an existing Tizen web application by performing the following steps:

1. Enable access to your server by inserting the following line into `config.xml`:

   ```
   <access origin="*" subdomains="true"></access>
   ```

2. Create an HTML5 unordered list for displaying the tweets:

   ```
   <ul id="listTweets" data-role="listview"></ul>
   ```

3. Create a JavaScript function that retrieves data from the sever:

   ```
   function getTweets() {
     $.ajax({
       type : 'GET',
   ```

4. Replace the value of `url` with the URL of your Twitter application:

   ```
        url : 'http://anavi.org/twitter.php',
        success : function(data) {
          var tweets = jQuery.parseJSON( data );
          for(var nIter in tweets.statuses) {
            var img = $( '<img>', {'src' : tweets.statuses[nIter].
   user.profile_image_url,
       'style':'float: left; padding-right: 4px;' } );
            var title = $( '<h2>'
               ).html('@'+tweets.statuses[nIter].
             user.screen_name);
            var text = $('<span>').html(tweets.statuses[nIter].text);
   ```

```
            var listItem = $('<li>').append($( '<p>'
              ).append(img, title, text));
                $('#listTweets').append(listItem);
         }
         $('#listTweets').listview('refresh');
       },
     error : function() {
         var listItem = $('<li>').html("Error");
         $('#listTweets').append(listItem);
         $('#listTweets').listview('refresh');
       }
     });
   }
```

5. Execute the JavaScript function to populate the HTML5 list:

    ```
    getTweets();
    ```

How it works

The PHP script deployed on the server retrieves tweets about #tizen using Twitter REST API v1.1 and the open source PHP library `TwitterOAuth`. The Tizen web applications receive the data from the PHP script and display it in a list as shown in the following screenshot. If this fails, an **Error** message is displayed to the user.

A Tizen web application showing the latest tweets about #tizen

Version 1.1 of the Twitter REST API provides a variety of methods for Twitter data management. In this recipe, `search/tweets` was used to return a collection of ten recent tweets about #tizen. According to the documentation of the API, the number of returned tweets and the hash tag are defined in GET parameters count and `q` of the URL:

```
https://api.twitter.com/1.1/search/tweets.
json?q=%23tizen&count=10&result_type=recent
```

The Tizen web application grabs data using `jQuery.ajax()`, iterates over the collection of tweets, and displays the text messages as well as the username and the profile picture of the author of each tweet.

See also

> ▸ Explore the official documentation to use the full capabilities of Twitter RESP API v1.1 at `https://dev.twitter.com/docs/api/1.1`

> ▸ Details about searching tweets using the API are also available at `https://dev.twitter.com/docs/using-search` and `https://dev.twitter.com/docs/api/1.1/get/search/tweets`

Developing a LinkedIn app in Tizen

LinkedIn is the most popular professional social network. It is an excellent tool for maintaining professional contacts. Although people rarely spend as much time on LinkedIn as on Facebook or Twitter, it is still very useful.

This recipe contains a tutorial on how to create a LinkedIn application, how to use the REST API, and how to develop a server-side script for management of access tokens.

Getting ready

The authentication of the LinkedIn API is based on OAuth 2.0 and it has a lot of similarities with Facebook. The only requirement to create a LinkedIn application is to have a LinkedIn account; so, before proceeding, please ensure that you are signed up for the professional social network.

How to do it...

Please create a LinkedIn application by performing the following easy steps:

1. Visit `https://www.linkedin.com/secure/developer`.
2. Click on **Add New Application**.
3. Type in the company information and application details.

4. Configure the OAuth permissions and set a redirect URL.

5. Click on **Save**.

Create a website for retrieving access tokens. Although this can be achieved with JavaScript due to security reasons, it is recommended to rely on server-side scripting languages because the API secret must be included at the source code. The following tutorial shows a simple implementation approach with PHP:

1. Create a PHP script that corresponds to the location pointed as a redirect URL and place in it the following source code:

```php
<?php
$sApiKey = '';
$sApiSecret = '';
$sAppState = '';
$sAppRedirectUri = '';
```

2. Replace the values of the previous four PHP variables with the API key and secret key, a long unique string for state, and the configured redirect URI:

```php
$sAuthoricationCode = (isset($_GET['code'])) ?
  $_GET['code'] : '';
$sState = (isset($_GET['state'])) ? $_GET['state'] : '';
if ($sAppState != $sState) {
  die('Cross-site request forgery detected.');
}
$sUrl =
  "https://www.linkedin.com/uas/oauth2/
  accessToken?grant_type=authorization_code&redirect_uri=
  {$sAppRedirectUri}&client_id={$sApiKey}&client_secret=
  {$sApiSecret}&code={$sAuthoricationCode}";
$data = file_get_contents($sUrl);
if (FALSE === $data) {
  die('Unable to retrieve access token');
}
$data = json_decode($data);
echo 'Access token: '.$data->access_token;
?>
```

3. Provide the following URL to the user to authenticate them:

   ❑ https://www.linkedin.com/uas/oauth2/
   authorization?response_type=code&client_id=<API
   key>&scope=<application's permissions>&state=<state>&red
   irect_uri=<redirect URI>

4. Replace `<API key>` and `<redirect URI>` with the generated key, set the redirect URI, and set a unique long string for `<state>`. Provide a list of permissions required by the application as a value of `<application permission>`. The permissions are divided by commas, for example, `scope=r_basicprofile,rw_nus`.

How it works

LinkedIn authentication is based on OAuth 2.0; so, the flow for the generation of an access token contains two steps. In the first step, the PHP script obtains an authorization code. After that, during the second step, the authorization code is exchanged for an access token.

> Please note that a similar authentication flow is also supported by Facebook, although we used a simpler but less secure solution known as an implicit authorization grant in the *Developing a Facebook app in Tizen* recipe. It is possible to apply authentication with exchange of code for an access token for Facebook as well.
>
> The implicit approach is less secure because an access token is directly issued to the client. This solution is optimized for clients implemented in web browsers with JavaScript or other scripting languages. For more information about the authorization grant, please explore the following section of the proposed OAuth 2.0 standard at `http://tools.ietf.org/html/rfc6749#section-1.3`.

The example relies on PHP only because of the personal preferences of the author. Feel free to implement similar solutions with any other server-side programming language if you want. Please review the code in this example as a proof of concept and improve it if you plan to use it in production.

The OAuth 2.0 redirects the URL saved in application settings, which must match the location of the server-side script. The state parameter of the initial URL is mandatory. It acts as a protection mechanism from cross-site request forgery. Its value should be a long string of text that is hard to be guessed. If there is a mismatch of the state value, the PHP script will exit with the **Cross-site request forgery detected** message.

On success, the PHP scripts print the retrieved access token on the screen. In case of error, the **Unable to retrieve access token** message is displayed.

As shown in the following screenshot, the user must grant privileges to the LinkedIn application when they start using it. The user is informed about all permissions required by the application:

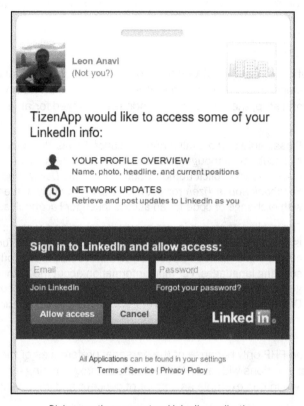

Dialog granting access to a LinkedIn application

Permissions depend on the API that will be used by the application. The full list of available programming interfaces and the permissions that they require can be viewed at `https://developer.linkedin.com/apis`.

See also

▶ LinkedIn provides a very good guide and a lot of examples about authentication to their API using OAuth 2.0. It is highly recommend that you extend the knowledge gained from this recipe by exploring the `https://developer.linkedin.com/documents/authentication` document.

Retrieving LinkedIn updates

This recipe contains an example usage of the LinkedIn REST API for retrieving shared content by the connections of the user. Instructions on how to integrate the API in a Tizen web application and to get the twenty most recent updates with shared information are included.

Getting ready

A LinkedIn application has to be created and an access token has to be obtained before proceeding with this recipe. If you have not yet created a LinkedIn application, please read the previous recipe to prepare.

How to do it...

The LinkedIn API can be integrated into a Tizen web application. For example, the following tutorial explains how to show a list of shared LinkedIn updates:

1. Allow access to websites by inserting the following line in `config.xml`:

   ```
   <access origin="*" subdomains="true"></access>
   ```

2. Place an unordered list to display LinkedIn updates in the HTML5 content of the application:

   ```
   <ul id="listUpdates" data-role="listview"></ul>
   ```

3. Implement JavaScript that retrieves data using the LinkedIn API, as shown in the following code:

   ```
   var sAccessToken = '';
   ```

   Replace the value of the previous JavaScript variable with the access token of the user:

   ```
   function showLinkedInUpdates() {
     $.ajax({
       type : 'GET',
       url :
       'https://api.linkedin.com/v1/people/~/network
       /updates?type=SHAR&count=20&oauth2_access_token=
       '+sAccessToken,
       headers : { 'x-li-format': 'json' },
       success : function(data) {
         for(var nIter in  data.values) {
           var person =
             data.values[nIter].updateContent.person;
           if (undefined != person.currentShare.content) {
             var img = $( '<img>', {'src' : person.pictureUrl,
               'style':'float: left; padding-right: 4px;' } );
   ```

```
                    var name = $( '<h2>' ).html(person.firstName + '
                      ' + person.lastName);
                    var text =
                      $('<span>').html(person.currentShare.
                      content.title+'<br
                      />'+person.currentShare.content.description+
                      '<br />'+person.currentShare.
                      content.shortenedUrl);
                    var listItem = $('<li>').append($( '<p>'
                      ).append(img, name, text));
                    $('#listUpdates').append(listItem);
                }
            }
            $('#listUpdates').listview('refresh');
          },
          error : function(data, textStatus) {
            var listItem = $('<li>').html("Error");
            $('#listUpdates').append(listItem);
            $('#listUpdates').listview('refresh');
          }
        });
    }
```

How it works

An asynchronous HTTPS request to the LinkedIn servers is performed using `jQuery.ajax()`. The URL is formatted according to the LinkedIn API documentation for share and network updates. The access token is appended to the end of the following URL:

```
'https://api.linkedin.com/v1/people/~/network/updates?type=SHAR&count
=20&oauth2_access_token='
```

The number of returned results is set as a value of the `count` parameter. The parameter type defines a filter of the updates. In this case, only sharing updates are selected. The full list of supported types is available at `https://developer.linkedin.com/documents/network-update-types`.

The `x-li-format` header is added to the HTTPS request to set JSON as the desired format of the response. If data is successfully retrieved, it is loaded in the unordered HTML5 list with ID `listUpdates`. The title, description, and the short URL of each shared item is displayed. The names of the author of the update as well as their profile image are also displayed. Otherwise, an error message is shown on the screen.

See also

▶ For all details regarding the full capabilities of the LinkedIn API for network updates and statistics, please check the official documentation at `https://developer.linkedin.com/documents/get-network-updates-and-statistics-api`

7
Managing the Address Book and Calendar

In this chapter, we will cover the following recipes:

- ▶ Retrieving all contacts
- ▶ Adding a new contact
- ▶ Deleting a contact
- ▶ Exporting a contact to vCard
- ▶ Retrieving all tasks
- ▶ Creating a new task
- ▶ Deleting a task
- ▶ Creating a new event
- ▶ Deleting an event
- ▶ Retrieving all events
- ▶ Setting an alarm

Introduction

The address book and the calendar are well-known applications on both feature phones and smartphones. Of course, Tizen is not an exception and these features and applications are built into the platform. Tizen web applications have full access to the data of these vital applications though a couple of APIs.

Tizen SDK brings Contacts and Calendar APIs to control the content of the address book and the calendar using JavaScript. Both APIs are capable of creating, updating, deleting, and reading items. Despite the powerful capabilities of the interfaces and their methods, the usage remains simple and it will be explained with a lot of examples in the following 11 recipes.

Retrieving all contacts

This recipe offers a tutorial on how to retrieve and display a list of contacts and their phone numbers using the Tizen Contacts API.

How to do it...

Perform the following steps to integrate the Contacts API in a Tizen web application and to load all contacts and their phone numbers inside an HTML5 list:

1. Add the following privilege to the `config.xml` file to allow the usage of the Contacts API:

   ❑ **http://tizen.org/privilege/contact.read**

2. Modify an appropriate HTML file of the application, for example, `index.html`, and add to it the content and an unordered list:

   ```
   <ul id="listContacts" data-role="listview"></ul>
   ```

3. Place the following source code into an existing file or create a new JavaScript file:

   ```
   function error(err) {
     var listItem = $('<li>').html('Error: '+ err.name + ':' +
       err.message);
     $('#listContacts').append(listItem);
     $('#listContacts').listview('refresh');
   }

   function showContacts(contacts) {
     $('#listContacts').empty();
     var addressBook = tizen.contact.getUnifiedAddressBook();

     for (var nIter in contacts) {
       var name = $( '<h2>' ).html(contacts[nIter].displayName);
       var contact =
         addressBook.get(contacts[nIter].displayContactId);
       var sPhones = '';
       for (var nPhoneIter in contact.phoneNumbers) {
         sPhones += contact.phoneNumbers[nPhoneIter].number +
           '<br />';
       }
       var phones = $( '<div>' ).html(sPhones);
   ```

```
        var listItem = $('<li>').append($( '<p>' ).append(name,
          phones));
        $('#listContacts').append(listItem);
      }
      $('#listContacts').listview('refresh');
    }

    function retrieveContacts() {
      try {
        tizen.contact.find(showContacts, error);
      } catch (err) {
        error(err);
      }
    }
```

4. Place a call to the JavaScript function to initialize the list with data at an appropriate state of the application, as shown in the following code:

```
retrieveContacts();
```

How it works

The JavaScript function `retrieveContacts()` invokes the `find()` method of the Tizen Contacts API and passes to it callback functions, which are triggered upon success or upon failure. The `contact.read` permission is required because without it, the operation will not be completed successfully. If a problem occurs, the previous sample implementation will display an error message in the HTML5 element with the ID `listContacts`.

List all contacts from the address book

See also

▶ Please refer to the subsequent recipes to learn how to add, update, delete, and export contacts from the address book. A project with the source code of a Tizen web application for the management of the contacts from the address book is provided with this book.

▶ Please read the documentation for more details regarding the Contacts API at `https://developer.tizen.org/dev-guide/2.2.1/org.tizen.web.device.apireference/tizen/contact.html`

Adding a new contact

The Tizen Contacts API offers a couple of different approaches for adding a new contact to the address book as well as for updating an existing contact. This recipe walks you through how to collect user details and to save them as a new contact. HTML5 is used to create a simple interface and JavaScript is used to validate user input and store the data in the address book.

Getting ready

Make sure that the following privilege has been added to `config.xml` of the Tizen web application before starting the tutorial for adding new content to the address book:

http://tizen.org/privilege/contact.write

This privilege is required by the `add()` method of the `AddressBook` interface, which saves contacts to the address book.

How to do it...

Perform the following steps to create a user interface for collecting contact details using HTML5 and to save them using JavaScript:

1. Create a page using the Tizen Web UI Framework by inserting the following HTML:

```
<div data-role="page" id="add">
  <div data-role="header" data-position="fixed">
    <h1>Add New Contact</h1>
  </div><!-- /header -->

  <div data-role="content">
    <div data-role="fieldcontain">
      <label for="contactFirstName">First name:</label>
      <input type="text" name="contactFirstName"
        id="contactFirstName" value=""  />
```

```
      </div>
      <div data-role="fieldcontain">
        <label for="contactLastName">Last name:</label>
        <input type="text" name="contactLastName"
id="contactLastName" value=""  />
      </div>
      <div data-role="fieldcontain">
        <label for="contactPhone">Phone:</label>
        <input type="tel" name="contactPhone"
          id="contactPhone" value=""  />
      </div>
      <a href="#" id="buttonSaveContact" data-
        role="button">Save</a>
      <a href="#list" data-direction="reverse" data-
        role="button">Back</a>
    </div><!-- /content -->

    <div data-role="footer" data-position="fixed">
      <h4>Tizen Cookbook</h4>
    </div><!-- /footer -->
  </div>
```

2. Create a dialog that will be displayed if any errors occur:

```
<div id="contactError" data-role="popup" class="center_info">
  <div class="ui-popup-text">
    <p id="dialogErrorText"></p>
  </div>
</div>
```

3. Implement a function that displays the dialog with some appropriate text:

```
function showErrorPopup(sMsg) {
  $('#popErrorText').text(sMsg);
  $('#contactError').popup('open');
}
```

4. Create a JavaScript function that saves the name and the phone number of a new contact:

```
function saveContact(sFirstName, sLastName, sTel) {
  var contact = new tizen.Contact(
    {name: new tizen.ContactName({firstName:sFirstName,
    lastName:sLastName}),
    phoneNumbers:[new tizen.ContactPhoneNumber(sTel)]});
  tizen.contact.getUnifiedAddressBook().add(contact);
}
```

5. In the function for initialization of the application, append the following source code:

```
$('#contactError').popup();

$('#buttonSaveContact').bind( "click", function(event, ui) {
   var sFirstName = $('#contactFirstName').val();
   var sLastName = $('#contactLastName').val();
   var sPhone = $('#contactPhone').val();
   try {
      if ( (0 == sFirstName.length) || (0 == sLastName.length) || (0
== sPhone.length) ) {
         throw new Error('Please enter a name and a phone.');
      }
      saveContact(sFirstName, sLastName, sPhone);
      $.mobile.changePage("#list");
   } catch(err) {
      showErrorPopup(err.message);
   }
});
```

 The page that was created in this recipe can be easily integrated in a Tizen web application that also contains a page with the list of all contacts. Take a look at the source code of the sample contacts application provided with this book.

How it works

The user interface implementation contains two components that are created in the first step of the tutorial: a page and a pop-up dialog. Input boxes for the first and the last name as well as for a phone number of the new contact are included on the page. The type of the input box for the phone number is set to `tel` so that a convenient keypad will be provided when the user enters information in this field. Take a look at the following screenshot. It is a screenshot that has been taken from the sample application source code, which is provided with the book.

The user interface for adding a new contact to the Tizen address book

The `saveContact()` function creates a JavaScript object from the `Contact` interface and saves it to the address book through the `add()` method of the `AddressBook` interface. In the last step of the tutorial, a code for handling buttons and initialization of the dialog is implemented. A function that validates the data and invokes `saveContact()` is bound to the button with the text `Save`. The same function catches all exceptions that may occur and displays their error messages to the user in a dialog. Upon success, the following code snippet transfers the user to the `#list` page, which has been created in the previous recipe:

```
$.mobile.changePage("#list");
```

As a consequence, the jQuery Mobile event `show` will be generated for the `#list` page. It is recommend to bind this event at the initialization of the application to a function that reloads the list of contacts, for example:

```
$('#list').bind('pageshow', retrieveContacts);
```

There's more

An alternative way to add a new contact is to create a JavaScript object from the `Contact` interface by specifying the contact details using the vCard format. For example, the following code snippet creates an object for a person with the name `Indiana Jones` and phone number `12345678` from data provided as vCard Version 3.0:

```
var contact = new tizen.Contact(
        "BEGIN:VCARD\n"+
        "VERSION:3.0\n"+
        "N:Jones;Indiana\n"+
        "FN:Indiana Jones\n"+
        "TEL;WORK:12345678\n"+
        "END:VCARD");
```

If you want to modify the contact details of a person from an address book, please use the `update()` function from the `AddressBook` interface. The usage is the same as for the `add()` function, and the JavaScript object from the `Contact` interface must be provided as an argument.

See also

▶ The example in this recipe saves only the name and a single phone number of a contact but the Tizen Contact API is not restricted only to this information. Refer to the following documentation to explore all available attributes of the Contact interface that can be saved into the address book: `https://developer.tizen.org/dev-guide/2.2.1/org.tizen.web.device.apireference/tizen/contact.html#::Contact::Contact`.

Deleting a contact

A good application has to be prepared for any apocalypse that may occur. Keep in mind that anything can happen and for example, the user might decide to delete the contact details of his ex-wife. Luckily, the Tizen Contact API is easy to use. This recipe explains how to remove a single contact or even a whole batch of contacts. It also includes a tutorial for the integration of a contact removal feature into the application developed following the instructions from the first recipe of this chapter, *Retrieving all contacts*.

Getting ready

Tizen web applications that have a feature for removing contacts from the address book must have the following privilege set in their `config.xml` file:

http://tizen.org/privilege/contact.write

The same privilege is required by the functions `remove()`, which deletes a single contact, and `removeBatch()`, which deletes several contacts at the same time.

How to do it...

Perform the following steps to improve the sample application from the previous recipe about retrieving all contacts and to delete the whole contact information of a person with a single click:

1. Launch a Tizen IDE and load the Tizen Web application to retrieve all contacts.

2. Edit `config.xml` and append the required privileges for contact removal. The following line should exist in the source of this file:

```
<tizen:privilege
  name="http://tizen.org/privilege/contact.write"/>
```

3. Create a JavaScript function that deletes a contact from the address book:

```
function deleteContact(contactId) {
    tizen.contact.getUnifiedAddressBook().remove(contactId);
}
```

4. Implement a JavaScript function that handles user selection and invokes the function created on the previous step with the ID of the selected contact:

```
function bindClick(item, contactId) {
  item.bind("click", function(event) {
    try {
      deleteContact(contactId);
      retrieveContacts();
    } catch(err) {
      showErrorPopup(err.message);
    }
  });
}
```

5. Modify the `retrieveContacts()` function and bind the click events of the list items to the handlers to delete a contact:

```
bindClick(listItem, contact.id);
```

How it works

The `bindClick()` function binds the click events to an anonymous function that tries to delete a person and all their contacts from the address book based on their ID. Upon success, the `retrieveContacts()` function is called to reload the list of all contacts. If an exception is caught, the error message will be displayed in a pop up.

To include the removal feature in the user interface of the application, you have to edit the `retrieveContacts()` function as described in the fifth step of the recipe. The `bindClick()` function expects two arguments: the object that represents the list item and the contact ID. It has to be invoked right after the creation of the list item:

```
var listItem = $('<li>').append($( '<p>' ).append(name, phones));
bindClick(listItem, contact.id);
$('#listContacts').append(listItem);
```

The Tizen Contact API provides the `remove()` function from the `AddressBook` interface for contact removal. The identifier of the contact is the only argument of this function. If the contact is not found or any other error is there, the function throws `WebAPIException`. Remember to add the exception handler anytime you use `remove()`, as shown in the previous example.

There's more

It is also possible to delete several contacts at the same time. Combining the functions `find()` and `removeBatch()` allows you to remove all contacts based on a specific filter. The following code snippet demonstrates how to delete all contacts with a specified first name:

```
function printError(err) {
   console.log('Error: '+err.message);
}

function contactsRemoved() {
   console.log('Contacts were removed');
}

function contactsFound(contacts) {
   try {
     var contactsToRemove = new Array();
     for (var nIter in contacts) {
       contactsToRemove.push(contacts[nIter].id);
     }
     addressbook.removeBatch(contactsToRemove, contactsRemoved,
printError);
   } catch (err) {
     printError(err);
   }
}

function removeAllContactsWithFirstName(sName) {
   addressbook = tizen.contact.getDefaultAddressBook();
```

```
    var filter = new tizen.AttributeFilter('name.firstName', 'CONTAINS',
  sName);
    try {
      addressbook.find(contactsFound, printError, filter);
    } catch (err) {
      printError(err);
    }
  }
```

The following example executes the function and deletes all the contacts of people with the first name `John`:

```
removeAllContactsWithFirstName('John');
```

The `contactsRemoved()` function is executed successfully. All errors that might occur are processed by the `printError()` function.

The applied instance of `AttributeFilter` is used with the matching flag `CONTAINS`, which ensures a case insensitive string comparison of the first name. The filter will select all contacts with the first name `John` as well all other names that contain John such as, Johnny. You can learn more about the filter and the other available matching flags from the official documentation at `https://developer.tizen.org/dev-guide/2.2.1/org.tizen.web.device.apireference/tizen/tizen.html#::Tizen::FilterMatchFlag`.

See also

▸ The example in this recipe depends on the source code from the previous recipes *Retrieving all contacts* and *Adding a new contact*. The source code of a sample application that combines the three recipes is provided with this book.

Exporting a contact to vCard

Have you transferred contacts to another device? Have you synchronized contacts from a mobile device with a computer or a cloud? Have you sent a contact to someone else as an e-mail or MMS? All these operations are basic for all smartphones and they require an export from the address book.

This recipe will guide you on how to serialize and export data from the address book using the Contact API for Tizen web applications.

Getting ready

The key word of this recipe is vCard. This is a standard file format for storing business card information. It appeared in the mid 90s and initially was used primarily in e-mails. Today, vCards are also used for contact data serialization on mobile devices and barcodes. Several versions of the format have been standardized: 2.1, 3.0, and 4.0.

Each vCard has a prefix of `BEGIN:VCARD` and suffix of `END:VCARD`. The version of the vCard should also be specified at the beginning of the vCard's text. The standards determine a set of predefined types such as `FN`, `TITLE`, `ADR`, and `TEL` and many more that are used to describe the full contact information. The most commonly known file extension for vCard is `.vcf`.

How to do it...

Retrieve a contact from the address book of Tizen and use the `convertToString()` function to export it, as shown in the following code snippet:

```
try {
  var vCard = contact.convertToString('VCARD_30');
  console.log(vCard);
} catch(err) {
  console.log('Error: '+err.message);
}
```

Please note that it in this case, `console.log` has been used only as a simple example. In a real application, you can do multiple things with a vCard. For example, you can share it with another application using the Tizen operation ID `http://tizen.org/appcontrol/operation/share`. The usage of this operation is similar to the one in the *Launching video in external player* recipe in *Chapter 5, Creating Multimedia Apps*.

How it works

The `convertToString()` method of the `Contact` interface has a single argument, which specifies the desired export format. It is optional. As of Tizen 2.2.1 SDK, the only supported format for export by Tizen Contacts API is vCard version 3.0 and it can be set using a string `VCARD_30`.

A sample output of an exported contact from **John Smith** with the phone number **12345678** is as follows:

```
BEGIN:VCARD
VERSION:3.0
N;CHARSET=UTF-8:Smith;John;;;
FN;CHARSET=UTF-8:John Smith
TEL;TYPE=VOICE;PREF;CHARSET=UTF-8:12345678
END:VCARD
```

Please note that the `convertToString()` function was not supported by the Tizen emulator provided with the SDK for older versions of the platforms such as Tizen 2.0 Magnolia. If you are targeting older Tizen releases, please test your application on a real device.

See also

▶ If you are interested in more information regarding the standard vCard format, you can explore the documents provided by the Internet Engineering Task Force (IETF) at `http://tools.ietf.org/html/rfc6868`

Retrieving all tasks

The Tizen calendar is capable of storing both tasks and events. This recipe as well as the subsequent two recipes are dedicated to tasks. The result of the combination of the three tutorials about finding all tasks, adding, and deleting a task is a Tizen web application for a `TO-DO` list for which source code is provided with the book.

Getting ready

The Tizen SDK provides a Tizen Calendar API for management of the tasks and events. Both of them are calendar items and share many properties. This recipe will not modify any data, so the only required privilege is `calendar.read`. The `calendar.write` privilege has to be added to applications that add, change, or remove tasks and/or events.

How to do it...

Perform the following steps to integrate the Calendar API into your Tizen web application and to show a list of all tasks:

1. Add the **http://tizen.org/privilege/calendar.read** privilege to read calendar items to the `config.xml` file of your Tizen web application.

2. Create an HTML list to display the tasks:

   ```
   <ul id="listTasks" data-role="listview"></ul>
   ```

3. Implement the following JavaScript function to retrieve and show all tasks:

   ```
   function error(err) {
       var listItem = $('<li>').html('Error: '+ err.message);
     $('#listTasks').append(listItem);
     $('#listTasks').listview('refresh');
   }
   ```

```
function showTasks(tasks) {
  $('#listTasks').empty();
  for (var nIter in tasks) {
    var taskDesc = $( '<h2>' ).html(tasks[nIter].description);
    var taskSummary = $( '<p>' ).html(tasks[nIter].summary);
    var listItem = $('<li>').append($( '<p>' ).append(taskDesc,
taskSummary));
    $('#listTasks').append(listItem);
  }
  $('#listTasks').listview('refresh');
}

function retrieveTasks() {
  try {
    tizen.calendar.getUnifiedCalendar("TASK").find(showTasks,
error);
  } catch (err) {
    error(err);
  }
}
```

4. Call the `retrieveTasks()` function to load the to-do list.

How it works

The `retrieveTasks()` function gets an aggregation of all calendars through the `getUnifiedCalendar()` function of the Calendar API on the operating system, which guarantees access to all available tasks. After that, `retrieveTasks()` calls the `find()` function and provides the functions `showTasks()` and `error()` as callbacks. Upon success, `showTasks()` iterates over an array of retrieved tasks and represents them graphically in an HTML unordered list with the ID `listTasks`, which was created in step 2. The Tizen web application created the file which includes the source code from this recipe should look just like the following screenshot:

Show all tasks

See also

▶ A lot of different features related to the calendar can be integrated in a Tizen web application. Study the documentation of the `Calendar` interface and its `find()` method to see all available options to define custom filters using an instance of `AbstractFilter` or to set ordering rules using an instance of `SortMode` at `https://developer.tizen.org/dev-guide/2.2.1/org.tizen.web.device.apireference/tizen/calendar.html#findidp349704`.

Creating a new task

The tutorial provided in this part of the chapter describes how to add a new task to a calendar. A simple user interface will be created using the Tizen Web UI framework and its purpose will be to prompt for task details. The source code in this recipe uses the Calendar API to access a calendar and store data in it.

How to do it...

Perform the following steps to create a user interface to collect details and create a new task:

1. Add a privilege for editing calendar events and tasks to `config.xml` of the application **http://tizen.org/privilege/calendar.write**.

2. Develop a user interface using HTML5 that will gather the information about the task. The following source code represents a single page created with the widgets provided by the Tizen Web UI Framework:

```
<div data-role="page" id="add">
  <div data-role="header" data-position="fixed">
    <h1>Add New Task</h1>
  </div><!-- /header -->

  <div data-role="content">
    <div data-role="fieldcontain">
      <label for="taskDesc">Description:</label>
      <input type="text" name="taskDesc" id="taskDesc"
        value=""  />
    </div>
    <div data-role="fieldcontain">
      <label for="taskSummary">Summary:</label>
      <input type="text" name="taskSummary" id="
        taskSummary" value=""  />
    </div>
    <div data-role="fieldcontain">
      <label for="taskDueDate">Due date:</label>
      <input type="date" name="taskDueDate" id="
        taskDueDate" value="" data-format="MMM dd yyyy hh:mm
          tt" value="2012-06-30T00:00:00+09:00"  />
    </div>

      <a href="#" id="buttonSaveTask" data-role="button">Save</a>
```

```
        <a href="#list" data-direction="reverse" data-
role="button">Back</a>
    </div><!-- /content -->

    <div data-role="footer" data-position="fixed">
      <h4>Tizen Cookbook</h4>
    </div><!-- /footer -->
  </div>
```

3. Implement a JavaScript function for storing tasks:

```
function showErrorPopup(sMsg) {
  $('#dialogErrorText').text(sMsg);
  $('#contactError').popup('open');
}


function saveTask(sTitle, sSummary, taskDate) {
  var task = new tizen.CalendarTask({description: sTitle,
            summary: sSummary,
            dueDate: taskDate });
  tizen.calendar.getUnifiedCalendar("TASK").add(task);
}


function clearForm() {
  $('#taskDesc').val('');
  $('#taskSummary').val('');
}
```

4. Append the following source code to the initialization function of the application:

```
$('#add').bind( "pageshow", clearForm);


$('#contactError').popup();
$("#taskDueDate").datetimepicker();


$('#buttonSaveTask').bind( "click", function(event, ui) {
  var sTaskDesc = $('#taskDesc').val();
  var sTaskSummary = $('#taskSummary').val();

  var dueDateRaw = $("#taskDueDate").datetimepicker("value");
  var dueDate = new tizen.TZDate(Date.parse(dueDateRaw));

  try {
    if ( (0 == sTaskDesc.length) || (0 == sTaskSummary.length) ) {
      throw new Error('Please set task details.');
    }
```

```
        saveTask(sTaskDesc, sTaskSummary, dueDate);
    } catch(err) {
        showErrorPopup(err.message);
    }
});
```

How it works

The user interfaces created in step 2 should look like the following screenshot:

Adding a new task to the Tizen calendar

The click event of the **Save** button is handled by a JavaScript anonymous function, which is implemented in the last step of the tutorial. This function gathers the values of entered information about a task summary, description, and date. The collected data is being validated and a `TZDate` object is constructed based on the value of the date. If the summary or the description is empty, a dialog with the error message **Please set task details** is displayed to the user.

The `saveTask()` function is called to create the new task. It obtains a JavaScript object for an aggregation of all calendars and passes an object of the type `CalendarTask` to its method `add()`.

Please note that according to the documentation, the `add()` method expects as an argument an instance of `CalendarItem`. Both interfaces `CalendarTask` and `CalendarEvent` implement `CalendarItem` so that their instances can be passed to `add()` as demonstrated in the code snippet of this recipe.

There's more...

The type of the task item in the Tizen calendar is defined by the `VTODO` format. It is also possible to create an object that represents a task using a string formatted following the rules of `VTODO`. For example:

```
var task = new tizen.CalendarTask("BEGIN:VCALENDAR\r\n" +
        "BEGIN:VTODO\r\n" +
        "DESCRIPTION:Champions league\r\n" +
        "SUMMARY:Buy tickets\r\n" +
        "DUE:20140130T134500Z\r\n" +
        "END:VTODO\r\n" +
        "END:VCALENDAR\r\n", "ICALENDAR_20");
```

See also

▶ If you need to change the details of an existing task, use the `update()` method of the `Calendar` interface and provide as an argument the object of the task that has to be modified. Other useful functions for creating or editing multiple calendar items at the same time are `addBatch()` and `updateBatch()`. Please check the documentation for details regarding any of these functions at `https://developer.tizen.org/dev-guide/2.2.1/org.tizen.web.device.apireference/tizen/calendar.html#::Calendar::Calendar`.

Deleting a task

The third and final recipe about calendar tasks in this chapter reveals how to remove an existing task.

How to do it...

Perform the following steps to implement the removal of a task upon click to the application developed following the instructions in the *Retrieving all tasks* recipe:

1. Edit `config.xml` of your Tizen web application and add the **http://tizen.org/ privilege/calendar.write** privilege, which allows the modification of calendar events.

2. Implement the JavaScript function that removes a task based on its name:

```
function deleteTask(taskId) {
    tizen.calendar.getUnifiedCalendar("TASK").remove(taskId);
}

function bindClick(item, taskId) {
    item.bind("click", function(event) {
        try {
            deleteTask(taskId);
            retrieveTasks();
        } catch(err) {
            showErrorPopup(err.message);
        }
    });
}

function showErrorPopup(sMsg) {
    $('#dialogErrorText').text(sMsg);
    $('#contactError').popup('open');
}
```

3. Connect click event upon a task with the `delete` function by appending the following line right after creation of list item in the `showTasks()` function:

```
bindClick(listItem, tasks[nIter].id);
```

How it works

The `remove()` function of the `Calendar` interface from the Calendar API is used to completely remove a task or an event from the calendar. As shown in the code snippet, the `deleteTask()` function is an aggregate instance of all available calendars on the devices are retrieved and after that the `remove()` function is executed. The ID of the task is specified as its argument.

In this recipe, the `bindClick()` function is utilized to connect a click event on any of the items of the list with the `deleteTask()` function through the `.bind()` method that is provided by jQuery.

See also

▶ The JavaScript source code for deleting a task using Calendar API in the previous example is integrated with the user interface created in the *Retrieving all tasks* recipe. Familiarize yourself with the other recipes related to the management of a calendar's tasks as well as with the official documentation of the `CalendarTask` interface at `https://developer.tizen.org/dev-guide/2.2.1/org.tizen.web.device.apireference/tizen/calendar.html#::Calendar::CalendarTask`.

Creating a new event

A couple of code snippets for adding a new event using the Tizen Calendar API are provided in this recipe. Events are described by the `CalendarEvent` interface. The interface has all the attributes of the `CalendarItem` interface as well as the additional attributes `endDate`, `availability`, and `recurrenceRule`.

Getting ready

The same functions of the Calendar API are used to add or update events and tasks. As expected, the same privilege has to be appended to the `config.xml` file of the Tizen web application, whether the application modifies events or tasks.

How to do it...

The Tizen Calendar API provides two options to add a new event. The first approach is to set the event details using JSON, as shown in the following code snippet:

```
var calendar = tizen.calendar.getUnifiedCalendar("EVENT");
var event = new tizen.CalendarEvent({description:'TuxCon',
  summary:'Conference about free and open source software',
  startDate: new tizen.TZDate(2014, 6, 28, 10, 0),
  duration: new tizen.TimeDuration(8, "HOURS"),
  location:'Plovdiv, Bulgaria'});
calendar.add(event);
```

The second approach relies on the VEVENT format. Implement and run the following source code to create an event from the string formatted following the rules of VEVENT:

```
var calendar = tizen.calendar.getUnifiedCalendar("EVENT");
var event = new tizen.CalendarEvent("BEGIN:VCALENDAR\r\n" +
    "BEGIN:VEVENT\r\n" +
    "DTSTAMP:20140422T1000Z\r\n" +
    "DTSTART:20140627T1900Z\r\n" +
    "DTEND:20140627T2330Z\r\n" +
    "SUMMARY:Friday beer event\r\n" +
    "CATEGORIES:MEETING\r\n" +
    "END:VEVENT\r\n" +
    "END:VCALENDAR", "ICALENDAR_20");
calendar.add(event);
```

See also

▶ Refer to the *Creating a new task* recipe for more information and example usage of the functions add() and update() of the Calendar interface

Deleting an event

This recipe shows how to use the remove() method provided with the Calendar API to remove an event.

Getting ready

The function used for removing events from the Tizen calendar requires the following privilege:

http://tizen.org/privilege/calendar.write

Please ensure that this privilege has been added to the configuration file of your application if it is supposed to delete events.

How to do it...

The following example implementation of the deleteEvent() function demonstrates how to remove an event for the unified calendar of Tizen:

```
function deleteEvent(nEventId) {
  try {
    var calendar = tizen.calendar.getUnifiedCalendar("EVENT");
    calendar.remove(nEventId);
```

```
  } catch (err) {
    console.log('Error: '+err.message);
  }
}
```

How it works

The usage of the `remove()` function for events is the same as for tasks. According to the documentation, the function expects an argument of the type `CalendarItemId`, which can be either `CalendarEventId` or `CalendarTaskId`. In this particular case, it must be `CalendarEventId` because the `deleteEvent()` function removes events. The `remove()` function may fail due to the wrong type of the argument, invalid identifier, security issue, missing event, or other unknown error. For each of these errors, an exception will be thrown and in the attached code snippet it will be caught and printed on the console.

See also

▶ Take another look at the *Deleting a task* recipe to see how the `remove()` function can be integrated into the user interface of a Tizen web application

Retrieving all events

This recipe provides instructions on how to find all events in your Tizen web application using the Calendar API. The provided sample code snippet is similar to the one in the recipe for retrieving all tasks. It shows how to list all events ordered alphabetically by their summary.

How to do it...

Perform the following steps to find all available events inside a Tizen web application:

1. Make sure that the application has the permission to read calendar events by adding the **http://tizen.org/privilege/calendar.read** privilege to its configuration file `config.xml`.

2. Insert an unordered list in the HTML5 content of the application:

   ```
   <ul id="listEvents" data-role="listview"></ul>
   ```

3. Implement JavaScript functions for retrieving and displaying basic information about events, as shown in the following code:

   ```
   function error(err) {
     var listItem = $('<li>').html('Error: '+ err.message);
     $('#listTasks').append(listItem);
     $('#listTasks').listview('refresh');
   }
   ```

```
function showEvents(events) {
  $('#listEvents').empty();
  for (var nIter in events) {
    var taskDesc = $( '<h2>' ).html(events[nIter].description);
    var taskSummary = $( '<p>' ).html(events[nIter].summary);
    var listItem = $('<li>').append($( '<p>' ).append(taskDesc,
taskSummary));
    $('#listEvents').append(listItem);
    deleteEvent(events[nIter].id);
  }
  $('#listEvents').listview('refresh');
}

function retrieveEvents() {
  try {
    var sort = new tizen.SortMode('summary', 'ASC');
    tizen.calendar.getUnifiedCalendar("EVENT").find(showEvents,
error, null, sort);
  } catch (err) {
    error(err);
  }
}
```

4. Execute the function at an appropriate moment, for example, at application startup using the following single line of code:

```
retrieveEvents();
```

How it works

The behavior of the Calendar API for retrieving events is almost the same as for tasks. As you can see, the names of the functions and variables in this recipe are similar to the ones from the *Retrieving all tasks* recipe.

The `retrieveEvents()` function gets a unified calendar and sorts events by their summary in ascending order. The callback functions `showEvents()` and `error()` are passed as the first and the second argument to the `find()` function. The other two arguments are optional. Null is passed as the third argument because all events should be retrieved. If you want to retrieve a subset of events based on any kind of criteria, please provide an instance of the `AbstractFilter` interface instead of `null`. Additionally, an object constructed from the `SortMode` interface defines the sorting properties.

Upon success, an array of the retrieved calendar events is passed to the `showEvents()` function, which loads their description and summary into the HTML5 unordered list with the ID `listEvents`. If a problem occurs, details about it are displayed in the same list by the `error()` function.

See also

▶ Have a look at the official documentation to study all the available attributes of each event that are specified by the `CalendarEvent` interface and the interface that it inherits `CalendarItem` at `https://developer.tizen.org/dev-guide/2.2.1/org.tizen.web.device.apireference/tizen/calendar.html`

Setting an alarm

The Tizen Calendar API allows developers to assign alarms to tasks and events. In this recipe, you will learn how to construct objects of the `CalendarAlarm` interface and how to use them.

Getting ready

Tizen web applications that set an alarm should have the `calendar.write` privilege. If the application has to find an existing calendar item and update its alarm, then the `calendar.read` privilege is also required. In this case, edit `config.xml` and add both the following privileges to ensure the application works properly:

▶ `http://tizen.org/privilege/calendar.read`

▶ `http://tizen.org/privilege/calendar.write`

How to do it...

Use the following code snippet to create an alarm using an absolute date and time:

```
var alarmDate = new tizen.TZDate(2014, 9, 24, 8, 0, 0);
var alarm = new tizen.CalendarAlarm(alarmDate, "SOUND", "Reminder: Buy
gifts!");
```

Alternatively, you can create an alarm using a relative time duration before the occurrence of an event or the due date of a task, for example:

```
var alarm = new tizen.CalendarAlarm(new tizen.TimeDuration(2,
"HOURS"), "DISPLAY", "Reminder: meeting in two hour!");
```

The alarm has to be attached to the attribute of an event or tasks. For example, an instance of `CalendarAlarm` named `alarm` can be assigned to an instance of `CalendarEvent` named `event`, as shown in the following code:

```
event.alarms = [alarm];
calendar.update(event);
```

How it works

As shown in this recipe, the Calendar API offers two different ways to create an instance of the interface `CalendarAlarm`. In the first example, an absolute value for date and time is provided as the `TZDate` object to the constructor of the `alarmDate` object. The second example defines a time duration before the event using an instance of the `TimeDuration` interface when a reminder should be triggered.

The notification method must also be explicitly specified as an argument of the constructor of `CalendarAlarm`. The available options are as follows:

 ▸ `SOUND`: The user is notified with a sound alarm

 ▸ `DISPLAY`: This shows a message on the screen of the device without playing any sound

A string with a description can be provided as an optional argument upon the creation of an alarm.

See also

 ▸ It is recommended that you have a look at the *Creating a new task* and *Creating a new event* recipes in this chapter. A good idea for a practical exercise is to develop Tizen web applications, which sets an alarm along with the creation of a calendar item.

 ▸ For full specifications of the interface `CalendarAlarm`, have a look at `https://developer.tizen.org/dev-guide/2.2.1/org.tizen.web.device.apireference/tizen/calendar.html#::Calendar::CalendarAlarm`.

8
Communication

In this chapter, we will cover the following recipes:

- ▸ Sending SMS messages
- ▸ Sending e-mail messages
- ▸ Receiving and displaying e-mail messages
- ▸ Browsing call history
- ▸ Using Bluetooth
- ▸ Using NFC and detecting other devices
- ▸ Sending NDEF messages
- ▸ Receiving NDEF messages
- ▸ Receiving push notifications

Introduction

Modern telecommunication technologies offer a rich set of wireless standards for data exchange. The recipes in this chapter will guide you on how to utilize Tizen APIs to create Tizen web applications that communicate over different channels using a variety of network bearers.

Each recipe provides simple examples. No source code for fancy user interfaces is included in any of the recipes, and the emphasis is on the usage of the APIs.

Sending SMS messages

The first SMS was sent in England on 3rd December 1992 by the software programmer Neil Papworth. Since then, the SMS has become the most popular text messaging service, and, nowadays, it is available for both feature and smartphones.

Due to historical reasons, I believe that SMS deserves the honor of being the first discussed communicational channel in this chapter of the book. In this recipe, you will learn how to use the Messaging API in Tizen web applications to send SMS messages.

Getting ready

The Messaging API provides tools to manage e-mails as well as messages transferred through telecommunication protocols, such as SMS and MMS. Tizen web applications that utilize it require additional privileges depending on the methods used. Two types of privileges have been defined based on the operations performed by the methods of the API, `http://tizen.org/privilege/messaging.read` to find messages and conversations as well as for listener settings related to messaging and `http://tizen.org/privilege/messaging.write` for any other operations, such as synchronization, sending and removing messages, and so on.

How to do it...

Perform the following steps to implement a JavaScript function to send SMS messages:

1. Edit the `config.xml` file, and append the following privilege:

   ```
   http://tizen.org/privilege/messaging.write
   ```

2. Create a global JavaScript object to store message details as follows:

   ```
   var message = { plainBody: "", to: [] };
   ```

3. Create the following callback functions:

   ```
   function logError(err) {
      console.log("Error: " + err.message);
   }

   function sentOK(recipients)
   {
     for (var nIter in recipients) {
       console.log("Message sent to " + recipients[nIter]);
     }
   }

   function retrieveServices(services) {
      var msg = new tizen.Message("messaging.sms", message);
      services[0].sendMessage(msg, sentOK, logError);
   }
   ```

4. Implement the function to send a text message to a single phone number as follows:

```
function sendSMS(sTxt, sPhone) {
  message.plainBody = sTxt;
  message.to.push(sPhone);
  tizen.messaging.getMessageServices("messaging.sms",
retrieveServices, logError);
}
```

5. Execute the function `sendSMS()` when you want to send a text message to a single recipient by specifying their phone number:

```
sendSMS("Hello", "12345678");
```

How it works...

The function `sendSMS()` gets as arguments a text message and a phone number and stores it in the global JavaScript object `message`. The text of the message is set in the attribute `plainBody` of the object `message`, and the phone number is saved as the first element of the attribute to which it is an array. After that, `sendSMS()` invokes the method `getMessageServices()` of the Messaging API and sets the functions, `retrieveServices()` and `logError()`, to be called on success or failure of the operations.

> Add more phone numbers to the attribute if you want to send the same message to multiple recipients.
>
> More details about all attributes of a message are available in the documentation of the `MessageInit` interface at `https://developer.tizen.org/dev-guide/2.2.1/ org.tizen.web.device.apireference/tizen/ messaging.html#::Messaging::MessageInit`.

The function `retrieveServices()` composes SMS messages and sends them using the method `sendMessage()`. This method requires the privilege `http://tizen.org/ privilege/messaging.write` that has been set at the first step of the tutorial.

Any issues that may occur during the execution of the error code are handled by the function `logError()`, which prints **Error** in the console followed by details about the problem.

Please note that standard text messaging charges, depending on your subscription plan, will be applied by the mobile network operator for each SMS sent. You will not be able to send SMS messages successfully if there is no network coverage or if the flight mode of the device is enabled.

See also

▶   Refer to the next recipe to learn how to use the same methods of the Messaging API to send e-mails.

Sending e-mail messages

The usage of the Messaging API to send e-mails is similar to the way SMSes are sent. This recipe will demonstrate how to send an e-mail and will discuss the differences between sending SMS messages and e-mails.

Getting ready

As of Tizen Version 2.2.1, the Messaging API is capable of sending SMS, MMS, and e-mail. These three options are defined at the enumerated type `MessageServiceTag`, which is defined by the API. Just as with the SMS method, `sendMessage()` has to be used to send an e-mail, and it also requires the `http://tizen.org/privilege/messaging.write` privilege.

Before you proceed, please ensure that an Internet connection is available and an e-mail account has been set up on the Tizen device and emulator.

To set up an e-mail, please launch the **Email** application that is present on the main screen of the device, or navigate to **Settings | Accounts | Add | Email**, and follow the onscreen instructions. Have a look at the following screenshot:

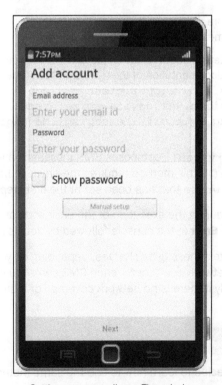

Setting up an e-mail on a Tizen device

How to do it...

Perform the following steps to send an e-mail from the Tizen web application:

1. Edit the `config.xml` file, and append the following privilege:

   ```
   http://tizen.org/privilege/messaging.write
   ```

2. Create a global JavaScript object capable of storing all the information in the message as follows:

   ```
   var msgEmail = { subject: "", plainBody: "", to: [], cc: [] };
   ```

3. Implement callback functions, as shown in the following code:

   ```
   function logError(err) {
       console.log("Error: " + err.message);
   }

   function sentOK(recipients)
   {
     for (var nIter in recipients) {
       console.log("Message sent to " + recipients[nIter]);
     }
   }

   function retrieveServices(services) {
     var msg = new tizen.Message("messaging.email",msgEmail);
     services[0].sendMessage(msg, sentOK, logError);
   }
   ```

4. Create a JavaScript function to send an e-mail:

   ```
   function sendEmail(sSubject, sTxt, sTo, sCC) {
     msgEmail.subject = sSubject;
     msgEmail.plainBody = sTxt;
     msgEmail.to.push(sTo);
     msgEmail.cc.push(sCC);
     tizen.messaging.getMessageServices("messaging.email",
   retrieveServices, logError);
   }
   ```

5. Specify the arguments required and invoke the function `sendEmail()` at an appropriate place on the application, for example:

   ```
   sendEmail("Hello", "Hello World", "foo@example.com", "bar@example.
   com");
   ```

How it works...

The previous example sends an e-mail with the subject **Hello** and content **Hello World** to foo@example.com and a carbon copy to bar@example.com. As you can see, the source code is very similar to the previous recipe for sending SMS messages. The major differences are in the attributes of the JavaScript object, `msgEmail`, the value of the first argument of the method `getMessageServices()`, and the constructor of `Message`, which has been set to `message.email`.

The structure of the object `msgEmail` follows the attributes described by the interface `MessageInit`. It is also possible to specify blind carbon copy e-mails using the attribute `bcc` or set HTML content for the e-mail using the attribute `htmlBody`. All of the attributes, to, cc, and bcc, are arrays, and any one of them can store multiple e-mails.

The API also allows attachments. All attached files must be provided to the attribute `attachments` of the instances of the interface `Message`, for example:

```
var msg = new tizen.Message("messaging.email",msgEmail);
msg.attachments = [new tizen.MessageAttachment("image.png", "image/
png"), new tizen.MessageAttachment("note.txt", "text/plain")];
```

An instance of `MessageAttachment` is created for each attachment. The files are described by their filenames and MIME types.

See also

> ▶ Explore the documentation of the Messaging API to find out more details about all interfaces, their attributes, and methods at `https://developer.tizen.org/dev-guide/2.2.1/org.tizen.web.device.apireference/tizen/messaging.html`

Receiving and displaying e-mail messages

It is possible to monitor and detect changes of messages, conversations, and message folders in the Tizen web application through the capabilities of the Messaging API. In this recipe, you will find guidelines on how to create an application to detect new e-mails.

Getting ready

An Internet connection should be available, and an e-mail account must be configured on the Tizen device to try out and verify the successful functioning of the application created in this recipe. If you have not set up an e-mail yet, please do it following the instructions from the previous recipe.

How to do it...

Perform the steps provided in the following tutorial to implement a listener for new e-mails in a Tizen web application:

1. Edit the `config.xml` file of the application, and add the following privilege to read messages:

    ```
    http://tizen.org/privilege/messaging.read
    ```

2. Declare the following global JavaScript variables:

    ```
    var gEmailListenerId, gEmailService;
    ```

3. Create JavaScript functions to show retrieved e-mails or an error that has occurred as follows:

    ```
    function showError(err) {
      console.log("Error: " + err.message);
    }

    function displayMessages(messages) {
      for (var nIter in messages) {
        var message = messages[nIter];
        console.log("From: " + message.from + " Subject: " +
          message.subject);
      }
    }
    ```

4. Implement JavaScript functions that initialize the e-mail service and listen for messages as follows:

    ```
    function registerEmailListener() {
      var messagesListener = {
        messagesadded : displayMessages,
        messagesupdated : function(messages) {},
        messagesremoved : function(messages) {},
      };
      gEmailListenerId = gEmailService.messageStorage.
    addMessagesChangeListener(mess
        agesListener);
    }

    function retrieveServices(services) {
      try
      {
        if (0 == services.length) {
          throw new Error("Email service not found.");
        }
        gEmailService = services[0];
        registerEmailListener();
    ```

```
        } catch (err) {
          showError(err);
        }
      }

      function initEmailService() {
        try {
          tizen.messaging.getMessageServices("messaging.email",
            retrieveServices);
        } catch (err) {
          showError(err);
        }
      }
```

5. Implement a function that unregisters the e-mail listener:

```
      function unregisterEmailListener() {
        try {
          gEmailService.messageStorage.removeChangeListener(gEmailListe
nerId);
        } catch (err) {
          showError(err);
        }
      }
```

6. Start listening for e-mails at an appropriate place in the source code of the application as follows:

```
      initEmailService();
```

 The code snippets provided are simple examples, and they are not related to any graphical user interface. The information about e-mail received or any errors is printed on the console.

How it works...

Three phases are required to monitor e-mails, as follows:

▶ To obtain an e-mail messaging service

▶ To listen for message changes

▶ To display messages

The first phase is performed by the function `initEmailService()`. If it is successful, the next step of the algorithm is to execute the function `registerEmailListener()`. The final phase is performed by the function `displayMessages()`, which is called as a callback by the method `addMessagesChangeListener()` of the interface `MessageStorage`. Please note that the code snippet from step four of the tutorial displays only messages that have been added to `MessageStorage`.

There's more...

Tizen's Messaging API provides methods to listen for changes related to conversations and message folders as well. Please note that conversations can represent e-mail correspondence or chat. They are grouped by the subject for e-mails and by the sender and recipient for chats.

The methods `addConversationsChangeListener()` and `addFoldersChangeListener()` of the interface `MessageStorage` should be utilized to detect changes related to conversations and folders. Their usage is similar to that of the method `addMessagesChangeListener()`, which was used in the code snippets of this recipe.

See also

▸ A sample Tizen web application based on the tutorial is provided alongside the book. It has a simple user interface that shows the sender and the subject of e-mails received as shown in the following screenshot. Explore the source code of the application for more details.

Sample application that displays a received e-mail

Browsing call history

In this recipe, you will learn how to use Tizen's Call History API to access and browse your call history. A sample application to retrieve the list of recently made outgoing calls is provided with the book.

How to do it...

Perform the following steps to implement the CallHistory API in the Tizen web application and to retrieve dialed phone numbers:

1. Add the following privilege to read the call log to `config.xml`:

   ```
   http://tizen.org/privilege/callhistory.read
   ```

2. Implement JavaScript functions to show call history and handle errors as follows:

   ```
   function showError(err) {
     console.log("Error: " + err.message);
   }

   function showCalls(calls) {
     try {
       for (var nIter in calls) {
         var call = calls[nIter];
         var sTel = (undefined != call.remoteParties[0]) ? call.
   remoteParties[0].remoteParty : '';
         console.log('TEL: ' + sTel + ' Date: ' + call.startTime.
   toLocaleTimeString() + " " + call.startTime.toLocaleDateString());
       }
     } catch (err) {
       showError(err);
     }
   }
   ```

3. Create the function that retrieves outgoing calls as follows:

   ```
   function getOutgoingCalls() {
     try {
       var filter = new tizen.AttributeFilter("direction", "EXACTLY",
   "DIALED");
       var order = new tizen.SortMode("startTime", "DESC");
       tizen.callhistory.find(showCalls, showError, filter, order,
   10);
     } catch(err) {
       showError(err);
     }
   }
   ```

4. Call the function `getOutgoingCalls()` at the launch of the application or any other appropriate place:

```
getOutgoingCalls();
```

How it works...

The function `getOutgoingCalls()` uses the method `find` of the interface `CallHistory` to retrieve the preceding ten outgoing calls. The results are ordered in descending order by their date and time. An instance of `AttributeFilter` is created to select only the `DIALED` numbers. The other options allowed for attribute direction are:

- ▶ `RECEIVED`: This is used for incoming calls
- ▶ `MISSEDNEW`: This is for not-yet-seen missed calls
- ▶ `MISSED`: This is for all missed calls
- ▶ `BLOCKED`: This is for calls that have been blocked
- ▶ `REJECTED`: This is for calls that have been rejected by the user

In the previous example, the function `showCalls()` is executed as a callback on success. Otherwise, on failure, the issue is handled by the function `showError()`.

A sample Tizen web application based on this recipe is provided with the book. It is integrated with the HTML5 user interface. The following screenshot is from this application. You may improve the sample application by combining it with the Contacts API that was analyzed in the previous chapter.

A list of the most recently dialed phone numbers

There's more...

Some Tizen web applications may need a capability to monitor calls. In these cases, you can use the methods `addChangeListener()` and `removeChangeListener()` of the interface `CallHistory`. An observer must be provided to the function `addChangeListener()`. On success, this function returns an identifier that is required for an argument of the function `removeChangeListener()` when the listener has to be removed.

See also

  ▶ For more details and information about all related interfaces, please refer to the documentation of the CallHistory API at `https://developer.tizen.org/dev-guide/2.2.1/org.tizen.web.device.apireference/tizen/callhistory.html`

Using Bluetooth

Bluetooth is a popular wireless standard for data transfer between devices at close range. The name of the standard comes from the nickname of the king of Denmark and Norway from the middle ages, Harald "Bluetooth" Gormsson.

This recipe provides details about the Bluetooth API for Tizen web applications and explains how to use it in the following cases:

  ▶ To discover Bluetooth devices

  ▶ To connect to another Bluetooth device

  ▶ To connect and transfer data over Bluetooth

Getting ready

The methods of the Bluetooth API used in this recipe require the following privileges:

  ▶ `http://tizen.org/privilege/bluetooth.admin`

  ▶ `http://tizen.org/privilege/bluetooth.gap`

  ▶ `http://tizen.org/privilege/bluetooth.spp`

Please append all privileges to the `config.xml` file of your Tizen web application before proceeding to the next section of the recipe.

How to do it...

Perform the following steps to discover, connect, and exchange data over Bluetooth in the Tizen web application:

1. Declare and initialize global JavaScript variables as follows:

```
var g_bluetoothAdapter = null;
var g_bIsServer = false;
```

The variable `bIsServer` is used only to determine whether the application is running as a server or as a client. Have a look at the following code:

```
var g_sUUID = '6BEE80ED-D05C-4B44-A329-E7441FEE9154';
```

The Bluetooth **Service Discovery Protocol** (**SDP**) defines a range of available UUIDs. Tizen developers working on computers with GNU/Linux or OS X can execute the command `uuidgen` in a console to generate **Universally Unique Identifier** (**UUID**).

If your application should connect and communicate to a Bluetooth serial board, you can try using the base UUID defined by SDP, `00000000-0000-1000-8000-00805F9B34FB`.

2. Create a simple function to log errors as follows:

```
function showError(err) {
  console.log("Error: " + err.message);
}
```

3. Turn on Bluetooth and retrieve a Bluetooth device as shown in the following sample code snippet:

```
function initBluetooth() {
  g_bluetoothAdapter = tizen.bluetooth.getDefaultAdapter();
  if(false == g_bluetoothAdapter.powered) {
    g_bluetoothAdapter.setPowered(true, run);
  }
  else
  {
```

At this point, the JavaScript function `run()` will be invoked. Its implementation is provided in the next steps of the recipe:

```
    run();
  }
}
```

You can also create a function that turns off Bluetooth. An example of the implementation of such a function is shown as follows:

```
function shutDownBluetooth() {
  if(true == g_bluetoothAdapter.powered) {
    g_bluetoothAdapter.setPowered(false);
  }
}
```

4. Create JavaScript data that reads data received from the Bluetooth socket. It will be used by both the server and client modes of the application. Have a look at the following code:

```
function readMessage(socket) {
  var data = socket.readData();
  var sResult = '';
  for (var nIter = 0; nIter < data.length; nIter++) {
    sResult += String.fromCharCode(data[nIter]);
  }
  $('#labelInfo').text(sResult);
}
```

5. Implement JavaScript functions that register a service, establish a connection with a client, and receive data if the application is running in server mode, as follows:

```
function registerServer(recordHandler) {
  console.log("Bluetooth services registered!");
  recordHandler.onconnect = function(socket) {
    console.log("Client connected: " + socket.peer.name + "," +
socket.peer.address);

    socket.onmessage = function() {
      readMessage(socket);
    };

    socket.onclose = function() {
      console.log('The socket was closed.');
    };
  };
}

function startService() {
  if (true == g_bIsServer) {
    g_bluetoothAdapter.registerRFCOMMServiceByUUID(g_sUUID,
"TizenCookbook",
        registerServer, showError);
  }
}
```

6. Implement JavaScript functions that scan and pair devices. These functions will be used when the application is running as a client. Have a look at the following code:

```
function paired(device) {
  try {
    console.log('Paired with device ' + device.name + '
      (address: ' + device.address + ')');
```

Please note that an exception will be thrown if the device found does not provide a service with the expected UUID. If everything is working as expected, the function `onSocketConnected()` will be invoked as a callback, as shown in the following code:

```
    if (-1 == device.uuids.indexOf(g_sUUID)) {
      throw new Error('UUID not found');
    }

    if (false == g_bIsServer) {
        device.connectToServiceByUUID(g_sUUID, onSocketConnected,
showError);
    }
  } catch (err) {
    showError(err);
  }
}
```

The following function tries to create a bond between two devices and, on success, invokes the function `paired()` as a callback:

```
function pairDevices(sAddress) {
  g_bluetoothAdapter.createBonding(sAddress, paired, showError);
}

function discoverBluetoothDevices() {
  try {
    console.log('searching...');
    var bluetoothDevices =
    {
      ondevicefound: function(device) {
        console.log('Bluetooth device: ' + device.name + '
address: ' + device.address);
        pairDevices(device.address);
      }
    };
    g_bluetoothAdapter.discoverDevices(bluetoothDevices,
showError);
```

```
    } catch (err) {
      showError(err);
    }
  }
```

7. Create a callback function that sends data from the client to the server as follows:

```
function onSocketConnected(socket) {
  console.log("Bluetooth socket created successfully.");
  socket.onmessage = function () { readMessage(socket); };
  socket.onclose = function() { };
  if ( (null != socket) && ("OPEN" == socket.state) ) {
    console.log('sending data to the server');
    var sMessage = 'Hello World';
    var sendData = [];
    for (var nIter = 0; nIter < sMessage.length; nIter++)
    {
      sendData[nIter] = sMessage.charCodeAt(nIter);
    }
    socket.writeData(sendData);
  }
}
```

8. Implement a function that runs the application as a server or as a client depending on the preferences set by the user as follows:

```
function run() {
  if (true == g_bIsServer) {
    console.log('running as a server...');
    startService();
  } else {
    console.log('running as a client...');
    discoverBluetoothDevices();
  }
}
```

9. Build and run the application on two different Tizen devices. Launch it in the server mode on the first device and in the client mode on the second device.

How it works...

A Tizen web application that uses the Bluetooth API, which can operate as the server and as the client, can be created following the instructions provided in this recipe. The following screenshot is taken from the sample application provided with the book:

Simple Bluetooth application for Tizen

In the server mode, the application registers a service with a unique UUID through the function `startService()`, receives text messages from the client, and displays them on the screen using the function `readMessage()`, which is executed as a callback.

When the application is running in client mode, it starts searching for any nearby Bluetooth devices using the method `discoverDevices()` of the interface `BluetoothAdapter`. The same interface also provides the method `getKnownDevices()`, which is capable of retrieving the list of known devices.

The function `paired()` bonds the two devices and establishes a connection only if the devices found offer services with the UUID that was configured in the first step of the recipe.

The methods `readData()` and `writeData()` of the interface `BluetoothSocket` are used to send and receive data over an opened Bluetooth socket. Text messages must be converted into arrays of bytes before sending, as shown in the function `onSocketConnected()`. The opposite operation is required when a message is received. For example, the code snippet in the function `readMessage()` transforms a byte array into a string.

In this example, the client sends just a single message, and its content is hardcoded as `Hello World`.

The code snippets from this recipe can be easily improved and adjusted to other use cases, such as chat over Bluetooth. Please note that the source code of the sample application is not production ready. Its main purpose is to demonstrate an easy way to use the Bluetooth API.

See also

- Have a look at the sample Bluetooth application that is provided with the book, and explore the documentation of the Bluetooth API for more details at `https://developer.tizen.org/dev-guide/2.2.1/org.tizen.web.device.apireference/tizen/bluetooth.html`

- Bluetooth specifications and a variety of other documents about the standard are available at `https://www.bluetooth.org/en-us/specification`

- For more technical information about the Bluetooth support in Tizen, please also explore the following page at the Tizen wiki at `https://wiki.tizen.org/wiki/Bluetooth`

Using NFC and detecting other devices

Near Field Communication (**NFC**) is a short-range wireless communication standard based on **radio-frequency identification** (**RFID**). NFC has several unique advantages compared to other communication technologies, such as Bluetooth. NFC does not require any setup to connect devices. The only requirement to establish a connection is a close proximity of about 4 cm (or less). Another valuable advantage of NFC is the lack of any requirements for power supply for passive tags.

NFC tags are also known as smart or info tags. They store data that can be easily read by users. In many cases, their usage is similar to QR codes and other types of barcodes. Anyone can buy an empty NFC tag and save customized information on it.

According to the standard, the usage of NFC can be grouped into three major categories depending on the modes, which are as follows:

- Reader/writer mode, which is appropriate to exchange data with passive, NFC-compatible tags. For example, QR codes on posters, stickers, and other promotional merchandise can be replaced by passive NFC tags.

- Peer-to-peer mode, which allows data exchange between devices.

- Card emulation mode, which allows the NFC device to be used as a card and accessed by external readers. For example, this feature might be convenient for contactless payments.

In this recipe, you will learn how to power on NFC devices and how to search for other devices in close range. The subsequent two recipes are dedicated to sending and receiving data.

Getting ready

Tizen web applications that use the NFC capabilities shown in this recipe must have the following privileges in their `config.xml` files:

- `http://tizen.org/privilege/nfc.common`
- `http://tizen.org/privilege/nfc.admin`

The following privilege is also required for applications that work in peer-to-peer mode:

- `http://tizen.org/privilege/nfc.p2p`

Applications that use the reader/writer mode should also include the following privilege:

- `http://tizen.org/privilege/nfc.tag`

How to do it...

Perform the following steps to establish peer-to-peer connection between two NFC-enabled devices in the Tizen web application using the NFC API:

1. Declare and initialize the global JavaScript variable for the NFC adapter and the NFC device that will be retrieved:

```
var g_nfcAdapter = null;
var g_nfcDevice = null;
```

2. Create an instance of the interface `NFCPeerDetectCallback`, which implements the methods `onattach()` and `ondetach()`, as follows:

```
var peerFound = {
    onattach : function(nfcPeer) {
        console.log("NFC Target found");
        },

    ondetach : function() {
        console.log("NFC Target is detached");
    }
};
```

3. Develop the JavaScript function to handle errors, for example:

```
function showError(err) {
  console.log("Error: " + err.message);
}
```

4. Create JavaScript functions that turn on the NFC device and search for other nearby NFC devices:

```
function findTarget() {
  try {
    g_nfcAdapter.setPeerListener(peerFound, showError);
  } catch (e) {
    showError(err);
  }
}

function initNFC() {
  try {
    g_nfcAdapter = tizen.nfc.getDefaultAdapter();
    g_nfcAdapter.setPowered(true, findTarget, showError);
  } catch (err){
    showError(err);
  }
}
```

5. Invoke the following function to start the procedure to establish an NFC connection:

```
initNFC();
```

The easiest way to debug a Tizen application that takes advantage of the NFC API is using **Event Injector**. Enable it by navigating to **Window | Show View | Event Injector** of the Tizen IDE and selecting the tab **Nfc**.

How it works...

The algorithm implemented in this recipe obtains an instance of the interface NFCAdapter, searches for other NFC devices using the method setPeerListener(), and establishes a connection with the detected device through the callback functions implemented in peerFound.

By the way, this JavaScript object is of the interface NFCPeerDetectCallback. The method onattach() is invoked when another NFC device is detected, and it receives as an argument an instance of the interface NFCPeer.

There's more...

Tizen web applications that have to connect to an NFC tag must use a similar approach. The only difference is that the method `setTagListener()` should be used instead of `setPeerListener()`, and the success callback is described by the interface `NFCTagDetectCallback`. Please note that the names of the methods of this interface match `NFCPeerDetectCallback`. In this case, however, the argument of `onattach()` is an instance of the interface `NFCTag`.

See also

▶ Please have a look at the upcoming recipes to understand how to send and receive NDEF messages. Please also do not forget to explore the documentation of the NFC API for more details at `https://developer.tizen.org/dev-guide/2.2.1/org.tizen.web.device.apireference/tizen/nfc.html`

Sending NDEF messages

The **NFC Data Exchange Format** (**NDEF**) is a binary format for the serialization of data transferred over NFC. This recipe demonstrates how to create an NDEF message, share it with another NFC device in peer-to-peer mode, or write it to a passive NFC tag.

Getting ready

Please include the privilege `http://tizen.org/privilege/nfc.p2p` if you plan to communicate in peer-to-peer mode and the privilege `http://tizen.org/privilege/nfc.tag` if you plan to write an NFC tag.

How to do it...

Perform the following steps to send an NDEF message:

1. Create an NDEF message. For example, the following function creates a text NDEF message with UTF-16 character encoding using instances of the interfaces `NDEFMessage` and `NDEFRecordText`:

```
function createNDEFMessage(sTxt) {
  var ndefRecord = new tizen.NDEFRecordText(sTxt, 'en-US',
'UTF16');
  var records = [ndefRecord];
  return new tizen.NDEFMessage(records);
}
```

The Tizen NFC API supports three different types of NDEF records; text, URI, and MIME. A separate interface is provided for each supported type. The interfaces `NDEFRecordText`, `NDEFRecordURI`, and `NDEFRecordMedia` implement the basic interface `NDEFRecord`.

2. Write or send the message. Use the method `writeNDEF()` of the interface to store information on an NFC tag as shown in the following code:

```
tag.writeNDEF(createNDEFMessage('foo'));
```

3. Use the method `sendNDEF()` of the interface to transfer information to another device in peer-to-peer mode. Take a look at the following example:

```
nfcPeer.sendNDEF(createNDEFMessage('bar'));
```

Please note that callback functions that will be invoked on success or failure can be optionally specified as arguments of both `writeNDEF()` and `sendNDEF()`. Both methods throw an exception upon error, so the try/catch block must be added when they are invoked.

See also

▸ For more details regarding the attributes of the interfaces `NDEFRecordText` and `NDEFMessage`, please refer to the following links:

□ `https://developer.tizen.org/dev-guide/2.2.1/`
`org.tizen.web.device.apireference/tizen/nfc.`
`html#::NFC::NDEFRecordText`

□ `https://developer.tizen.org/dev-guide/2.2.1/org.tizen.`
`web.device.apireference/tizen/nfc.html#::NFC::NDEFMessage`

▸ NDEF technical specifications as well as other documents related to NFC are available for download at the NFC Forum at `http://members.nfc-forum.org/` `specs/spec_list/`

Receiving NDEF messages

The previous two recipes demonstrated how to establish a connection with NFC and to write/send data. The next logical step is to explore the capabilities of the Tizen NFC API to read/receive data.

Getting ready

The privilege `http://tizen.org/privilege/nfc.p2p` is required when an NDEF message is received in NFC's peer-to-peer mode. If you plan to implement a feature to read data from passive NFC tags, you have to include the privilege `http://tizen.org/privilege/nfc.tag` in the `config.xml` file. Please note that as described in the previous recipe, the same privileges are required to send messages and to write information to a tag.

How to do it...

Please use the method `readNDEF()` provided by the interface `NFCTag` to read data from passive NFC tags as demonstrated in the following example:

1. Create a function that will be invoked as a callback if a supported NDEF is found as follows:

```
function readMessage(message)
{
  console.log("Number of retrieved records: " + message.
recordCount);
}
```

2. Implement a function to handle any errors that may occur as follows:

```
function printError(err) {
  console.log("Error: " + err.message);
}
```

3. Read the content of the tag using the following code snippet:

```
try {
  if (tag.isSupportedNDEF) {
    tag.readNDEF(readMessage, printError);
  }
} catch (err) {
  printError(err);
}
```

In Tizen web applications that communicate in the NFC peer-to-peer mode, it is possible to listen for incoming NDEF messages. For example, the following code snippet extends the source code from the second step of the *Using NFC and detecting other devices* recipe:

```
var peerFound = {
    onattach : function(nfcPeer) {
      console.log("NFC Target found");
      nfcPeer.setReceiveNDEFListener({
        onsuccess: function(message) {
```

```
            console.log("Number of retrieved records: " + message.
    recordCount);
            }
        });
    },

    ondetach : function() {
        console.log("NFC Target is detached");
    }
};
```

The new lines of code that have been appended are shown in bold. The method
`setReceiveNDEFListener()` is used to listen to incoming NDEF messages.
An anonymous JavaScript function, which receives an instance of the interface
`NDEFMessage` as an argument, is assigned to the `onsuccess` method.

How it works...

The second argument of `readNDEF()` is optional but is recommended to handle errors that
might occur during its execution. It is also recommend that you surround the method with
try/catch blocks, as it may throw an exception.

In the example to read a passive NFC tag, an instance of `NDEFMessage` will be provided as
an argument of the function `readMessage()`. An instance of the same class is provided
to the function, which is invoked on success in peer-to-peer mode. The attribute records of
`NDEFMessage` contain an array with instances of `NDEFRecord`. The specified type of each
record can be checked through the attribute `tnf`, which stores the 3-bit value for **Type Name
Field** (**TNF**). According to the documentation, at least the following values are supported:

- ▶ NFC_RECORD_TNF_EMPTY
- ▶ NFC_RECORD_TNF_WELL_KNOWN
- ▶ NFC_RECORD_TNF_MIME_MEDIA
- ▶ NFC_RECORD_TNF_URI
- ▶ NFC_RECORD_TNF_EXTERNAL_RTD
- ▶ NFC_RECORD_TNF_UNKNOWN
- ▶ NFC_RECORD_TNF_UNCHANGED

See also

- ▶ Please explore the information available at the following link for more information
  about the interface `NDEFRecord` at `https://developer.tizen.org/dev-guide/2.2.1/org.tizen.web.device.apireference/tizen/nfc.html#::NFC::NDEFRecord`

Receiving push notifications

Tizen provides a mechanism to trigger events from an application server and the delivery of these events on Tizen devices. Tizen web applications that have to receive notifications for these events must utilize and take advantage of the Push API.

For example, if you want to send a notification from your website to your Tizen web application, which is running on the user's device, you have to send the notification to a push service, which will forward it to the Tizen device. Once the notification is received on the device, your Tizen application should handle the message.

Getting ready

The push service in Tizen is provided by Samsung. You have to request access to the service before you start with the application development.

According to the procedure for *Push Service Request*, the developer must send an e-mail to `push.tizen@samsung.com`. The request should contain developer and application information. Please read the up-to-date information and details about the request form for Tizen web applications in the documentation at `https://developer.tizen.org/dev-guide/2.2.1/org.tizen.native.appprogramming/html/guide/messaging/push_service_request.htm`.

How to do it...

Perform the following steps to integrate the Push API into a Tizen web application:

1. Add the privilege `http://tizen.org/privilege/push` to `config.xml`, and allow access from the domain of the Push server as follows:

```
<tizen:privilege name="http://tizen.org/privilege/push"/>
<access origin="https://{region}.push.samsungosp.com:8088"
subdomains="true"/>
```

> Replace `{region}` and set a value that corresponds to the location of the used server depending on the first two digits of `regID`. Please read the official documentation for more details at `https://developer.tizen.org/dev-guide/2.2.1/org.tizen.native.appprogramming/html/guide/messaging/push_server_api.htm`.

2. Create a JavaScript function to handle errors and exceptions as follows:

```
function printError(err) {
  console.log("Error: " + err.message);
}
```

3. Create a JavaScript function to handle successful registration of the push service as follows:

```
function registerServiceOK(id)
{
    console.log('Service with id: ' + id + ' registered.');
}
```

4. Register for the service using the following code:

```
var service = null;
try {
    service = new tizen.ApplicationControl("http://tizen.org/
appcontrol/operation/push_test");
    tizen.push.registerService(service, registerServiceOK,
printError);
} catch (err) {
    printError(err);
}
```

5. Create a JavaScript function to handle incoming notifications as follows:

```
function notificationReceived(notification)
{
    console.log("Notification received: " + notification.
alertMessage);
}
```

6. Connect to the push service and receive messages as follows:

```
try {
    tizen.push.connectService(notificationReceived, printError);
} catch (err) {
    printError(err);
}
```

How it works

The notification received will be handled immediately if it is received while the application is running. If the application is not running or if it is running in the background, a ticker message will be displayed, and a badge with the number of unread notifications will appear next to the application's icon.

To take advantage of the Push API and receive push notifications, you must first register the push service on the devices in the Tizen web application using the method `registerService()` of the interface `PushManager`.

After that, the application must be connected to the service using the method `connectService()` of the same interface. In the previous code snippet, an instance of `PushMessage` is passed to the function `notificationReceived()` for each message received. The function `notificationReceived()` is invoked as a callback by `connectService().connectiService()`.

There's more...

To send a notification for a website or service to the server of the Push API, execute the HTTPS POST request to `https://{region}.push.samsungosp.com:8088/spp/pns/api/push`. Please replace `{region}` following the guide provided in the first step of the recipe. The header of the request should include information about the ID (`appID`) and the secret (`appSecret`) of the application. The body must contain `regID`, `requestID`, `message`, and `appData`.

For example, the following code snippet demonstrates how to send a HTTPS POST request to the push server using JavaScript and jQuery:

```
jQuery.ajax({
  type: 'POST',
  contentType: 'json',
  url: 'https://euwest.push.samsungosp.com:8088/spp/pns/api/push',
  headers: { "appID": sAppId, "appSecret": sAppSecret },
  data: JSON.stringify({ "regID": sRegId, "requestID":"000001", "mess
age":"badgeOption=SET&badgeNumber=10&action=ALERT&alertMessage=Foo",
"appData":"Bar" }),
  dataType: 'json',
})
```

The notification is sent to the Tizen server in the EU West region, and it includes the text **Bar** and the ticker message **Foo**. The value of the application's ID and secret is provided through the JavaScript variables `sAppId` and `sAppSecret`. The variable `sRegId` stores the registration identification of the application.

For more details regarding the integration of websites and services with the push server, please visit `https://developer.tizen.org/dev-guide/2.2.1/org.tizen.native.appprogramming/html/guide/messaging/push_server_api.htm`.

 By the way, the Tizen Push API uses the same servers as the push messaging service in Bada. This coincidence is not a surprise, because in 2013, Samsung merged its Bada OS into the second major version of the open source platform Tizen.

See also

▶ Please explore the Push API documentation for more details about the interfaces provided, their methods, and attributes at `https://developer.tizen.org/dev-guide/2.2.1/org.tizen.web.device.apireference/tizen/push.html`

9
Using Sensors

In this chapter, we will cover the following topics:

- ▶ Using location-based services to display current location
- ▶ Getting directions
- ▶ Geocoding
- ▶ Reverse geocoding
- ▶ Calculating distance
- ▶ Detecting device motion
- ▶ Detecting device orientation
- ▶ Using the Vibration API

Introduction

The data provided by the hardware sensors of Tizen devices can be useful for many mobile applications. In this chapter, you will learn how to retrieve the geographic location of Tizen devices using the assisted GPS, to detect changes of the device orientation and motion as well as how to integrate map services into Tizen web applications.

Most of the examples related to maps and navigation use Google APIs. Other service providers such as **Nokia HERE**, **OpenStreetMap**, and **Yandex** also offer APIs with similar capabilities and can be used as an alternative to Google in Tizen web applications.

It was announced that Nokia HERE joined the Tizen association at the time of writing this book. Some Tizen devices will be shipped with built-in navigation applications powered by Nokia HERE. The smart watch Gear S is the first Tizen wearable device from Samsung that comes of the box with an application called Navigator, which is developed with Nokia HERE. Explore the full capabilities of Nokia HERE JavaScript APIs if you are interested in their integration in your Tizen web application at `https://developer.here.com/javascript-apis`.

OpenStreetMap also deserves special attention because it is a high quality platform and very successful community-driven project. The main advantage of OpenStreetMap is that its usage is completely free. The recipe about Reverse geocoding in this chapter demonstrates address lookup using two different approaches: through Google and through OpenStreetMap API.

Using location-based services to display current location

By following the provided example in this recipe, you will master the HTML5 Geolocation API and learn how to retrieve the coordinates of the current location of a device in a Tizen web application.

Getting ready

Ensure that the positioning capabilities are turned on. On a Tizen device or Emulator, open **Settings**, select **Locations**, and turn on both **GPS** (if it is available) and **Network position** as shown in the following screenshot:

Enabling GPS and network position from Tizen Settings

How to do it...

Follow these steps to retrieve the location in a Tizen web application:

1. Implement JavaScript for handling errors:

```
function showError(err) {
    console.log('Error ' + err.code + ': ' + err.message);
}
```

2. Implement JavaScript for processing the retrieved location:

```
function showLocation(location) {
    console.log('latitude: ' + location.coords.longitude + '
        longitude: ' + location.coords.longitude);
}
```

3. Implement a JavaScript function that searches for the current position using the HTML5 Geolocation API:

```
function retrieveLocation() {
    if (navigator.geolocation) {
        navigator.geolocation.getCurrentPosition(showLocation,
            showError);
    }
}
```

4. At an appropriate place in the source code of the application, invoke the function created in the previous step:

```
retrieveLocation();
```

How it works

The `getCurrentPosition()` method of the HTML5 Geolocation API is used in the `retrieveLocation()` function to retrieve the coordinates of the current position of the device. The functions `showLocation()` and `showError()` are provided as callbacks, which are invoked on success or failure. An instance of the `Position` interface is provided as an argument to `showLocation()`. This interface has two properties:

▶ `coords`: This specifies an object that defines the retrieved position

▶ `timestamp`: This specifies the date and time when the position has been retrieved

The `getCurrentPosition()` method accepts an instance of the `PositionOptions` interface as a third optional argument. This argument should be used for setting specific options such as `enableHighAccuracy`, `timeout`, and `maximumAge`. Explore the Geolocation API specification if you are interested in more details regarding the attributes of the discussed interface at `http://www.w3.org/TR/geolocation-API/#position-options`.

There is no need to add any specific permissions explicitly in `config.xml`. When an application that implements the code from this recipe is launched for the first time, it will ask for permission to access the location, as shown in the following screenshot:

A request to access location in Tizen web application

If you are developing a location-based application and want to debug it using the Tizen Emulator, use the Event Injector to set the position.

There's more...

A map view provided by Google Maps JavaScript API v3 can be easily embedded into a Tizen web application. An Internet connection is required to use the API, but there is no need to install an additional SDK or tools from Google. Follow these instructions to display a map and a marker:

1. Make sure that the application can access the Google API. For example, you can enable access to any website by adding the following line to `config.xml`:

   ```xml
   <access origin="*" subdomains="true"></access>
   ```

2. Visit `https://code.google.com/apis/console` to get the API keys.

3. Click on **Services** and activate **Google Maps API v3**.

4. After that, click on **API** and copy **Key for browser apps**. Its value will be used in the source code of the application.

5. Implement the following source code to show a map inside `div` with the ID `map-canvas`:

   ```
   <style type="text/css">
     #map-canvas { width: 320px; height: 425px; }
   </style>
   <script type="text/javascript" src="https://maps.googleapis.com/
   maps/api/js?key=<API Key>&sensor=false"></script>Replace <API
   Key> in the line above with the value of the key obtained on the
   previous step.

   <script type="text/javascript">
   function initialize(nLatitude, nLongitude) {
     var mapOptions = {
       center: new google.maps.LatLng(nLatitude, nLongitude),
       zoom: 14
     };
     var map = new google.maps.Map(document.getElementById("map-
   canvas"), mapOptions);

     var marker = new google.maps.Marker({
       position: new google.maps.LatLng(nLatitude,
         nLongitude),
       map: map
     });
   }
   </script>
   ```

6. In the HTML of the application, create the following `div` element:

   ```html
   <div id="map-canvas"></div>
   ```

7. Provide latitude and longitude to the function and execute it at an appropriate location. For example, these are the coordinates of a location in Westminster, London:

```
initialize(51.501725, -0.126109);
```

The following screenshot demonstrates a Tizen web application that has been created by following the preceding guidelines:

Google Maps in a Tizen web application

Combine the tutorial from the *How to do it* section of the recipe with these instructions to display a map with the current location.

See also

▶ The source code of a simple Tizen web application is provided alongside the book following the tutorial from this recipe. Feel free to use it as you wish.

▶ More details are available in the W3C specification of the HTML5 Geolocation API at `http://www.w3.org/TR/geolocation-API/`.

▶ To learn more details and to explore the full capabilities of the Google Maps JavaScript API v3, please visit `https://developers.google.com/maps/documentation/javascript/tutorial`.

Getting directions

Navigation is another common task for mobile applications. The Google Directions API allows web and mobile developers to retrieve a route between locations by sending an HTTP request. It is mandatory to specify an origin and a destination, but it is also possible to set way points. All locations can be provided either by exact coordinates or by address. An example for getting directions and to reach a destination on foot is demonstrated in this recipe.

Getting ready

Before you start with the development, register an application and obtain API keys:

1. Log in to Google Developers Console at `https://code.google.com/apis/console`.

2. Click on **Services** and turn on **Directions API**.

3. Click on **API Access** and get the value of **Key for server apps**, which should be used in all requests from your Tizen web application to the API.

For more information about the API keys for the Directions API, please visit `https://developers.google.com/maps/documentation/directions/#api_key`.

How to do it...

Use the following source code to retrieve and display step-by-step instructions on how to walk from one location to another using the Google Directions API:

1. Allow the application to access websites by adding the following line to `config.xml`:

```
<access origin="*" subdomains="true"></access>
```

2. Create an HTML unordered list:

```
<ul id="directions" data-role="listview"></ul>
```

3. Create some JavaScript that will load retrieved directions:

```
function showDirections(data) {
  if (!data || !data.routes || (0 == data.routes.length)) {
    console.log('Unable to provide directions.');
    return;
  }
  var directions = data.routes[0].legs[0].steps;
  for (nStep = 0; nStep < directions.length; nStep++) {
    var listItem = $('<li>').append($( '<p>'
      ).append(directions[nStep].html_instructions));
    $('#directions').append(listItem);
  }
  $('#directions').listview('refresh');
}
```

4. Create a JavaScript function that sends an asynchronous HTTP (**AJAX**) request to the Google Maps API to retrieve directions:

```
function retrieveDirection(sLocationStart, sLocationEnd){
  $.ajax({
    type: 'GET',
    url: 'https://maps.googleapis.com/maps/api/directions/json?',
    data: { origin: sLocationStart,
      destination: sLocationEnd,
      mode: 'walking',
      sensor: 'true',
      key: '<API key>' },
```

Do not forget to replace <API key> with the **Key for server apps** value provided by Google for the Directions API. Please note that a similar key has to be set to the source code in the subsequent recipes that utilize Google APIs too:

```
    success : showDirections,
    error : function (request, status, message) {
      console.log('Error');
    }
  });
}
```

5. Provide start and end locations as arguments and execute the `retrieveDirection()` function. For example:

```
retrieveDirection('Times Square, New York, NY, USA', 'Empire State Building, 350 5th Avenue, New York, NY 10118, USA');
```

How it works

The first mandatory step is to allow access to the Tizen web application to Google servers. After that, an HTML unordered list with ID directions is constructed. An origin and destination is provided to the JavaScript function `retrieveDirections()`. On success, the `showDirections()` function is invoked as a callback and it loads step-by-step instructions on how to move from the origin to the destination. The following screenshot displays a Tizen web application with guidance on how to walk from Times Square in New York to the Empire State Building:

The Directions API is quite flexible. The mandatory parameters are `origin`, `destination`, and `sensor`. Numerous other options can be configured at the HTTP request using different parameters. To set the desired transport, use the parameter `mode`, which has the following options:

- `driving`
- `walking`
- `bicycling`
- `transit` (for getting directions using public transport)

By default, if the mode is not specified, its value will be set to `driving`.

The unit system can be configured through the parameter `unit`. The options `metric` and `imperial` are available. The developer can also define restrictions using the parameter `avoid` and the addresses of one or more directions points at the `waypoints` parameter. A pipe (|) is used as a symbol for separation if more than one address is provided.

There's more...

An application with similar features for getting directions can also be created using services from Nokia HERE. The REST API can be used in the same way as Google Maps API. Start by acquiring the credentials at `http://developer.here.com/get-started`.

An asynchronous HTTP request should be sent to retrieve directions. Instructions on how to construct the request to the REST API are provided in its documentation at `https://developer.here.com/rest-apis/documentation/routing/topics/request-constructing.html`.

The Nokia HERE JavaScript API is another excellent solution for routing. Make instances of classes `Display` and `Manager` provided by the API to create a map and a routing manager. After that, create a list of way points whose coordinates are defined by an instance of the `Coordinate` class. Refer to the following example provided by the user's guide of the API to learn details at `https://developer.here.com/javascript-apis/documentation/maps/topics/routing.html`.

The full specifications about classes `Display`, `Manager`, and `Coordinate` are available at the following links:

▶ `https://developer.here.com/javascript-apis/documentation/maps/topics_api_pub/nokia.maps.map.Display.html`

▶ `https://developer.here.com/javascript-apis/documentation/maps/topics_api_pub/nokia.maps.routing.Manager.html`

▶ `https://developer.here.com/javascript-apis/documentation/maps/topics_api_pub/nokia.maps.geo.Coordinate.html`

See also

▶ All details, options, and returned results by the Google Directions API are available at `https://developers.google.com/maps/documentation/directions/`.

Geocoding

Geocoding is the process of retrieving geographical coordinates associated with an address. It is often used in mobile applications that use maps and provide navigation. In this recipe, you will learn how to convert an address to longitude and latitude using JavaScript and AJAX requests to the Google Geocoding API.

Getting ready

You must obtain keys before you can use the Geocoding API in a Tizen web application:

1. Visit Google Developers Console at `https://code.google.com/apis/console`.
2. Click on **Services** and turn on **Geocoding API**.
3. Click on **API Access** and get the value of **Key for server apps.** Use it in all requests from your Tizen web application to the API.

For more details regarding the API keys for the Geocoding API, visit `https://developers.google.com/maps/documentation/geocoding/#api_key`.

How to do it...

Follow these instructions to retrieve geographic coordinates of an address in a Tizen web application using the Google Geocoding API:

1. Allow the application to access websites by adding the following line to `config.xml`:

   ```
   <access origin="*" subdomains="true"></access>
   ```

2. Create a JavaScript function to handle results provided by the API:

   ```
   function retrieveCoordinates(data) {
     if (!data || !data.results || (0 == data.results.length)) {
       console.log('Unable to retrieve coordinates');
       return;
     }
     var latitude = data.results[0].geometry.location.lat;
     var longitude = data.results[0].geometry.location.lng;
     console.log('latitude: ' + latitude + ' longitude: ' +
       longitude);
   }
   ```

3. Create a JavaScript function that sends a request to the API:

   ```
   function geocoding(address) {
     $.ajax({
       type: 'GET',
   ```

```
        url:
'https://maps.googleapis.com/maps/api/geocode/json?',
      data: { address: address,
        sensor: 'true',
        key: '<API key>' },
```

As in the previous recipes, you should again replace <API key> with the
Key for server apps value provided by Google for the Geocoding API.

```
      success : retrieveCoordinates,
      error : function (request, status, message) {
      console.log('Error: ' + message);
      }
    });
}
```

4. Provide the address as an argument to the geocoding() function and invoke it.
   For example:

```
geocoding('350 5th Avenue, New York, NY 10118, USA');
```

How it works

The address is passed as an argument to the geocoding() function, which sends a request
to the URL of Google Geocoding API. The URL specifies that the returned result should be
serialized as JSON. The parameters of the URL contain information about the address and the
API key. Additionally, there is a parameter that indicates whether the device has a sensor. In
general, Tizen mobile devices are equipped with GPS so the parameter sensor is set to true.

A successful response from the API is handled by the retrieveCoordinates() function,
which is executed as a callback. After processing the data, the code snippet in this recipe
prints the retrieved coordinates at the console. For example, if we provide the address of the
Empire State Building to the geocoding() function on success, the following text will be
printed: **latitude: 40.7481829 longitude: -73.9850635**.

See also

▶ Explore the Google Geocoding API documentation to learn more details regarding the
  usage of the API and all of its parameters at https://developers.google.com/
  maps/documentation/geocoding/#GeocodingRequests.

▶ Nokia HERE provides similar features. Refer to the documentation of its Geocoder
  API to learn how to create the URL of a request to it at https://developer.
  here.com/rest-apis/documentation/geocoder/topics/request-
  constructing.html.

Reverse geocoding

Reverse geocoding, also known as address lookup, is the process of retrieving an address that corresponds to a location described with geographic coordinates.

The Google Geocoding API provides methods for both geocoding as well as reverse geocoding. In this recipe, you will learn how to find the address of a location based on its coordinates using the Google API as well as an API provided by OpenStreetMap.

Getting ready

The same keys are required for geocoding and reverse geocoding. If you have already obtained a key for the previous recipe, you can directly use it here again. Otherwise, you can perform the following steps:

1. Visit Google Developers Console at `https://code.google.com/apis/console`.

2. Go to **Services** and turn on **Geocoding API**.

3. Select **API Access**, locate the value of **Key for server apps**, and use it in all requests from the Tizen web application to the API.

If you need more information about the Geocoding API keys, visit `https://developers.google.com/maps/documentation/geocoding/#api_key`.

How to do it...

Follow the described algorithm to retrieve an address based on geographic coordinates using the Google Maps Geocoding API:

1. Allow the application to access websites by adding the following line to `config.xml`:

   ```
   <access origin="*" subdomains="true"></access>
   ```

2. Create a JavaScript function to handle the data provided for a retrieved address:

   ```
   function retrieveAddress(data) {
     if (!data || !data.results || (0 == data.results.length)) {
       console.log('Unable to retrieve address');
       return;
     }
     var sAddress = data.results[0].formatted_address;
     console.log('Address: ' + sAddress);
   }
   ```

3. Implement a function that performs a request to Google servers to retrieve an address based on latitude and longitude:

```
function reverseGeocoding(latitude, longitude) {
  $.ajax({
    type: 'GET',
    url: 'https://maps.googleapis.com/maps/api/geocode/json?',
    data: { latlng: latitude+','+longitude,
        sensor: 'true',
        key: '<API key>' },
```

Pay attention that `<API key>` has to be replaced with the **Key for server apps** value provided by Google for the Geocoding API:

```
    success : retrieveAddress,
    error : function (request, status, message) {
    console.log('Error: ' + message);
    }
  });
}
```

4. Provide coordinates as arguments of function and execute it, for example:

```
reverseGeocoding('40.748183', '-73.985064');
```

How it works

If an application developed using the preceding source code invokes the `reverseGeocoding()` function with latitude 40.748183 and longitude -73.985064, the printed result at the console will be **350 5th Avenue, New York, NY 10118, USA**. By the way, as in the previous recipe, the address corresponds to the location of the Empire State Building in New York.

The `reverseGeocoding()` function sends an AJAX request to the API. The parameters at the URL specify that the response must be formatted as JSON. The longitude and latitude of the location are divided by commas and set as a value of the `latlng` parameter in the URL.

There's more...

OpenStreetMap also provides a reverse geocoding service. For example, the following URL will return a JSON result of a location with the latitude 40.7481829 and longitude -73.9850635:

```
http://nominatim.openstreetmap.org/reverse?format=json&lat=40.7481829
&lon=-73.9850635
```

The main advantage of OpenStreetMap is that it is an open project with a great community. Its API for reverse geocoding does not require any keys and it can be used for free.

Leaflet is a popular open source JavaScript library based on OpenStreetMap optimized for mobile devices. It is well supported and easy to use, so you may consider integrating it in your Tizen web applications. Explore its features at `http://leafletjs.com/features.html`.

See also

> ► All details regarding the Google Geocoding API are available at `https://developers.google.com/maps/documentation/geocoding/#ReverseGeocoding`

> ► If you prefer to user the API provided by OpenStreetMap, take a look at `http://wiki.openstreetmap.org/wiki/Nominatim#Reverse_Geocoding_.2F_Address_lookup`

Calculating distance

This recipe is dedicated to a method for calculating the distance between two locations. The Google Directions API will be used again. Unlike the *Getting directions* recipe, this time only the information about the distance will be processed.

Getting ready

Just like the other recipe related to the Google API, in this case, the developer must obtain the API keys before the start of the development. Please follow these instructions to register and get an appropriate API key:

1. Visit Google Developers Console at `https://code.google.com/apis/console`.
2. Click on **Services** and turn on **Geocoding API**.
3. Click on **API Access** and save the value of **Key for server apps.** Use it in all requests from your Tizen web application to the API.

If you need more information about the API keys for Directions API, visit `https://developers.google.com/maps/documentation/directions/#api_key`.

How to do it...

Follow these steps to calculate the distance between two locations:

1. Allow the application to access websites by adding the following line to `config.xml`:

    ```
    <access origin="*" subdomains="true"></access>
    ```

2. Implement a JavaScript function that will process the retrieved data:

    ```
    function retrieveDistance(data) {
      if (!data || !data.routes || (0 == data.routes.length)) {
        console.log('Unable to retrieve distance');
        return;
      }
      var sLocationStart =
        data.routes[0].legs[0].start_address;
      var sLocationEnd = data.routes[0].legs[0].end_address;
      var sDistance = data.routes[0].legs[0].distance.text;
      console.log('The distance between ' + sLocationStart + '
        and ' + sLocationEnd + ' is: ' +
        data.routes[0].legs[0].distance.text);
    }
    ```

3. Create a JavaScript function that will request directions using the Google Maps API:

    ```
    function checkDistance(sStart, sEnd) {
      $.ajax({
        type: 'GET',
        url: 'https://maps.googleapis.com/maps/api/directions/json?',
        data: { origin: sStart,
            destination: sEnd,
            sensor: 'true',
            units: 'metric',
            key: '<API key>' },
    ```

4. Remember to replace <API key> with the **Key for server apps** value provided by Google for the Direction API:

    ```
        success : retrieveDistance,
        error : function (request, status, message) {
        console.log('Error: ' + message);
        }
      });
    }
    ```

5. Execute the `checkDistance()` function and provide the origin and the destination as arguments, for example:

    ```
    checkDistance('Plovdiv', 'Burgas');
    ```

Geographical coordinates can also be provided as arguments to the function
`checkDistance()`. For example, let's calculate the same distances but this time by
providing the latitude and longitude of locations in the Bulgarian cities Plovdiv and Burgas:

```
checkDistance('42.135408,24.74529', '42.504793,27.462636');
```

How it works

The `checkDistance()` function sends data to the Google Directions API. It sets the
origin, the destination, the sensor, the unit system, and the API key as parameters of
the URL. The result returned by the API is provided as JSON, which is handled in the
`retrieveDistance()` function.

The output in the console of the preceding example, which retrieves the distance between the
Bulgarian cities Plovdiv and Burgas, is `The distance between Plovdiv, Bulgaria`
`and Burgas, Bulgaria is: 253 km.`

See also

▶ For all details about the Directions API as well as a full description of the returned
   response, visit `https://developers.google.com/maps/documentation/`
   `directions/`.

Detecting device motion

This recipe offers a tutorial on how to detect and handle device motion in Tizen web
applications. No specific Tizen APIs will be used. The source code in this recipe relies
on the standard W3C `DeviceMotionEvent`, which is supported by Tizen web applications
as well as any modern web browser.

How to do it...

Please follow these steps to detect device motion and display its acceleration in a Tizen
web application:

1. Create some HTML components to show device acceleration, for example:

    ```
    <p>X: <span id="labelX"></span></p>
    <p>Y: <span id="labelY"></span></p>
    <p>Z: <span id="labelZ"></span></p>
    ```

2. Create a JavaScript function to handle errors:

    ```
    function showError(err) {
      console.log('Error: ' + err.message);
    }
    ```

3. Create a JavaScript function that handles motion events:

```
function motionDetected(event) {
   var acc = event.accelerationIncludingGravity;
   var sDeviceX = (acc.x) ? acc.x.toFixed(2) : '?';
   var sDeviceY = (acc.y) ? acc.y.toFixed(2) : '?';
   var sDeviceZ = (acc.z) ? acc.z.toFixed(2) : '?';

   $('#labelX').text(sDeviceX);
   $('#labelY').text(sDeviceY);
   $('#labelZ').text(sDeviceZ);
}
```

4. Create a JavaScript function that starts a listener for motion events:

```
function deviceMotion() {
   try {
      if (!window.DeviceMotionEvent) {
         throw new Error('device motion not supported.');
      }
      window.addEventListener('devicemotion', motionDetected,
         false);
   } catch (err) {
      showError(err);
   }
}
```

5. Invoke a function at an appropriate location of the source code of the application:

```
deviceMotion();
```

How it works

The deviceMotion() function registers an event listener that invokes the motionDetected() function as a callback when device motion event is detected. All errors, including an error if DeviceMotionEvent is not supported, are handled in the showError() function. As shown in the following screenshot, the motionDetected() function loads the data of the properties of DeviceMotionEvent into the HTML5 labels that were created in the first step. The results are displayed using standard units for acceleration according to the international system of units (**SI**)—metres per second squared (m/s^2). The JavaScript method toFixed() is invoked to convert the result to a string with two decimals:

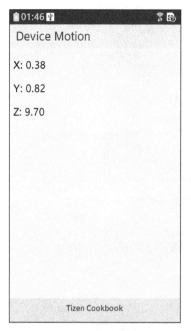

A Tizen web application that detects device motion

See also

▶ Notice that the device motion event specification is part of the `DeviceOrientationEvent` specification. Both are still in draft. The latest published version is available at `http://www.w3.org/TR/orientation-event/`.

▶ The source code of a sample Tizen web application that detects device motion is provided along with this book. You can import the project of the application into the Tizen IDE and explore it.

Detecting device orientation

In this recipe, you will learn how to monitor changes of device orientation using the HTML5 `DeviceOrientation` event as well as get the device orientation using the Tizen SystemInfo API. Both methods for retrieving device orientation have advantages and work in Tizen web applications. It is up to the developer to decide which approach is more suitable for their application.

How to do it...

Perform the following steps to register a listener and handle device orientation events in your Tizen web application:

1. Create a JavaScript function to handle errors:

```
function showError(err) {
   console.log('Error: ' + err.message);
}
```

2. Create a JavaScript function that handles changes of the orientation:

```
function orientationDetected(event) {
   console.log('absolute: ' + event.absolute);
   console.log('alpha: ' + event.alpha);
   console.log('beta: ' + event.beta);
   console.log('gamma: ' + event.gamma);
}
```

3. Create a JavaScript function that adds a listener for the device orientation:

```
function deviceOrientation() {
   try {
     if (!window.DeviceOrientationEvent) {
        throw new Error('device motion not supported.');
     }
     window.addEventListener('deviceorientation',
        orientationDetected, false);
   } catch (err) {
     showError(err);
   }
}
```

4. Execute the JavaScript function to start listening for device orientation events:

```
deviceOrientation();
```

How it works

If `DeviceOrientationEvent` is supported, the `deviceOrientation()` function binds the event to the `orientationDetected()` function, which is invoked as a callback only on success. The `showError()` function will be executed only if a problem occurs.

An instance of the `DeviceOrientationEvent` interface is provided as an argument of the `orientationDetected()` function. In the preceding code snippet, the values of its four read-only properties `absolute` (a Boolean value, `true` if the device provides orientation data absolutely), `alpha` (motion around the *z* axis), `beta` (motion around the *x* axis), and `gamma` (motion around the *y* axis) are printed in the console.

There's more...

There is an easier way to determine whether a Tizen device is in landscape or portrait mode. In a Tizen web application, in this case, it is recommended to use the SystemInfo API.

The following code snippet retrieves the device orientation:

```
function onSuccessCallback(orientation) {
  console.log("Device orientation: " + orientation.status);
}

function onErrorCallback(error) {
  console.log("Error: " + error.message);
}

tizen.systeminfo.getPropertyValue("DEVICE_ORIENTATION",
onSuccessCallback, onErrorCallback);
```

The status of the orientation can be one of the following values:

- `PORTRAIT_PRIMARY`
- `PORTRAIT_SECONDARY`
- `LANDSCAPE_PRIMARY`
- `LANDSCAPE_SECONDARY`

See also

- The `DeviceOrientationEvent` specification is still a draft. The latest published version is available at `http://www.w3.org/TR/orientation-event/`.
- For more information on the Tizen SystemInfo API, visit `https://developer.tizen.org/dev-guide/2.2.1/org.tizen.web.device.apireference/tizen/systeminfo.html`.

Using the Vibration API

Tizen is famous for its excellent support of HTML5 and W3C APIs. The standard Vibration API is also supported and it can be used in Tizen web applications. This recipe offers code snippets on how to activate vibration on a Tizen device.

How to do it...

1. Use the following code snippet to activate the vibration of the device for three seconds:

```
if (navigator.vibrate) {
  navigator.vibrate(3000);
}
```

2. To cancel an ongoing vibration, just call the `vibrate()` method again with zero as a value of its argument:

```
if (navigator.vibrate) {
  navigator.vibrate(0);
}
```

3. Alternatively, the vibration can be canceled by passing an empty array to the same method:

```
navigator.vibrate([]);
```

How it works

The W3C Vibration API is used through the JavaScript object, `navigator`. Its `vibrate()` method expects either a single value or an array of values. All values must be specified in milliseconds. The value provided to the `vibrate()` method in the preceding example is `3000` because 3 seconds is equal to 3000 milliseconds.

There's more...

The W3C Vibration API allows advanced tuning of the device vibration. A list of time intervals (with values in milliseconds), during which the device will vibrate, can be specified as an argument of the `vibrate()` method. For example, the following code snippet will make the device vibrate for 100 ms, stand still for 3 seconds, and then again vibrate, but this time just for 50 ms:

```
if (navigator.vibrate) {
  navigator.vibrate([100, 3000, 50]);
}
```

See also

- ▸ For more information on the vibration capabilities and the API usage, visit `http://www.w3.org/TR/vibration/`.

- ▸ Tizen native applications for the mobile profile have exposure to additional APIs written in C++ for light and proximity sensors. Explore the source code of the sample native application SensorApp which is provided with the Tizen SDK to learn how to use these sensors. More information about them is available at `ttps://developer. tizen.org/dev-guide/2.2.1/org.tizen.native.appprogramming/html/ guide/uix/light_sensor.htm` and `https://developer.tizen.org/dev- guide/2.2.1/org.tizen.native.appprogramming/html/guide/uix/ proximity_sensor.htm`.

Part 3

Porting and Debugging

Porting Apps to Tizen

Debugging Apps in Tizen

Porting Tizen to Hardware Devices

10
Porting Apps to Tizen

In this chapter, we will cover the following topics:

- ► Porting web apps
- ► Installing the PhoneGap or Cordova SDK
- ► Creating Tizen web applications with PhoneGap or Cordova
- ► Deploying Cordova and PhoneGap applications to the Tizen device or Emulator
- ► Bringing Android apps to Tizen
- ► Porting the Android UI to Tizen UI Framework
- ► Setting Qt for Tizen
- ► Deploying Qt applications on Tizen

Introduction

This chapter provides options and hints for porting the existing Web (Firefox OS, Chrome OS, webOS, and so on), Android, or Qt apps to Tizen. Tutorials for running Android applications on Tizen using the compatibility layer as well as for complete porting of Android applications to HTML5 are included.

Details about the community port Qt for Tizen that allows deployment of existing Qt mobile applications for Android, iOS, MeeGo/Harmattan, Symbian, SailfishOS, and BlackBerry 10 on Tizen devices will also be covered in this chapter.

Tizen is among the supported platforms of the leading developer tool vendors such as Marmalade, Appcelerator Titanium, Intel XDK, Project Anarchy, Sencha Touch, and many more. The tools and technologies provided by these vendors simplify the development process and allow cross-platform compatibility. The latest information regarding partner tools for Tizen is available at `https://www.tizen.org/about/partner-tools`.

Porting web apps

Web applications are first-class citizens in Tizen as well on several other popular mobile platforms such as Firefox OS, webOS, Chrome, and BlackBerry 10. Although it must be clarified that on BlackBerry 10, the native applications are created with C++ and Qt/QML. Despite this, BlackBerry WebWorks also provides all the required tools to develop and deploy an HTML5 application with a native look and feel on BlackBerry 10 devices.

On the other hand, Android and iOS do not provide generic tools for packaging HTML5 applications for distribution through application stores. Third-party software such as Cordova or PhoneGap can be used to create a hybrid application and to deploy HTML5 projects as standalone applications on Android and iOS (iPhone, iPad) devices.

Depending on the technologies and the development tools, we can divide web applications for mobile devices into three categories: packaged web applications, hosted web applications, and hybrid web applications.

The main focus of this recipe is on hosted web applications. We will go through the most common challenges when an HTML5 application built for another platform is ported to Tizen. From the subsequent two recipes, you can learn in detail the process of setting and porting hybrid (Cordova and PhoneGap) web applications to Tizen.

Getting ready

Before you start porting a web application to Tizen, take a moment and explore the existing structure and source code of your application. A good analysis at the beginning can save you a lot of time and help you solve issues easily during the porting process.

As you already know, the extension of the Tizen web application installation package is `wgt`. Different platforms have different package formats and file extensions, as detailed in the following list:

- `xpi` for Mozilla's FirefoxOS
- `crx` for Google's Chrome OS
- `ipk` for webOS
- `bar` for BlackBerry 10
- `xap` for web applications for Windows Phone

Each Tizen web application has two mandatory components: a configuration file and a main file (`index.html`). Optionally, an icon can be set with the recommended filename `icon.png` as well as the following directories:

- `js` for string JavaScript files
- `css` to store CSS files
- `img` to store images

The configurations are described in the XML file, which has to be called `config.xml`. It is possible to set custom names of all of the optional resources at the configuration file.

If you are using Cordova or PhoneGap, you should not worry because these tools will automatically generate an appropriate structure for packaging when you enable Tizen support. Otherwise, explore the structure of your existing application and locate the corresponding files. You may need to modify them manually to meet the requirements for packaging Tizen web applications.

How to do it...

The following guidelines specify the required actions to port an existing standalone web application to Tizen:

1. Create a `config.xml` file and set all settings as well as any permissions that your application needs to work on Tizen devices.

    If you are porting an application from Firefox OS, then `config.xml` is equivalent to `manifest.webapp`. The name of the configuration file for Chrome applications is `manifest.json`. On webOS, it is `appinfo.json`, `package.appxmanifest` on Windows Phone applications, and `config.xml` for BlackBerry WebWorks applications.

2. If your applications communicate with a server, specify their domains in the configuration file. For example, the following setting allows the Tizen web application to access `www.google.com`:

   ```
   <access origin="http://google.com"
     subdomains="true"></access>
   ```

   Although it is not highly recommended, due to security reasons, you can also allow access to any server by adding the following line:

   ```
   <access origin="*" subdomains="true"></access>
   ```

3. Add any permission that your application needs to use `config.xml`.

4. Create an icon following the Tizen guideline for icons at `https://developer.tizen.org/documentation/ux-guide/visual-style/icons`.

5. Build and run your application on the Tizen device or Emulator. Keep in mind that inconsistent behavior and bugs in the user interfaces might appear. Carefully test the application. You might need to debug and adjust the HTML, CSS, and JavaScript files.

See also

▶ In general, it is highly recommended to rely only on HTML5 specifications in the platform documentation. However, in certain cases, you may find it useful, especially for hosted web applications, to compare HTML5 of different platforms and their browsers at `http://html5test.com/`.

Installing the PhoneGap or Cordova SDK

PhoneGap and Cordova are popular tools for development of cross-platform HTML5 applications for mobile devices. The main advantage is that multiple mobile platforms are targeted with a single code base. All of the most popular mobile operating systems are supported: Android, iOS, Windows Phone, BlackBerry 10, and of course Tizen. Even older platforms that are not popular nowadays such as Symbian and webOS are supported.

Additionally, PhoneGap and Cordova allow web developers to use their existing knowledge and to develop high quality mobile applications without learning Java, Objective C, or C++.

Both Cordova and PhoneGap are open source projects. Cordova is available under Apache 2.0 License. PhoneGap is a fork of Cordova, and since 2011, it is owned and maintained by Adobe. Because of this, sometimes Cordova is referenced as an engine behind PhoneGap or as an Adobe distribution of Cordova.

The mobile applications developer with PhoneGap and Cordova are bundled as standard installation packages that are deployed on mobile devices. For example, installation files for Android have the extension `.apk` and for Tizen, it is `.wgt`.

In this recipe, you will learn how to install PhoneGap or Cordova and in the subsequent recipe, you will learn how to set up and deploy applications for Tizen.

Getting ready

Make sure that you have successfully installed Tizen SDK by following the instructions in the first chapter. Both PhoneGap and Cordova rely on its tools to build and package applications for Tizen. Also make sure that you have installed **npm** (Node Package Manager) before proceeding further.

If you are using Ubuntu, run the following commands to add a repository for Cordova and to ensure that the information for all repositories is up to date:

```
sudo apt-add-repository ppa:cordova-ubuntu/ppa
sudo apt-get update
sudo apt-get install cordova-cli
```

How to do it...

The installation of both Cordova and PhoneGap is very simple. Open a terminal and execute the following command to install the latest version of Cordova:

```
npm install -g cordovaRun the command below to install the latest version
of PhoneGap:
```

```
npm install -g phonegap
```

As you have probably noticed, both commands contain a parameter, -g. It specifies that this is a global installation.

How it works

The installation of both Cordova and PhoneGap is done through Node Package Manager, which is a software for management of Node.js packages. It is written entirely using JavaScript and the Node.js platform.

> Node.js and npm are open source projects. Node.js is available under MIT license, but it is provided bundled with components under other open source licenses. The source code of Node Package Manager is available under the Apache License 2.0.

See also

▶ The following recipes provide instructions on how to integrate PhoneGap and/or Cordova with the Tizen SDK as well as how to create and deploy applications to Tizen.

Creating Tizen web applications with PhoneGap or Cordova

In this recipe, you will learn how to create web applications for Tizen with PhoneGap and Cordova through the Tizen IDE.

Getting ready

Make sure that you have already installed the Tizen SDK as well as Cordova or PhoneGap. Instructions on the Tizen SDK installation are available in the first chapter of the book. Tutorials for setting up Cordova and PhoneGap are provided in the previous recipe.

Version 3.5 or older of both Cordova and PhoneGap do not provide support for Tizen of the command-line-interface (CLI). Several of the provided with Cordova and PhoneGap sample applications are used as templates to create Tizen projects. Ensure that you have these samples on your computer. You can obtain their latest version from the Apache public Git server. Type the following command to clone them on your computer:

```
git clone git://git.apache.org/cordova-tizen.git
```

How to do it...

Follow these steps to create a Cordova or PhoneGap application for Tizen using the Tizen IDE:

1. Launch the Tizen IDE.
2. Navigate to **File | Import | Tizen Web Project** and click on **Next**.
3. Click on **Browse...** to browse the root directory of a sample Cordova project.
4. Select **Copy projects into workspace**:

Importing a Cordova sample application into the Tizen IDE

5. Click on **Finish**.

How it works

The main purpose of projects such as Cordova and PhoneGap is to provide easy-to-use tools for development of mobile applications with the web technologies HTML, CSS, and JavaScript. Web applications are first class citizens in Tizen, so it is a very appropriate platform for Cordova and PhoneGap projects as well.

The Tizen IDE can be used directly to import, develop, debug, and deploy Cordova or PhoneGap applications. On the third step of the preceding tutorial, the sample Cordova application is used as a template. It is important to make sure that the **Copy project into workspace** option is checked as described in the fourth step. The IDE will duplicate the application and save it in the current workspace.

See also

▶ Have a look at the next recipe to learn how to deploy applications created with Cordova or PhoneGap to the Tizen device or Emulator. Have a look at the official documentation of PhoneGap for more details on Tizen applications at `http://docs.phonegap.com/en/edge/guide_platforms_tizen_index.md.html#Tizen%2520Platform%2520Guide`.

Deploying Cordova and PhoneGap applications to the Tizen device or Emulator

After creating or importing a new or existing Cordova/PhoneGap application into the workspace Tizen IDE, it is time to deploy it. In this recipe, you will learn how to use the options of the Tizen IDE to deploy a Cordova or PhoneGap application to a Tizen device or Emulator.

Getting ready

My preferred way for building and deploying Cordova application on an Android device or Emulator is by typing in the console the following command:

```
Cordova run android
```

Unfortunately, at the time of the writing of this book, the command-line interface (CLI) was not available for Tizen in both PhoneGap and Cordova. As you can see, regarding these circumstances, the easiest way to develop and deploy Cordova or PhoneGap applications for a Tizen device or Emulator is through the user interface of the IDE.

Before you proceed, make sure that you have connected a Tizen device to your computer or you have launched a Tizen Emulator on it.

How to do it...

Follow these simple instructions to deploy and run your Cordova or PhoneGap application on a Tizen Emulator:

1. Navigate to the **Project Explorer** view in the Tizen IDE.
2. Right-click on the project.
3. Navigate to **Run As | Tizen Web Simulator Application**.

The process for deployment of the application on a real device is almost the same. Make sure that the Tizen device is successfully connected to the computer and perform the following actions to run the application:

1. Navigate to the **Project Explorer** view in the Tizen IDE.
2. Right-click on the right mouse button over the project.
3. Navigate to **Run As | Tizen Web Application**.

How it works

The Tizen IDE is convenient for manual work but it might be an obstacle if you want to create continuous integration and testing of a Tizen web application created with Cordova and PhoneGap. The Tizen IDE relies on Tizen-centric tools such as SDB to deploy the application. In rare cases, when you have to deploy the application through the console instead of typing `cordova run`, use `sdb install` followed by the full name of the `wgt` file of the application.

See also

> ▶ If you are looking for options on how to deploy a Cordova or PhoneGap application on the Tizen device and Emulator through the console, refer to the recipe about Smart Development Bridge in the first chapter of the book for more details about SDB usage.

Bringing Android apps to Tizen

The Tizen smartphone has similar capabilities and hardware buttons as Android devices. The user interface of Tizen smartphones manufactured by Samsung is similar to TouchWiz—the frontend touch interface of the existing Samsung devices powered by Android

Android has been ruling the smartphone market for several years and millions of Android mobile applications exist. Several alternative platforms such as BlackBerry 10 and SailfishOS offer runtime for running an Android application. The same approach allows us to run Android applications on Tizen as well. The most popular solution in the Tizen ecosystem is the **Application Compatibility Layer** (**ACL**) provided by OpenMobile. In this recipe, the basic steps that are required to get started with ACL will be revealed.

Getting ready

Please prepare the APK (application package file) file of your Android application. Make sure that you have a valid bank account or a PayPal account if you plan to submit a paid application.

How to do it...

Follow these instructions to sign up for OpenMobile Developer Program and to port your Android applications to Tizen using their services:

1. Visit the website OpenMobile and register as an AppMall content provider at http://www.openmobileww.com/#!content-provider-registration/cuwc.

2. You will receive an e-mail with your username and password within 24 hours.

3. After receiving the e-mail, log in to http://manager.openmobileappmall.com.

4. Click on the **Profile** form and enter your preferred payment methods. Payments through PayPal and wire transfer are supported.

5. Go to **My Apps** and click on **Add App**:

Add new application to OpenMobile AppMall

6. Fill all the details in the **Overview** tab.

7. Go to the tab **Version / Files** and upload your Android application:

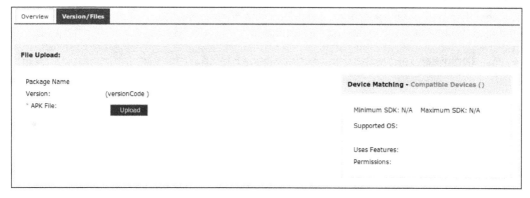

Uploading the APK file

How it works

The Application Compatibility Layer of OpenMobile is based on Google's **Android Open Source Project** (**AOSP**). Based on this, the ACL integrates the graphical stacks, the media, the **Inter-Process Communication** (**IPC**) and notifications of Android applications with Tizen. Using ACL, Android applications can be launched from the Tizen desktop just like any other Tizen web or native application. Just like all other applications, the Android applications on Tizen are also shown in the Task Manager of the operating system.

OpenMobile will convert your `apk` to `tpk`, validate, and publish it to Tizen Store. OpenMobile will also sign `tpk` and handles the whole administration of the application at Tizen Store Seller Office. Application download reports as well as revenues will be shared with the developer regularly.

See also

> ▶ More information and details regarding the terms of use of OpenMobile are available at `http://www.openmobileww.com/`.

Porting an Android UI to Tizen UI Framework

The information provided in this recipe will be useful if you decide to port an Android application to a Tizen web application. Pay attention that a lot of development will be required because you will have to rewrite from scratch your Java code to HTML5 and JavaScript. This chapter provides an overview and comparison of Android and Tizen widgets. It should be a good starting point for developers who intend to port Android applications.

How to do it...

The complete port of an application developed with Android SDK to HTML5 requires a lot of work and the following actions must be performed:

1. Completely rewrite the user interface using HTML5.
2. Port the existing Java source code to JavaScript.

Build and debug the application on the Tizen device or Emulator. The following is a list of the most popular Android UI components from the Java package `android.widget` and brief instructions on how to replace them in a Tizen web application, which relies on Tizen Web UI Framework:

- `Button`: Tizen Web UI Framework offers a widget with the same name and behavior. There are several ways to create it. Here is an approach using the `a` element and `data-role="button"`:

```
<a id="myBtn" href="#" data-role="button">Button 1</a>
```

- `EditText`: This is an editable text field. In Tizen web applications, the same user experience for gathering information from the user can be achieved using text inputs, for example:

```
<div data-role="fieldcontain">
  <label for="name">Text:</label>
  <input type="text" name="txt" id="txt" value=""  />
</div>
```

- `CheckBox`: Both the Tizen UI framework and jQuery Mobile offer a component `Checkbox`, which allows to replace the Android component in an HTML5 application.

- `ToggleButton`: This type of button allows the user to quickly change a setting from one state to another. Notice that only two states are allowed. Tizen Web UI Framework offers the same feature at the component Flip Toggle Switch. It can be created as shown in the following code snippet:

```
<select id="SwitchBtn" data-role="slider">
  <option value="off">Off</option>
  <option value="on">On</option>
</select>
```

- `Spinner`: This Java class provides a component for quick selection of a value from a list in Android. In an HTML5 application, it can be replaced with a `select` component with multiple options.

▸ `DatePicker` and `TimePicker`: Tizen Web UI Framework offers the following widgets for gathering user input about date and time: Date Picker, Time Picker, and Date Time Picker. For example, a Tizen widget for date selection can be achieved with the following HTML:

```
<div>
  <input type="date" name="datePicker" id="datePicker" data-
    format="dd MMM yyyy" />
</div>
```

A sample Tizen web application with date picker

▸ `Toast`: In Android, this component is used to show messages to the user in a small pop up, which does not require any interaction. In Tizen web applications, it can be replaced by the `Notification` widget.

▸ `AlertDialog`: This pop up widget should be used in Tizen web applications as a replacement of the `AlertDialog` in Android. Use a `div` element with the attribute `data-role="popup"` to create it.

How it works

After creating the user interface with HTML, you will need to rewrite the logic of the application. The following is a comparison between a Java code snippet for handling button clicks in an Android application and a JavaScript code for the same use case in Tizen web applications.

The sample Java source code from Android applications handles button clicks with the ID `myBtn`:

```
final Button button = (Button) findViewById(R.id.myBtn);
button.setOnClickListener(new View.OnClickListener() {
  public void onClick(View v) {
    //do something
  }
});
```

The following JavaScript code handles the `click` event of a button with the ID `myBtn`:

```
$('#myBtn').bind( "click", function(event, ui) {
  //do something
});
```

As you can see, the concept is the same but there are major differences in the syntax because of the nature of the Java and JavaScript programming languages. In both cases, the button has ID myBtn and from a user's perspective, a click on it in the Tizen web application will work just like the one in the Android application.

See also

▶ Refer to *Chapter 3, Building a UI*, as well as the official Tizen documentation to explore the widgets provided by Tizen Web UI Framework. A list of all available widgets is available at `https://developer.tizen.org/dev-guide/2.2.1/org.tizen.web.uiwidget.apireference/html/widgets/widget_reference.htm`.

Setting Qt for Tizen

Qt is a popular cross-platform framework for development of applications, primarily fascinating graphical user interfaces. The main programming languages are C++ and QML but other programming languages such as Python can also be used through language bindings.

The Qt project has a long story. Its development started in 1991 in Sweden and until 2008, the framework was developed by Trolltech. After that, Nokia bought Qt. Initially, Qt was available under commercial and GPL licenses. In 2009, Qt also became available under LGPL. Two years later, Nokia sold the commercial licensing business with Qt to Digia.

The latest major version of the project is Qt 5 and it was released at the end of 2012. A year later, Tomasz Olszak and Jarosław Staniek founded an open source project for porting Qt 5 to Tizen. I am proud that Philippe Coval, who is a reviewer of this book, and, I were among the first contributors of the project and we were able to help the leading developer of the project, Tomasz Olszak, with the testing of Qt for Tizen on different reference devices and code reviews.

In this recipe, you will learn how to install and configure the development environment to build Qt applications for Tizen mobile devices.

Getting ready

The tutorial provided in this recipe has been tested only on Ubuntu. Ensure that you have fulfilled the following four requirements before proceeding with the next section of the recipe.

- ▶ Ensure that you have successfully installed Tizen SDK. The process for setting up Qt for Tizen requires Qt to be built from source and to install Qt Creator so please make sure that you have at least 5 GB free disk space.

- ▶ Run `apt-get` and make sure that the packages from the following long list are installed because they are needed to build Qt:

```
sudo apt-get install perl python git build-essential libqt4-
dev "^libxcb.*" libx11-xcb-dev libxkbcommon-dev libglu1-mesa-dev
libxrender-dev libdbus-1-dev libfontconfig1-dev libfreetype6-dev
libatspi2.0-dev flex bison gperf libicu-dev libcups2-dev libxslt-
dev ruby libsqlite3-dev libgstreamer0.10-dev libgstreamer-plugins-
base0.10-dev libssl-dev libpulse-dev libasound2-dev libgtk2.0-dev
libpng12-dev libjpeg8-dev libjpeg-dev chrpath
```

- ▶ Install GBS. The first step you should do is to add a Tizen repository that corresponds to your distribution to `/etc/apt/sources.list`. After that, run the following commands:

```
sudo apt-get update
sudo apt-get install gbs
```

> An up-to-date installation guide for Tizen development tools is available at `https://source.tizen.org/documentation/developer-guide/getting-started-guide/installing-development-tools`.

- ▶ Make sure that you have a valid author certificate. Please refer to the recipe *Setting Active Secure Profile* from the first chapter for more details.

How to do it...

The following instructions explain how to install Tizen development tools, build Qt from source, install Qt Creator, and to set up the Tizen plugin for it.

1. Create a directory to store the source code of Qt.

2. Download the source code to your computer by cloning it from the Git repository of the project:

```
git clone -b alpha6 git://gitorious.org/tizenbuildtools/
tizenbuildtools.git
cd tizenbuildtools
git checkout v_alpha6.2
```

3. Go to the desktop directory and build Qt:

```
cd desktop
MAKE_THREADS=4 ./downloadAndBuildAll.sh
```

> Replace the number of threads with a number that matches the count of cores of the processor.
>
> Alternatively, you can include the following commands, which will retrieve the number of cores automatically:
>
> ```
> MAX_THREAD=$(grep 'Core' /proc/cpuinfo | wc -l
> ) ./downloadAndBuildAll.sh
> ```

4. Go to the `emulator` directory and prepare the emulator of Qt for Tizen:

```
cd ../emulator
./prepare_developer_tools.sh
```

5. Change the current directory again but this time to directory mobile. Prepare Qt to make Tizen run on devices:

```
cd ../mobile
./prepare_developer_tools.sh
```

6. Visit `http://qt-project.org/downloads#qt-creator` and download Qt Creator.

7. Install Qt Creator. On Linux, the installation can be started through the command line using the following command:

```
chmod u+x ./qt-creator-linux-...run
./qt-creator-linux-...run
```

8. Build the Tizen plugin for Qt Creator:

```
cd ../qtcreator
export PATH=$HOME/dev/src/tizenbuildtools/desktop/qt5hostInstall/
bin:$PATH
QTC_BUILD=$HOME/qtcreator-3.0.1 ./build_and_deploy_tizen_plugin.sh
```

There's more...

Follow these steps to integrate the Tizen SDK into Qt Creator:

1. Launch Tizen **Emulator Manager**.
2. Launch Qt Creator.
3. Navigate to **Tools | Options**.
4. Select **Tizen**.
5. Navigate to **Tizen SDK Path**, click on **Browse** to find Tizen SDK installation directory, and after that click on **OK**.
6. Navigate to **Author certificate** and again click on **Browse** to select a certificate. The default path for storing author certificates on Linux is `$HOME/tizen-sdk-data/keystore/author/`.
7. Type in the password of the certificate.

You are almost done. Now, you have to configure the Tizen Emulator for Qt Creator:

1. Go to **Devices** from the **Options** dialog and select **tizen**.
2. Type the name that will help you in future to easily distinguish that this is Tizen Emulator.
3. From **Options**, go to **Build & Run**, select the tab **Qt Versions** and click on **Add**.
4. Choose **qmake** for Tizen Emulator builds and click on **Apply**. By default, the path should be `$HOME/dev/src/tizenbuildtools/emulator/qt5CrossCompileTools/bin/qmake`.
5. Go to the tab **Kits**, click on **Add**, and type the appropriate name, for example, `Tizen Emulator`.
6. Click on **Add**.
7. Select **Tizen Device** as a **Device type**, **Tizen GCC (x86)** for the **Compiler**, and the Qt version for Emulator in the **Qt Version** field.
8. Click on **Apply**.

See also

▶ The development of Qt for Tizen is entirely transparent. To get in contact with Tomasz, Jarosław or any other contributor, please use the communication channels described at `http://qt-project.org/wiki/Tizen`.

▶ For more information on building Qt for Tizen, refer to the latest version of the official guidelines at Qt's wiki `http://qt-project.org/wiki/Build-Qt-for-Tizen`.

Deploying Qt applications on Tizen

This recipe will explain how to prepare, build, and deploy Qt application on Tizen Emulator or devices.

Getting ready

Before you start, ensure that you have successfully set up Qt for Tizen on your computer. As we already discussed at the beginning of the book for Tizen, smartphones support both native applications created with C++ and extension `.tpk`, as well as web applications with extension `.wgt`. Qt is a framework based on C++, so the port for Tizen relies on the tools for `.tpk` files.

How to do it...

Follow these step-by-step instructions to develop new or port existing Qt applications to Tizen using Qt Creator:

1. Create a directory with the name `tizen` in the project of your Qt application.

2. Copy `manifest.xml` from the `helloworld` project, which is provided with `qtquickcontrols-tizen` to the directory that you have created in the previous step.

3. Edit `manifest.xml` and set the application ID in it.

4. Open the `.pro` file of the application and enable Tizen support by adding the following rules:

```
tizen {
  tizen_shared.files = shared/res
  CONFIG += TIZEN_STANDALONE_PACKAGE
  TIZEN_BUNDLED_QT_LIBS=Qt5Core Qt5DBus Qt5Qml Qt5Quick
    Qt5Widgets Qt5Gui Qt5Network
  load(tizen_app)
}
```

5. Open `main.cpp` and implement the following source code for the method `OspMain()`, which is the entry point for Tizen native applications:

```
extern "C" int OspMain(int argc, char *argv[]) {
  return main(argc, argv);
}
```

 This recipe has been tested on the Tizen mobile profile. It will not work on Tizen IVI and other profiles on which native application development is not present.

6. Build the application and deploy it to Tizen Emulator or device through Qt Creator.

How it works

The `helloworld` application provided with `qtquickcontrols-tizen` is used as a template. Actually, the first step of this recipe is almost the same as the first step for creating Tizen applications with Cordova or PhoneGap. Although these technologies create web applications, the first step for them is to import and use a sample application as a template.

The second and the third steps are dedicated to `manifest.xml`. This is a configuration file. Each Tizen native application must have just a single manifest file that must comply with the XML standard.

The next step is again dedicated to editing the configuration file. The `.pro` extension is specific for the project files of Qt applications. This file must contain all the information required by **qmake** to build the application.

In the fifth step, the method that acts as an entry point of Tizen native applications is instructed to run the main method of the Qt application. All arguments provided to `OspMain()` are provided to `main()`. The prefix of `OspMain()` stands for Open Service Platform and its origins lead to Bada that was merged into Tizen 2.

See also

▶ Tomasz Olszak, the co-founder and the leading developer of Qt for Tizen, maintains an article at Qt wiki about development of Qt applications for Tizen. For more information, visit `http://qt-project.org/wiki/Creating-Hello-World-Application`.

▶ Tutorials and documentation related to Qt 5 are available at `http://qt-project.org/`.

▶ A good starting point if you are not familiar with QML is `http://qt-project.org/doc/qt-5/qml-tutorial.html`.

11
Debugging Apps
in Tizen

In this chapter, we will cover the following topics:

- ▶ Running an application in Tizen Web Simulator
- ▶ Running an application in Tizen Emulator
- ▶ Running an application on a device
- ▶ Debugging in Tizen Web Simulator
- ▶ Debugging in Tizen Emulator
- ▶ Debugging on a device
- ▶ Using Samsung Remote Test Lab
- ▶ Tracking JavaScript bugs
- ▶ Unit testing with QUnit

Introduction

Quality assurance is among the most important processes during the development of an application because it ensures less issues and better user experience for end users. A lot of great mobile applications have failed to achieve commercial success due to bugs. Even if an application has a great user interface and offers good user experience, it is not enough to be sure that it will be successful.

In general, users have low tolerance to bugs. A user might never open your application again if it has crashed just once.

The recipes in this chapter bring ideas and tutorials on how to test applications and to provide good quality. In this chapter, you will learn about how to run and debug Tizen applications, as well as exploring JavaScript unit testing of web applications.

This chapter also includes a recipe on Samsung **Remote Test Lab** (**RTL**) with a tutorial on how to deploy and test applications on physical Tizen devices located remotely. Although there is no separate recipe for Selenium, you might consider using this tool for functional and user acceptance testing of web applications compatible with Tizen. To get started with it, please visit http://www.seleniumhq.org/.

Running an application in Tizen Web Simulator

You should be already familiar with Tizen Web Simulator for web applications, which was revealed in the first chapter of this book. In this recipe, you will learn in detail how to use it.

Getting ready

A Tizen web application can be launched in the simulator from the Tizen IDE. All you have to do has been explained in the first chapter of the book, but it is summarized here:

- Select the project in the **Project Explorer** view. Right-click on the project to activate the context menu and navigate to **Run As | Tizen Web Simulator Application**.

- Go to the **Run** menu of the Tizen IDE and navigate to **Run As | Tizen Web Simulator Application**.

- Alternatively, just click on the **Run** button from the toolbar of the Tizen IDE.

How to do it...

It is possible to configure the device information and the system settings of the simulator. Follow these instructions to configure the Simulator:

1. Launch the Simulator using any of the three available options.
2. Click on the **Configuration** button in the right-upper corner of the Simulator.

3. Adjust the device, system, and network settings, as shown in the following screenshot:

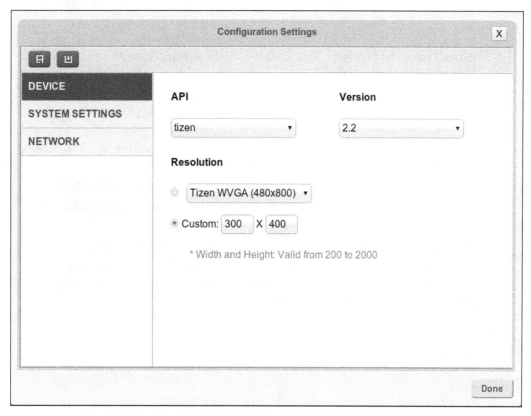

Configuration settings of Tizen Web Simulator

Furthermore, you can adjust the visible panels by clicking on the **Panel Settings** button that is located next to the **Configuration** button.

There's more

Tizen Web Simulator offers numerous panels to simulate various events. These are the available panels listed in their order of appearance in the simulator:

▸ **Orientation and zooming**: This panel allows you to change the orientation of the simulator from portrait to landscape and vice versa. As an additional feature, you can adjust the zoom level from the same panel.

▸ **System summary**: This panel provides basic information about the system and the application.

▸ **Notification**: A list of the received notifications is available in this panel.

- ▶ **Sensors**: This panel is extremely valuable for the simulation of events related to the accelerometer and the gyroscope. It offers options for the adjustment of the position of the device as well as to the simulator.

- ▶ **Geolocation**: This panel is used for setting the current time zone, location, and routes. It is useful for testing location-based Tizen web applications without a real GPS device in the simulator.

- ▶ **Application configuration**: This panel shows information regarding the application configuration and its installation package. Basically, it displays the content of the `config.xml` file.

- ▶ **Communications**: From this panel, the developer can simulate the handling of calls and messages as well as reception of push notifications.

- ▶ **Power manager**: This panel changes the battery level and simulates low battery.

- ▶ **Network management**: This panel controls the network units of the simulator: NFC, Bluetooth, Wi-Fi, and cellular network.

- ▶ **Download**: This panel manages the download resources of the simulator.

- ▶ **Packages and applications**: This panel shows the list of installed packages and applications on the simulator. Furthermore, this panel provides the capability to delete the installed package or application.

See also

- ▶ Specifications of all available features of the simulator can be found at `https://developer.tizen.org/dev-guide/2.2.1/org.tizen.web.` `appprogramming/html/ide_sdk_tools/simulator_features.htm`.

Running an application in Tizen Emulator

Using this recipe, you will recall how to launch Tizen Emulator and you will learn how to run applications and to simulate events using **Event Injector**.

How to do it...

A couple of options are available to start Tizen Emulator. Both of them have already been presented in the first chapter of the book with instructions on how to create a virtual Tizen device. Before you proceed, make sure that you have already set a virtual machine.

The easiest way to start Tizen Emulator from a user's point of view is using the Emulator Manager. The following is a quick recap of the required actions:

1. Start the application Tizen Emulator, which comes with the installation of the Tizen SDK.

2. Select the desired configuration and click on the **Play** button to launch it.

An alternative option for launching Tizen Emulator is to type the following command in the terminal:

```
./emulator-x86 --skin-args <skin options> --qemu-args <QEMU options>
```

Once the emulator is running, you can install and launch the Tizen application in it directly from the Tizen IDE. There are three ways to do this. Pick the one that suits you the best:

*   Go to **Project Explorer** view, open a project, right-click on it, and navigate to **Run As | Tizen Web Application**

*   Navigate to the **Run** menu in the Tizen IDE and navigate to **Run As | Tizen Web Application**

*   Click on the **Run** button in the toolbar of the Tizen IDE

While your application is running on the emulator, you can simulate various events to test it using Event Injector. The following events can be created and sent to the emulator through the Event Injector view in the Tizen IDE or through the console:

*   **Sensor**: This event indicates values related to any of the following sensors: acceleration, magnetic, gyro, proximity, or light.

*   **Motion**: This event simulates motion events such as shake.

*   **Battery**: This event adjusts the current battery level as well as the state of the charger.

*   **Earjack**: This event controls the state of the headset.

*   **USB**: This event manages the state of the USB connector of the virtual device.

*   **RSSI (Received signal strength indication)**: This event simulates different signal strength. Note that if you set the RSSI to 0, then the events for text messaging and calls will not work.

*   **SD card**: This event sets the state of the indicator for the SD card.

*   **Location**: This event simulates a fake position of the device for testing purposes.

*   **SMS**: This event simulates sending text messages.

*   **Call**: This event handles simulated calls.

*   **NFC**: This event manages NFC tags, for example, NDEF messages, NFC tags, and so on.

See also

▶ The official documentation shipped with the SDK reveals all the capabilities of the Event Injector at `https://developer.tizen.org/dev-guide/2.2.1/org.tizen.gettingstarted/html/dev_env/event_injec.htm`.

▶ It is also possible to inject events through the console. This feature is extremely valuable for scripts used in automated testing. A user's guide of this console tool is available at `https://developer.tizen.org/dev-guide/2.2.1/org.tizen.gettingstarted/html/dev_env/using_event_injector.htm`.

▶ Of course, the official documentation offers basic instructions for running application on the emulator at `https://developer.tizen.org/dev-guide/2.2.1/org.tizen.web.appprogramming/html/app_dev_process/running_widget_emulator.htm`.

Running an application on a device

In the previous chapters of the book, we have already discussed SDB and how applications can be run on an emulator or devices. The purpose of this recipe is to consolidate this knowledge.

Getting ready

Perform the following actions to set the run configuration of a connected device:

1. Make sure that the Tizen device is successfully connected to the computer and that it is recognized in the **Connection Explorer** of the Tizen IDE.

2. Adjust the configurations before the first start of the application using any of the following approaches:

   ❑ Navigate to **Run | Run Configurations** from the main menu of the Tizen IDE.

   ❑ Locate the project in the **Project Explorer** view. Right-click on the project and from the context menu and navigate to **Run As | Run Configurations**.

How to do it...

Make sure that you have adjusted the run configuration and used any of the following methods to run the application on a connected Tizen device:

1. Navigate to the **Project Explorer** view, mark the project, and right-click on it. A context menu will appear. Select **Run As | Tizen Web Application**.

2. In the Tizen IDE menu, go to **Run | Run As | Tizen Web Application**.

3. Click on the **Run** button from the toolbar of the Tizen IDE.

No matter which method you choose, you will get the same result. Use the method that suits you best.

How it works

The algorithm for running an application on a Tizen device includes five major steps. The first step is to build the application. After that, it must be packaged as `.wgt` if it is a web application, or `.tpk` if it is a native application. In the third step, the package is transferred to the connected device. The next step is to install the package and finally to launch the application on the device.

See also

- ▶ Complete guidelines for connecting a Tizen device and running an application through the Tizen IDE on it are available as part of the official documentation of the SDK at `https://developer.tizen.org/dev-guide/2.2.1/org.tizen.web.appprogramming/html/app_dev_process/running_widget_target.htm`.

Debugging in Tizen Web Simulator

This recipe offers guidelines on how to run and debug a Tizen web application using the Web Simulator and its web inspector.

How to do it...

Follow these instructions to run a Tizen web application in the Web Simulator and to debug it:

1. Launch the application in the simulator following any of the methods described in the recipe *Running an application in the simulator*.
2. Hit *F12* to open the Web Inspector.
3. Click on **Console** to have a look at the log messages.
4. Click on **Sources**, select some JavaScript, and set and control the breakpoints for debugging of the application.

How it works

Tizen Web Simulator works in a Google Chrome browser. When you start it from Tizen IDE, it automatically launches a new Chrome window and loads a local URL in it. All debugging tools of Chrome are available in the simulator.

See also

▶ For more information about the simulator and its usage, visit `https://developer.`
    `tizen.org/dev-guide/2.2.1/org.tizen.web.appprogramming/html/`
    `app_dev_process/running_widget_simulator.htm`

Debugging in Tizen Emulator

In this recipe, you will learn how to install and run Tizen applications in the debug mode on
the emulator and how to debug them with the **Remote Inspector**.

Getting ready

The tool for debugging applications in the emulator is called Remote Inspector and it requires
Google Chrome. Ensure that you have successfully installed Chrome on the computer that is
used for development before you proceed.

How to do it...

Follow these steps to debug Tizen applications using the Emulator:

1. Launch the Tizen IDE and Tizen Emulator.

2. Select the application from the **Project Explorer** and use any of the following
    methods to launch it on the emulator:

    ❑ Right-click on the project and navigate to **Debug as | Tizen web application**

    ❑ Click on the **Debug** button on the toolbox of the Tizen IDE

    ❑ From the menu of the Tizen IDE, navigate to **Run | Debug As | Tizen
        Web Application**

How it works

The emulator provides the full stacks of the platform and it is convenient for testing Tizen
native and web applications. It is well integrated with the Tizen IDE. The application gets
copied to the emulator. After that, it is automatically installed and launched. A new Chrome
window is opened for the Remote Inspector.

See also

▶   A tutorial about the usage of the Remote Inspector is available in the subsequent recipe about tracking JavaScript bugs. More information about the process of launching applications on emulator can be found in the previous recipes as well in the official documentation available at `https://developer.tizen.org/dev-guide/2.2.1/org.tizen.web.appprogramming/html/app_dev_process/running_widget_emulator.htm`.

Debugging on a device

Debugging on a real Tizen device is almost the same as on an emulator. This recipe will only reveal the minor differences of the process when it is performed with a device.

Getting ready

The requirements for debugging Tizen applications on a real device are the same as for emulator. Google Chrome must be installed on your development machine because it is required by the Remote Inspector.

How to do it...

Follow these instructions to install and debug applications on the Tizen device through the Tizen IDE:

1.   Launch the Tizen IDE.
2.   Connect the device and make sure that it is recognized and displayed in **Connection Explorer** in the Tizen IDE.
3.   Start the application on the device in the debug mode using any of these methods:
     ❑   Right-click on the project and choose **Debug as | Tizen web application**
     ❑   Click on the **Debug** button in the toolbox of the Tizen IDE
     ❑   From the menu of the Tizen IDE, navigate to **Run | Debug As | Tizen Web Application**

As you can see from the preceding tutorial, the steps are almost the same as for debugging applications on Tizen Emulator.

There's more

Building, copying, and installing an application to the Tizen device can be an annoying process if you have to do it hundred of times each day. Do you want to save the development time and accelerate your debugging process?

Tizen **Rapid Development Support** (**RDS**) to the rescue! Using it, the application is fully packaged, copied, and installed on the device only at its first run. After that, the step for packaging is skipped and only the modified files are transferred to the device. RDS has a built-in watchdog that monitors the process and if it fails then normal installation of the application is performed.

By default, RDS is enabled. If you need to disable it, go to the **Windows** menu of the Tizen IDE and select **Preferences | Tizen SDK | Rapid Development Support**:

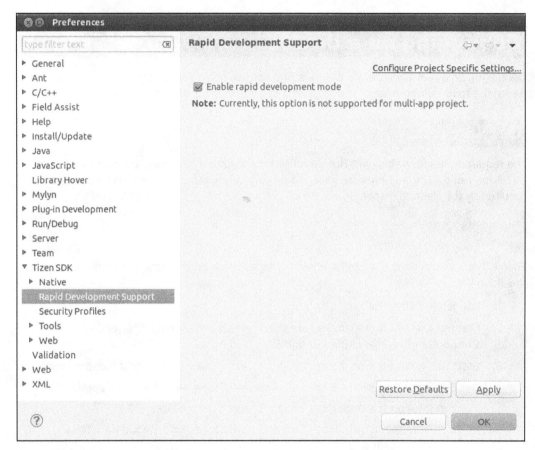

Enable or disable Rapid Development Support

See also

> ▶   More information about RDS is available at `https://developer.tizen.org/dev-guide/2.2.1/org.tizen.web.appprogramming/html/app_dev_process/rapid_dev_support.htm`

> ▶ Explore the next recipe to learn how to take advantage of the Remote Inspector or dig into the official documentation about it at `https://developer.tizen.org/dev-guide/2.2.1/org.tizen.web.appprogramming/html/app_dev_process/debugging_widget.htm`

Using Samsung Remote Test Lab

Samsung offers a free service for remote testing of applications on mobile and wearable devices with Android and Tizen. The service is called Samsung **Remote Test Lab** (**RTL**). It is a convenient and affordable way to try out an application on a physical device without having a real hands-on experience with it.

Getting ready

You need to be a registered Samsung developer to take the advantage of RTL. If you do not have an account, you can sign up for free at `http://developer.samsung.com/signup`.

RTL has several technical requirements that you must fulfill:

> ▶ A modern web browser (Firefox v2+,Internet Explorer v7+, Opera v9.6+, Chrome 7+, or Safari v3+)
>
> ▶ JavaScript, enabled in the web browser
>
> ▶ Java Web Start

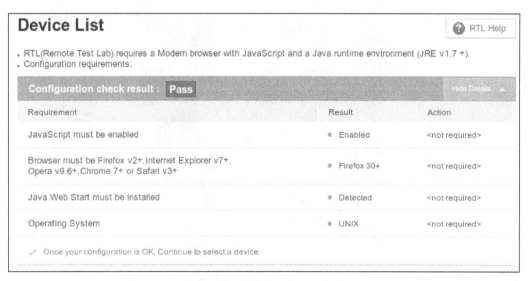

Requirements for Remote Test Lab

The service can be used on computers with GNU/Linux, Mac OS X, and Microsoft Windows. You should also prepare the installation file of your application.

How to do it...

Follow this step-by-step guide to access a Tizen device using RTL and to launch your application on it:

1. Sign in using your Samsung Developer credentials at `https://account.samsung.com/account/check.do`.

2. Visit Samsung Remote Test Lab at `http://developer.samsung.com/remotetestlab/rtlDeviceList.action`.

3. Go to the **Tizen** tab and select the device, OS version, and duration of the reservation.

4. Click on **Start** and wait until the RTL client loads.

5. Right-click on the top of the RTL client and navigate to **Test | Install Application**, as shown in the following screenshot:

Installing a Tizen application

6. Upload the installation file of your application and click on **Install**.

7. Upon success, the following message will be displayed: **App was successfully installed.**

How it works

The RTL client application has been installed on your computer and provides an environment and a connection to a physical Tizen device that can be used remotely. The devices are situated in different locations around the world: South Korea, Poland, India, UK, US, and Russia.

If there is a free device, you can use it immediately. Alternatively, you can make a reservation and use it later. Although the service is free, there are some limitations and you need credit to use a device. Each Samsung developer receives 20 credits per day. One credit allows you to use a device for 15 minutes and the minimal reservation period is half an hour (2 credits).

You should leave the device in the same condition as you found it, so keep in mind that you have to remove all the applications that you have installed. You may choose the screen quality: **Low**, **Normal**, and **High**. It is recommended to use low quality if your Internet connection is slow. The RTL client also allows you to change the device orientation through its context menu. Other useful features are the options to capture a screenshot and to record a video.

See also

▶   For more information, sign in with your Samsung Developers' account and refer to the following article:

▶   `http://developer.samsung.com/remotetestlab/rtlHelpDevice.action`

Tracking JavaScript bugs

In this recipe, we will discuss two different techniques for tracking JavaScript bugs. Tutorials about the JavaScript log console and debugging by break points in the Remote Inspector will be revealed.

How to do it...

The most primitive and easy debugging approach is to write messages in the console. The following methods of the JavaScript object `console` can be used:

▶   `console.log`
▶   `console.info`
▶   `console.warn`
▶   `console.error`
▶   `console.debug`

Messages logged with any of the preceding methods will be displayed in the JavaScript Log Console of the Tizen IDE. It starts automatically with the launch of a Tizen web application.

The technique to debug through logging in the console is not efficient in all cases. Debugging the code with breakpoints is more useful in many cases.

Follow these instructions to launch the Remote Inspector and to track JavaScript bugs by setting breakpoints in the source code:

1. Launch the Remote Inspector for a Tizen web application that runs on Tizen Emulator and device. Instructions on how this step is provided in the previous recipes.

2. Click on the **Sources** button from the main toolbar:

The Sources button in the Remote Inspector

3. Click on the button in the left-upper corner below the main toolbar to show the navigator.

4. Select and open a JavaScript file.

5. Click on the line number to set a breakpoint. Multiple breakpoints can be defined.

6. Use the control buttons to navigate through the breakpoints and the source of the application:

Buttons to manage and move through breakpoints in the Remote Inspector

For example, have a look at the following screenshot, which has been taken during the debugging of the Hello World application in Tizen Emulator. Three breakpoints have been set in the main.js file to track the behavior of the hardware back button, as shown in the following screenshot:

Tracking JavaScript bugs with Tizen Emulator and Remote Inspector

How it works

The Remote Inspector is integrated in the Tizen IDE. As you have seen, it provides powerful tools for debugging Tizen web applications running on Tizen Emulators and devices. With this tool, you can not only debug JavaScript, but also inspect the resources, the styles, and the DOM structure of the HTML files.

The Remote Inspector is based on WebKit Web Inspector but it includes additional features for remote debugging. A separate window of the Chrome browser opens automatically when the Remote Inspector is launched. The communication between Tizen Emulator and the Remote Inspector for debugging Tizen web applications goes entirely through HTTP.

See also

For more information, visit the following links and visit the following pages:

- ▶ `https://developer.tizen.org/dev-guide/2.2.1/org.tizen.web.` `appprogramming/html/ide_sdk_tools/javascript_log_console.htm`
- ▶ `https://developer.tizen.org/dev-guide/2.2.1/org.tizen.web.` `appprogramming/html/app_dev_process/debugging_widget.htm`

Unit testing with QUnit

Unit testing is an approach for automated verification of the software by testing individual units of it. Unit testing is the backbone of the concept for test-driven development according to which tests must be written before the source code of the application.

A lot of JavaScript frameworks for unit testing are available under an open source license but in this recipe, we will focus on QUnit. It is a jQuery unit testing framework that makes it very appropriate for Tizen web applications built with Tizen Web UI Framework or jQuery Mobile. Another advantage of QUnit is its license, because it is available under MIT license.

This recipe reveals the required steps to integrate QUnit in a Tizen web application and to create several basic tests.

Getting ready

Visit and get the latest version of QUnit. At the time of writing this book, the latest version was Version 1.14.0.

How to do it...

Follow these instructions on how to create a new Tizen web application from scratch and to integrate QUnit in it. After that, based on the knowledge gained in this tutorial, you will be able to perform unit tests in any other Tizen web application.

1. Launch Tizen IDE and create a new Tizen web application.
2. Find the application in the **Project Explorer** and right-click on it. From the context menu that will appear, navigate to **New | Folder**.
3. Type in `tests` as the name of the new folder and click on **Finish**.
4. Copy the downloaded QUnit file inside the new folder.
5. Again, right-click on the name of the project in the **Project Explorer** view and this time navigate to **New | File**.
6. Save the file `tests.js` in the folder `tests`.

7. Open `tests.js` and insert a couple of test cases:

```
QUnit.test( "Tizen Test 1", function( assert ) {
  assert.ok( 1 == "1", "1 is 1" );
});

QUnit.test( "Tizen Test 2", function( assert ) {
  assert.equal( 0, 0, "0 is 0" );
  assert.notEqual( 2, 1, "2 is not 1" );
});
```

8. By following the same procedure, create another file called `tests.html` and place it in the root directory of the project.

9. Open `tests.html` and insert the following code:

```
<!DOCTYPE html>
<html>
<head>
  <meta charset="utf-8">
    <title>QUnit Tests</title>
```

The following line must be included in the source code of the frontend to guarantee that the test results will fit into the size of the screen on Tizen Emulator or device.

```
  <meta name="viewport" content="width=device-width,user-
    scalable=no"/>
  <link rel="stylesheet" href="tests/qunit-1.14.0.css">
</head>
<body>
  <div id="qunit"></div>
  <div id="qunit-fixture"></div>
  <script src="tests/qunit-1.14.0.js"></script>
  <script src="tests/tests.js"></script>
</body>
</html>
```

10. Edit `config.xml` and set `tests.html` as the main page by changing the value of the `content` tag:

```
<content src="tests.html"/>
```

11. Launch the application in the emulator or device to see the results of the tests.

How it works

Test results are directly displayed on the screen of the device or emulator when the application is launched. This is caused by the changed HTML for the entry at tenth step of the tutorial.

We have created only two basic test cases in `tests.js`. The first test case verifies that `1` is equal by value to `"1"` in JavaScript. The second test case shows the usage of the `equal()` assert method. Both unit tests will pass successfully; so, on the screen, a report similar to the one in the following screenshot will be displayed:

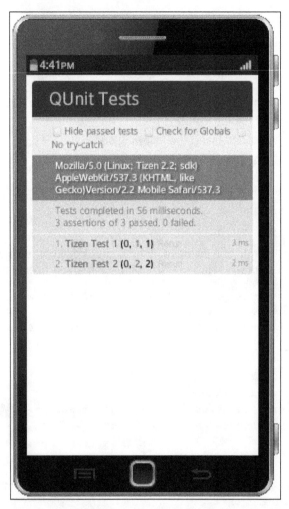

A QUnit report on Tizen Emulator with successfully completed tests

Let's make a minor change in the first test case to demonstrate the QUnit report with the failed test. Change the test by replacing `==` with `===`, so its code will become:

```
QUnit.test( "Tizen Test 1", function( assert ) {
  assert.ok( 1 === "1", "1 is 1" );
});
```

This minor modification completely changes the relation. In JavaScript, the comparison operator === checks not only the values but also the types. This time the test will fail because the operand on the left is numeric and the one of the right side is a string. Have a look at the following screenshot to see how a failed test case is reported:

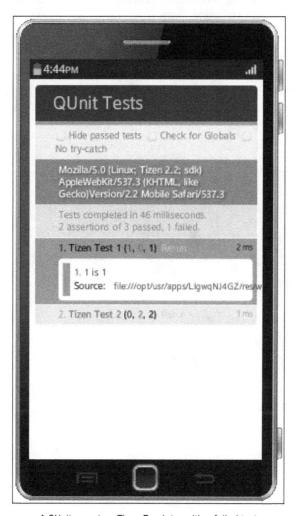

A QUnit report on Tizen Emulator with a failed test

In this recipe, only two assert methods have been used. The full list of all assert methods is available at http://api.qunitjs.com/category/assert/.

Along with this book, you can find a sample Tizen web application with integrated unit tests using QUnit. It is created by following the tutorial provided in this recipe. Import it in the Tizen IDE and run it to see the test results of the screen of your emulator or device.

See also

- With the examples in this recipe, you have taken a sneak peek in QUnit; so, you can continue by exploring the resources available in its API documentation at `http://api.qunitjs.com/`.

- Furthermore, the QUnit cookbook is an excellent article for getting started. It is available online at `http://qunitjs.com/cookbook/`.

- Keep in mind that a lot of other good tools for creating JavaScript unit tests exist. Facebook recently published on GitHub the source code of their product for painless unit testing called Jest at `http://facebook.github.io/jest/`.

12

Porting Tizen to Hardware Devices

In this chapter, we will cover:

- ▶ Setting up a platform development environment
- ▶ Installing development tools in Ubuntu or Debian
- ▶ Installing development tools in openSUSE
- ▶ Installing development tools in Fedora and CentOS
- ▶ Building Tizen platform images
- ▶ Flashing a Tizen image to mobile devices
- ▶ Enabling 3D acceleration and OpenGL
- ▶ Booting Tizen on Intel NUC
- ▶ Booting Tizen on Allwinner devices
- ▶ Hacking a tablet and booting Tizen on it

Introduction

Congratulations! You made it to the last chapter of this book! So far, we have covered Tizen application development and kept the focus on web applications. I hope you had fun. It's time to move to the next level—Tizen platform development.

This chapter offers just a sneak peek into the enormous possibilities that Tizen platform development opens for both individual developers and companies. I hope your Tizen journey will not finish with the last recipe of this chapter and you will continue experimenting with the platform.

This is definitely the most advanced and complex chapter of the book. It offers guidelines to build embedded control systems powered by Tizen. Brief tutorials to build Tizen platform images and booting them on ARM and x86 devices are included. The information provided is useful for the development or porting of new or existing embedded control systems, such as IVI or home automation, to the Tizen software platform. Based on all the recipes in this chapter, you should be able to start the development of your own wearable devices and the Internet of Things powered by Tizen.

Setting up a platform development environment

The Tizen project uses the online code review system Gerrit and the version control system Git. This recipe reveals how to obtain access to and configure both systems.

Getting ready

If you still do not have a user account for `https://www.tizen.org/`, complete the registration form at `https://www.tizen.org/user/register`. An Internet connection and a Linux computer are also needed for this recipe. Tizen is a Linux-based platform, and the tools for platform development are compatible with popular Linux distributions.

Ensure that you have installed Git. If it is not present on your system, you can use the following commands to install it:

- On Ubuntu or Debian, use the following command:

  ```
  sudo apt-get update
  sudo apt-get install git
  ```

- On Fedora or CentOS, use the following command:

  ```
  yum install git-core
  ```

- On OpenSUSE, use the following command:

  ```
  zypper install git
  ```

How to do it...

Follow these instructions to configure SSH for Gerrit access:

1. Generate RSA keys by running the following command in a terminal and follow the onscreen instructions:

   ```
   ssh-keygen
   ```

2. Using your favorite text editor, for example, vim, create an SSH configuration file at `~/.ssh/config`, and place it inside the following settings:

```
Host tizen review.tizen.org
Hostname review.tizen.org
IdentityFile ~/.ssh/id_rsa
User <username>
Port 29418
```

 Do not forget to replace `<username>` with your Gerrit account name.

3. Copy the entire content of the file generated in the previous step to the clipboard. By default, the file is stored at `~/.ssh/id_rsa.pub`.

4. Open a web browser, and log in to `http://review.tizen.org/gerrit/`.

5. Click on your username in the upper-right corner of the web pages, and select **Settings**.

6. Click on **SSH Public Keys** from the menu of the **Settings** page, which is as follows:

Settings

Profile
Preferences
Watched Projects
Contact Information
SSH Public Keys
HTTP Password
Identities
Groups

Gerrit settings

7. Paste the content of ~/.ssh/id_rsa.pub from the clipboard to the input box with the label **Add SSH Public Key**, and click on the button **Add**, as follows:

Add SSH Public Key
▶ How to Generate an SSH Key

Clear | Add | Close

8. Verify that you have successfully configured SSH for Gerrit access by running the following command in the terminal:

    ```
    ssh tizen
    ```

9. Upon successful access, you should see a welcome message as follows:

    ```
    **** Welcome to Gerrit Code Review ****
    ```

After that, proceed to the next part of the recipe, and configure Git for Gerrit access by performing the following actions after the last two steps:

1. Replace First_Name and Last_Name shown in the following command, and execute it to configure the username for Git:

    ```
    git config --global user.name <First_Name Last_Name>
    ```

2. Replace <Email> with the e-mail that you used to register at tizen.org, and run the following command to set it for Git:

    ```
    git config --global user.email "<Email>"
    ```

How it works

The source code of the Tizen project is hosted using the distributed version control system Git. This is an open source solution initially created by Linux Torvalds in 2005 as a tool for the development of the Linux kernel. It quickly became popular and its usage spread among the majority of open source projects. The services provided by GitHub and Gitorious played an important role in the Git penetration among developers.

The last two steps of this recipe are dedicated to the global options of Git. The `git config` command takes two arguments. The first argument is the setting, which should be updated, and the second argument is a new value.

The other system that was configured in this recipe is Gerrit. This is another open source tool. It is a web-based code review system that is tightly integrated with Git. Gerrit is very convenient for large projects, because it enables more centralized usage of Git. Some of the other well-known, large open source projects that rely on Git and Gerrit are Qt, Android, CyanogenMod, Eclipse, LibreOffice, and MediaWiki.

See also

▸ For more information as well as instructions on how to configure a working environment through proxy, take a look at `https://source.tizen.org/documentation/developer-guide/environment-setup`.

Installing development tools in Ubuntu or Debian

Tizen platform development tools are available for several Linux distributions. Their installation is different for each distribution, but it is done using their standard installation mechanisms. This recipe provides a step-by-step installation guide for Ubuntu and Debian using `apt-get`.

How to do it...

Follow these instructions if you are using Ubuntu or Debian:

1. Open the file `/etc/apt/sources.list` in a text editor with appropriate permissions, for example:

   `sudo vim /etc/apt/sources.list`

2. Append the repository for Tizen development tools that corresponds to the version of Ubuntu or Debian that you are using. For example, the repository for Ubuntu 14.04 is:

   `deb http://download.tizen.org/tools/latest-`
   `release/Ubuntu_14.04/ /`

 Please note the slash at the end of the line, and do not forget to write it when you specify the repository. The full list of available repositories for the different Linux distributions can be browsed at `http://download.tizen.org/tools/latest-release/`.

3. Run the following command to update the index of the packages and to synchronize with the repository that was added in the previous step:

```
sudo apt-get update
```

4. Install the mandatory development tools, GBS and MIC, with the following command:

```
sudo apt-get install gbs mic
```

How it works

Debian is known as a stable distribution with an enormous database of supported packages. Ubuntu is built on Debian and recently has become the third most used platform (in the terms of operating systems) behind Mac OS X and Microsoft Windows.

The powerful command-line tool for package management `apt-get` is used in both Debian and Ubuntu. Packages can be installed, upgraded, or removed with it. The whole process in this recipe is absolutely standard, as it follows the common workflow for package installation on Ubuntu and Debian. The first and second steps are Tizen-specific, because the URL of the appropriate repository of the development tools must be set.

There's more...

It is highly recommended that you keep the version of the Tizen development tools up to date. In Ubuntu and Debian, it is possible to obtain the latest version of all packages by executing `apt-get` with the following parameters:

```
sudo apt-get update
sudo apt-get upgrade
```

Alternatively, a single package or a list of packages can be upgraded to the newest version with the following command:

```
sudo apt-get install <package>Replace <package> with the name of the
package or the list of packages separated by space if you want to upgrade
more than one package. For example, if you have already installed GBS run
sudo apt-get install gbs to get its version up to date.
```

See also

▸ This article is based on the information from the developer guide at `tizen.org`. Visit the following link for more information:

▸ `https://source.tizen.org/documentation/developer-guide/getting-started-guide/installing-development-tools`

Installing development tools in openSUSE

OpenSUSE is a free, Linux-based general purpose operating system. The development of this distribution is pushed forward by a community project with the same name that is sponsored by SUSE. The mission of this recipe is to facilitate openSUSE users with the installation of a Tizen development tool.

How to do it...

Perform these steps to install GBS and MIC on openSUSE:

1. Add a repository of Tizen development tools that matches the version of your openSUSE. For example, the following commands add a repository compatible with openSUSE 13.1:

   ```
   sudo zypper addrepo http://download.tizen.org/tools/latest-
   release/openSUSE_13.1/ tools
   ```

    If you are using a different version of openSUSE, browse and find an appropriate Tizen developer tools repository for it at `http://download.tizen.org/tools/latest-release/`.

2. Download the metadata of the repository that has just been added as follows:

   ```
   sudo zypper refresh
   ```

3. Download and install GBS and MIC using the following command:

   ```
   sudo zypper install gbs mic
   ```

How it works

The installation process on openSUSE is similar to the one for Ubuntu and Debian, but the commands are different. In openSUSE, the name of the command-line tool for package management is Zypper. The algorithm for the installation is still the same as in the previous recipe but requires even fewer manual interactions. The first step is to add a repository, and the second step is to update the metadata of the new repository. The last step is to install GBS, MIC, or any of the other tools.

There's more...

Run the following commands if Tizen development tools on your computer are outdated and you want to get the latest version:

```
sudo zypper refresh
sudo zypper update <package>
```

Replace `<package>` with the name of the package that you want to upgrade. For example, gbs or `mic`.

See also

▶ Tizen development tools can be also installed on Ubuntu, Debian, Fedora, and CentOS. Check out the preceding recipe and the next recipe if you want to install these tools on other distributions, or have a look at the official guides at `https://source.tizen.org/documentation/developer-guide/getting-started-guide/installing-development-tools`.

Installing development tools in Fedora and CentOS

You have already seen how to install Tizen development tools on Ubuntu, Debian, and openSUSE from the previous recipes. Now, it is time to discuss Fedora and CentOS. The installation processes on these Linux distributions are the same, because both Fedora and CentOS are based on **Red Hat Enterprise Linux** (**RHEL**). Both distributions use RPM packages, which are managed by the command-line tool **YUM** (Yellowdog Updater, Modified).

Fedora is owned by Red Hat, but the project is supported by the community, and a lot of volunteers are involved in the development and the maintenance of the source code. New versions of Fedora are released every six months.

Unlike Fedora, the governance of CentOS is independent from Red Hat although it is sponsored by the company. The first edition of CentOS was released in May 2004.

How to do it...

Please follow the steps in the following tutorial to install Tizen development tools on Fedora or CentOS using YUM:

1. Add the repository of Tizen development tools by downloading it using `wget` to `/etc/yum.repos.d`. Let's add the repository for Fedora 20 as an example:

   ```
   sudo wget -O /etc/yum.repos.d/tools.repo http://download.tizen.org/tools/latest-release/Fedora_20/tools.repo
   ```

    If you are using CentOS or another version of Fedora, please browse and retrieve the repo file that matches your operating system at: `http://download.tizen.org/tools/latest-release/`

2. Execute the following command to update the metadata of the repositories:

   ```
   sudo yum makecache
   ```

3. Install GBS and MIC as follows:

   ```
   sudo yum install gbs mic
   ```

How it works

If you have read the previous two recipes, you will already be familiar with the algorithm of the installation. The same procedure with different tools is specific for Fedora and CentOS.

Just as in the case of Ubuntu, Debian, and openSUSE, the first step again is to add the repository of the Tizen development tools. After that, the metadata of the new repository has to be downloaded. Finally, the packages from this repository are downloaded with `yum`.

There's more...

To keep Tizen development tools up to date and to upgrade them to the latest version, please run the following commands:

```
sudo yum makecache
```
```
sudo yum update <Package>
```

Replace `<Package>` with the exact name of the package that has to be upgraded, for example, `gbs` or `mic`.

See also

▶ The official guide for the installation of Tizen development tools is available at `https://source.tizen.org/documentation/developer-guide/getting-started-guide/installing-development-tools`.

Building Tizen platform images

This recipe reveals the ingredients and the steps required to cook Tizen platform images. A step-by-step tutorial as well as a lot of external links are provided. Based on this information, you will be able to build Tizen platform images and, after that, to boot them on compatible devices, you will need to follow the instructions in the following recipes.

Getting ready

You are about to start a time-consuming process. Make sure that you have a powerful computer to build Tizen platform images; otherwise, prepare to wait for a long time. Although Tizen platform images can also be built on systems with less impressive specifications, my personal experience shows that the recommended system requirements are a new Intel Core i7 processor and 8 GB RAM.

A platform development environment should be set, and the platform development tools should be properly installed as explained in the previous recipes.

How to do it...

Follow these guidelines to build a Tizen platform image from scratch:

1. Create a directory, `~/bin/` ,and include it in PATH as follows:

   ```
   mkdir ~/bin/
   PATH=~/bin:$PATH
   ```

2. Download the repo script, and add permissions for its execution by running the following commands:

   ```
   cd ~/bin/
   wget http://commondatastorage.googleapis.com/git-repo-downloads/repo
   sudo chmod a+x ~/bin/repo
   ```

3. Create a new directory where the Tizen source code will be downloaded as follows:

   ```
   mkdir ~/tizen
   cd ~/tizen
   ```

The name of the directory in the preceding example is `tizen`. Set a name of the directory that suits you best.

4. Replace `<user>` with your Gerrit username, and execute the following two commands to download the source code of Tizen Common over SSH:

   ```
   repo init -u ssh://<user>@review.tizen.org:29418/scm/manifest -b
   tizen -m common.xml
   
   repo sync
   ```

    Change the manifest to `ivi.xml` to download the source code of the IVI profile or to `mobile.xml` for the mobile profile. The full list of available branches and remote repositories can be found at `https://source.tizen.org/documentation/developer-guide/getting-started-guide/building-packages-locally-gbs#available-branches-and-the-corresponding-remote-repos`.

5. Open `.gbs.conf` in your favorite text editor, and configure it. For example, this is the default configuration for Tizen Common:

   ```
   [general]
   tmpdir=/var/tmp/
   profile = profile.tizen3.0_common
   work_dir=.
   
   [repo.tizen3.0_x86]
   url=${work_dir}/pre-built/toolchain-x86/
   
   [repo.tizen3.0_arm]
   url=${work_dir}/pre-built/toolchain-arm/
   
   [profile.tizen3.0_common]
   repos=repo.tizen3.0_x86,repo.tizen3.0_arm
   buildconf=${work_dir}/scm/meta/build-config/build.conf
   ```

   Select one of the following options, and remove # from the beginning of its line to enable it:

   ```
   # For wayland ia32
   # buildconf=${work_dir}/scm/meta/build-config/build-ia32-wayland.
   conf
   # For emulator32 wayland
   # buildconf=${work_dir}/scm/meta/build-config/build-emulator32-
   wayland.conf
   # For wayland x86_64
   ```

```
# buildconf=${work_dir}/scm/meta/build-config/build-x86_64-
wayland.conf
# For wayland arm32
# buildconf=${work_dir}/scm/meta/build-config/build-arm-wayland.
conf
# For wayland arm64
# buildconf=${work_dir}/scm/meta/build-config/build-arm64-wayland.
conf
```

> The default configurations for the IVI and the mobile profile are available at `https://source.tizen.org/ documentation/developer-guide/getting- started-guide/building-packages-locally-gbs`.

6. Build all packages using GBS with a command that matches the targeted CPU architecture as follows:

   ❑ For i586, use the following:

   ```
   gbs build -A i586 --threads=4 --clean-once
   ```

> If you are building a Tizen 2 platform image, append `--ex clude=gcc,cmake,filesystem,aul,libmm- sound,libtool` to the preceding command.

   ❑ For armv7l, use the following commands:

   ```
   accel_pkgs="bash,bzip2-libs,c-ares,cmake,coreutils,dif
   futils,eglibc,elfutils-libelf,elfutils-libs,elfutils,fd
   upes,file,findutils,gawk,gmp,gzip,libacl,libattr,libcap
   ,libcurl,libfile,libgcc,liblua,libstdc++,make,mpc,mpfr
   ,ncurses-libs,nodejs,nspr,nss-softokn-freebl,nss,openss
   l,patch,popt,rpm-build,rpm-libs,rpm,sed,sqlite,tar,xz-
   libs,zlib,binutils,gcc"

   gbs build -A armv7l --threads=4 --clean-once
   --exclude=${accel_pkgs},filesystem,aul,libmm-sound,libtool
   ```

7. Download an appropriate kickstart file from `http://download.tizen.org`. For example, the following command will download the kickstart file to build Tizen 2.2.1 for RD-PQ:

   ```
   wget http://download.tizen.org/releases/2.2.1/tizen-2.2.1/
   builddata/image-configs/RD-PQ-REF.ks
   ```

8. Edit the repo section, and change the value of the `--baseurl` argument to point to the local builds. In this case, the value must start with the prefix `file://` followed by the absolute path.

9. Finally, run the following command to create a Tizen image using the kickstart file:

```
gbs createimage –ks-file=RD-PQ-REF.ks
```

 Append `--tmpfs` as an additional argument if more than 4 GB RAM is available on the system.

How it works

Tizen is an open source software platform, and anyone can download its source code for free and build it from scratch. The process is time-consuming, but it is not that difficult.

The main tools used are **Git Build System** (**GBS**) and **MeeGo Image Creator** (**MIC**). GBS is a command-line tool to build Tizen packages. MIC is a tool inherited from MeeGo to create images. Nowadays, its features are embedded into GBS, and images can be created directly by running `gbs createimage`. Alternatively, you can still invoke MIC directly with the `create` argument.

The steps of this recipe are pretty much self-explanatory. First, you must get the source code, then build packages, and finally prepare a Tizen image with MIC and an appropriate kickstart file.

Tizen images can be built for both ARMv7 and i586 compatible processors. Depending on the targeted device, you need to use an appropriate configuration as shown in the sixth step.

See also

► Tizen platform development contains a lot of hidden gems. To build Tizen platform images, this recipe covers only the basics. For more information and advanced tutorials, please explore the resource available at `https://source.tizen.org/`.

► Detailed instructions to clone the source code of different Tizen versions and profiles are available at `https://source.tizen.org/documentation/developer-guide/getting-started-guide/cloning-tizen-source`.

► Visit the following link to learn more about building packages with GBS on your computer at `https://source.tizen.org/documentation/developer-guide/getting-started-guide/building-packages-locally-gbs`.

► Details regarding the final step in creating images from the local packages built with GBS can be found at `https://source.tizen.org/documentation/developer-guide/getting-started-guide/creating-tizen-images-mic`.

► Information about Tizen packaging guidelines is available at `https://wiki.tizen.org/wiki/Packaging/Guidelines`.

Flashing a Tizen image to mobile devices

The first Tizen reference device was RD-210, and it was announced at the Tizen Developer Conference in 2012. Nowadays, it is outdated, and new versions of the Tizen mobile profile are no longer released for it. Its successor was released a year later under the code name RD-PQ, and as of the time of this writing, it is still compatible with all the latest Tizen releases. RD-PQ is based on Samsung Galaxy S3, and it has similar hardware specifications.

This recipe provides guidelines to flash both of these Tizen reference devices. Please note that the flashing process is simple but potentially risky. Read carefully all instructions as well as the information in the links provided before performing any actions on the device.

Getting ready

The flashing process is very delicate. Prepare well, because even a minor mistake may lead to permanent poor results, and in the worst case to brick the device.

Make sure that you have a Tizen-compatible device and that its battery is fully charged. Also, you will require a USB cable that will be used to connect the device to the computer.

A personal computer with Linux distribution is required. The flashing process depends on a tool called `lthor`. Ensure that you can set up resource a Tizen development tools repository successfully on your distribution, and run the following commands to install `lthor`:

```
sudo apt-get update
sudo apt-get install lthor
```

As a precaution, it is highly recommended that you use a computer with backup power supply, for example, a laptop with a fully charged battery, to minimize the risk of electrical outage during the flashing process.

How to do it...

The following tutorial describes the flashing process of Tizen reference devices, such as RD-PQ and RD-210:

1. Build an appropriate Tizen image for your device, or download it from `http://download.tizen.org/releases/`.
2. Turn off the device.
3. Press the volume down and the power hardware buttons simultaneously to boot the device into the download mode.
4. Connect the device to a computer via a USB cable.

5. Flash the image to the device by replacing `<Tizen image>` with the name of the downloaded file in the following command, and execute it:

```
sudo ./lthor <Tizen image>
```

 Additional actions are required if you are planning to update RD-210 with Tizen 1.0 Larkspur to a newer version. Please refer to the following link for more information: `https://source.tizen.org/documentation/reference/flash-device#RD-PQ_RD-210`.

There's more...

On Ubuntu, the last step of the flashing process may fail due to any of the following errors:

- A handshake failed error:

```
USB port is detected: /dev/ttyACM0

line 328: failed to read signature bytes
line 603: handshake failed
line 922: failed to open port (null)
```

- A port open error:

```
USB port is detected : /dev/ttyACM0

port open error!!
: Device or resource busy
line 954: failed to open port (null)
```

Both issues have been discussed numerous times during the Tizen mailing list. They are caused by `modemmanager`, which tries to communicate with the attached device on the USB port and prevents the normal work of `lthor`.

If you experience any of the preceding errors, please uninstall `modemmanager` from your computer using the following command and `lthor` again:

```
sudo apt-get purge modemmanager
```

Alternatively, if you want to keep `modemmanager`, please perform the following actions:

1. Remove or move to another location the configuration file of the D-BUS service for `modemmanager` as follows:

```
sudo mv /usr/share/dbus-1/system-services/org.freedesktop.
ModemManager.service ~/org.freedesktop.ModemManager.service
```

2. Terminate all instances of `modemmanager` that are running at the moment via the following commands:

   ```
   sudo stop modemmanager
   sudo killall modem-manager
   ```

For more troubleshooting tips and tricks related to `lthor`, visit `https://wiki.tizen.org/wiki/Troubleshooting_lthor_on_Ubuntu`.

See also

▶ Up-to-date information and details about flashing Tizen reference mobile devices are available at `https://source.tizen.org/documentation/reference/flash-device#RD-PQ_RD-210`.

Enabling 3D acceleration and OpenGL

This recipe will guide you on how to enable 3D acceleration and OpenGL on Tizen devices with Mali GPU immediately after flashing Tizen on them.

Getting ready

If you have a flashed Tizen reference device, for example, RD-PQ, upon following the instructions in the previous recipe, you will notice a warning immediately after booting the platform as shown in the following screenshot:

Compositor warning after booting Tizen 2 for the first time on RD-PQ

The warning is displayed due to missing drivers for 3D acceleration and OpenGL. It affects a lot of built-in applications and interferes with their normal work. Third-party drivers for Mali DDK have to be installed to solve the issue.

The installation process is fairly easy. It requires a computer with an installed Tizen SDB, an Internet connection, and of course, the Tizen device.

How to do it...

There are several ways to install Mali DDK. The final result is the same no matter which way you choose. The following methodology to enable hardware acceleration is pretty straightforward:

1. Download the Mali DDK compatible with the version of Tizen that has been flashed on the devices. The following Mali DDK versions are available for Tizen 2:

    ❑ Tizen 2.0 (`https://source.tizen.org/mali-ddk`)

    ❑ Tizen 2.1 (`http://source.tizen.org/mali-ddk-2.1`)

    ❑ Tizen 2.2 (`http://source.tizen.org/mali-ddk-2.2`)

    > The source code of Mali DDK is not open. Visit `https://source.tizen.org/` to find out the binaries of the latest available versions.

2. Extract the downloaded files on your computer, for example:

    ```
    tar -xvzf hw_accel.tar.gz
    ```

3. Connect the Tizen device to your computer, and copy the extracted files in it using SDB. The commands in the following example will copy the files to `/home/` directory:

    ```
    sdb -d root on
    sdb -d push libdrm-exynos-gem-*.rpm /home/
    sdb -d push libump-*.rpm /home/
    sdb -d push opengl-es-mali400mp-*.rpm /home/
    ```

4. Log in to the devices, and go to the directory where you have copied the files, for example, `/home/`, as follows:

    ```
    sdb -d shell
    cd /home/
    ```

5. Remove old packages as follows:

    ```
    rpm -e --nodeps opengl-es-virtual-drv
    ```

6. Install new packages to enable hardware acceleration as follows:

    ```
    rpm -ivh --force *.rpm
    ```

7. Finally, flush the filesystem buffers, and reboot the Tizen device by executing the following commands:

    ```
    sync
    reboot
    ```

Alternatively, you can even decrease the manual interactions of the described process if you first copy the downloaded tarball and directly extract it on the Tizen device.

How it works

The Tizen reference device RD-PQ has Mali 400-MP4 GPU. Its drivers are provided as a tarball of RPM files, because Tizen, as a platform, uses the RMP package manager. SDB is required to copy the files to the device and, after that, to install the packages. The changes take effect only after the device has been rebooted.

See also

▶ More information about enabling 3D acceleration and OpenGL on Tizen devices
is available on the Tizen wiki page at `https://wiki.tizen.org/wiki/`
`Enable_3D_Acceleration_on_Tizen`

Booting Tizen on Intel NUC

Tizen is a software platform that supports both ARM and x86 architectures. Intel, as one of the leading contributors of the Tizen project, is putting in a lot of effort for the support of x86 architecture, which powers their processors. This architecture was introduced more than 40 years ago, in the late 70s. The 64-bit version of x86 was released in 2003.

This recipe is dedicated to the process of flashing Tizen images compatible with the x86 architecture on devices with Intel processors. There are a lot of compatible devices on the market, but the focus of this recipe is on Intel NUC with the Intel Atom processor, model E3815.

Getting ready

A tool to flash Tizen images is required for this recipe. It is provided by the package `bmap-tools`. Install it by following the guidelines for the installation of Tizen development tools. For example, on Ubuntu, it can be installed using the following command:

```
sudo apt-get install bmap-tools
```

You will also need a USB memory stick with at least 4 GB disk space and a compatible computer, such as Intel NUC. A Tizen image will be flashed on the USB memory stick, and all other data will be completely erased from it. To prevent any loss of data, please make sure that you have a backup of the data from your USB memory stick before you proceed.

How to do it...

Perform the described actions to create a bootable USB memory stick with Tizen:

1. Plug the USB memory stick into your computer.

2. Identify the device using `fdisk -l` or by going through the log of `dmesg`.

3. Unmount the device. On Unix-based systems, this can be achieved as follows. Replace X with the ID of the USB memory device:

    ```
    umount /dev/sdX*
    ```

4. Use `bmaptool` to download a Tizen image, and copy it on the USB drive. If you are not sure which image to download, bet on milestone release, as follows:

    ```
    bmaptool <Tizen> /dev/sdX
    ```

Replace `<Tizen>` with the image present on your local drive or with the URL to an image.

Once you have a bootable USB memory stick with Tizen, you can proceed to booting it on a compatible device with an Intel processor:

1. Plug the USB memory stick into Intel NUC.

2. Turn on the device.

3. Enter its BIOS by hitting *F2*.

4. Modify the boot order, and set the USB memory stick with the highest priority.

5. Save changes and proceed. If everything works fine, Tizen will boot shortly.

How it works

Tizen is divided into several profiles. Tizen IVI and Common are preferred for Intel architectures. In this recipe, we have used a milestone release of Tizen Common. This type of release should be stable, and it is recommended that you rely on them if you are not sure which version to pick.

There's more...

By following the preceding process, you created a bootable USB memory stick with Tizen, which you can copy to the persistent memory of the device.

The following tutorial describes one of the ways to copy Tizen to the built-in storage of Intel NUC. A second USB stick will be needed.

1. Plug in the second memory stick in your computer, and copy the same Tizen image as a raw file on it. After that, unplug this USB stick.

2. Plug the second USB memory stick into Intel NUC while Tizen is running from the first USB stick.

3. Launch the Tizen terminal and log in as root.

4. Detect the second USB memory stick and the internal eMMC storage using `fdisk -l`.

5. Unmount the internal eMMC storage using `umount`.

6. Copy the Tizen image from the second USB memory stick to the eMMC. Use the following command, and replace `<Tizen image>` with the file from the second USB memory stick, and replace `<storage>` with the eMMC, for example, `/dev/mmcblk0`:

```
bzcat <Tizen image> | dd of=<storage> bs=512k oflag=sync
conv=sparse
```

7. Turn off the device, unplug all the USB memory sticks and boot it again.

8. Make sure that the device will boot from the internal memory, and if everything works fine, Tizen will boot shortly.

Alternatively, instead of using a second USB memory stick, you can boot Tizen on Intel NUC and enable a network connection. After that, you can copy a Tizen image to the USB memory stick on which the operating system runs.

See also

▶ For more information about booting Tizen on Intel devices, you can visit `https://source.tizen.org/documentation/reference/flash-device#intel`

Booting Tizen on Allwinner devices

Allwinner is a Chinese company, the core business of which is related to the development of SoC. The company was established in 2007, and it became popular worldwide in 2010 with the launch of their SoC with Cortex-A8 processor, which is known as A10. In 2013, Allwinner released A20, which features a dual core Cortex-A7 ARM processor.

In April 2013, Allwinner received the ARM award for being the number one in Android tablet AP shipment worldwide. A lot of popular single-board computers, such as OLinuXino, Cubieboard, and Banana Pi also use Allwinner processors with ARMv7 compatible architecture. All devices with Allwinner processors are also called Sunxi.

Because of their low prices, Sunxi devices with Android have excellent penetration on the market. They are important for the Tizen ecosystem as well, because they open the road to a lot of owners of Sunxi devices. Additionally, open source hardware devices with Allwinner processors, such as the boards from the OLinuXino series, provide excellent opportunities for innovation to start-up companies and enthusiasts with limited budgets.

This recipe provides a complete guideline to port Tizen to Sunxi devices. Please note that there are thousands of devices with Allwinner SoCs. Each device has different specifications, so you should adjust the tutorial depending on your device and the version of Tizen that you use.

Getting ready

Prepare for the most advanced recipe in this book. The provided instructions are generic for Sunxi devices. Adapt them to match the exact specifications of the vendor of the devices that you target.

This tutorial is provided as is, without warranty of any kind. Do it at your own risk. Read all the instructions very carefully and obey the recommendations and guidelines of the hardware vendors. Be aware that any mistake may brick the device or cause other unwanted behavior.

To successfully complete this recipe, you need a Linux computer, Sunxi device with a slot for microSD card, and you must have the following:

- ► Tizen platform development environment setup
- ► Installed Tizen platform development tools
- ► A Tizen image for ARMv7 compatible devices

If you fail to comply with any of the preceding requirements, refer to the previous recipes.

How to do it...

The following tutorial is about building a Linux-sunxi kernel, U-Boot loader, flashing Tizen on a microSD card, and booting it on a Sunxi device:

1. Set up the tool chain to build kernel and bootloader by running the following commands:

   ```
   sudo apt-get update
   sudo apt-get install gcc-4.7-arm-linux-gnueabihf ncurses-dev
   uboot-mkimage build-essential git
   ```

    Debian users might need to add the repositories from http://www.emdebian.org/debian to /etc/apt/sources.list.

2. Make a directory and download in it the source code of the U-Boot loader using Git:

   ```
   mkdir sunxi/
   cd sunxi/
   git clone -b sunxi https://github.com/linux-sunxi/u-boot-sunxi.git
   ```

It is highly recommended that you use a revision of the source code that has been verified by the vendor of your device.

3. Enter the directory that has been created by `git clone`:

   cd u-boot-sunxi/

4. Build a U-Boot loader from scratch using the GNU `make` utility. For example, the following command will build U-Boot using a **makefile** for the open source hardware development board, A20-OLinuXino-MICRO:

   make a20-olinuxino_micro CROSS_COMPILE=arm-linux-gnueabihf-

5. Check whether the files `spl/sunxi-spl.bin u-boot.bin u-boot-sunxi-with-spl.bin` exist to verify that the build of U-Boot loader was successful.

6. Go back to the major directory, and prepare to build the Linux-sunxi kernel by downloading its source code.

   cd ..

   git clone https://github.com/linux-sunxi/linux-sunxi

7. Enter the directory `linux-sunxi`, and build the kernel using appropriate `<defconfig>` for the targeted platform with the following command:

   cd linux-sunxi/

   make ARCH=arm <defconfig>

All defconfig files included in the project are located in the directory `linux-sunxi/arch/arm/configs/`. It is recommended that you place any third-party defconfig files in the same directories. Some vendors, such as Olimex, provide their own defconfig files.

8. Optionally, you can build kernel modules using the following commands:

   make ARCH=arm CROSS_COMPILE=arm-linux-gnueabihf- -j4 INSTALL_MOD_PATH=out modules

   make ARCH=arm CROSS_COMPILE=arm-linux-gnueabihf- -j4 INSTALL_MOD_PATH=out modules_install

9. Insert a microSD card into your computer and identify it. Pay attention to the fact that all the information on the microSD card will be erased completely, and Tizen will be overwritten on it.

10. Replace `<X>` with the ID of the microSD card, and launch `fdisk`:

    sudo fdisk /dev/sd<X>

11. Retrieve the total size of the microSD card by running the p command in `fdisk`. This is a sample output for a 4 GB microSD card:

```
Command (m for help): p


Disk /dev/sdc: 4026 MB, 4026531840 bytes
```

12. Calculate the number of cylinders by dividing the size retrieved in the previous step by the size of a single cylinder, which is equal to the number of heads multiplied by the number of sectors and the size of a single sector.

 The size of a single cylinder with 255 heads, 63 sectors, and 512 bytes per sector is 8225280 bytes. So, if, for example, the total size of the microSD card is 4026531840 bytes, then the number of cylinders is 489.

13. Delete the existing partition with the d command at `fdisk` as shown in the following example. Repeat the action until all partitions are deleted:

```
Command (m for help):  d

Partition number (1-4): 1
```

14. Configure the heads, sectors, and cylinders of the microSD card as follows; replace `<cylinders>` with the value calculated in step 12:

```
Command (m for help): x
Expert command (m for help): h
Number of heads (1-256, default 30): 255
Expert command (m for help): s
Number of sectors (1-63, default 29): 63
Warning: setting sector offset for DOS compatibility
Expert command (m for help): c
Number of cylinders (1-1048576, default 2286): <cylinders>
```

15. Create a boot partition, and leave the rest for Linux partitions:

```
Expert command (m for help): r
Command (m for help): n
Command action
e extended
p primary partition (1-4)
p
Partition number (1-4): 1
First cylinder (1-123, default 1):
Using default value 1
```

```
Last cylinder or +size or +sizeM or +sizeK (1-123, default 123):
+64M (see note above)
Command (m for help): n
Command action
e extended
p primary partition (1-4)
p
Partition number (1-4): 2
First cylinder (10-123, default 10):
Using default value 10
Last cylinder or +size or +sizeM or +sizeK (10-123, default 123):
Using default value 123
```

16. Set the FAT32 filesystem for the boot partition:

```
Command (m for help): t
Partition number (1-4): 1
Hex code (type L to list codes): c
Changed system type of partition 1 to c (W95 FAT32 (LBA))
* You have to format 1st partitions with vfat32 filesystem.
Command (m for help): a
Partition number (1-4): 1
```

17. Verify that the partitions are correct by running the p command again.

18. Save all changes using the w command:

```
Command (m for help): w
The partition table has been altered!

Calling ioctl() to re-read partition table.
```

19. Replace <X> with the identifier of the microSD card, and format the partitions as follows:

```
sudo mkfs.vfat -F 32 -n boot /dev/sd<X>1
sudo mkfs.ext4 -L rootfs /dev/sd<X>2
sudo mkfs.ext4 -L data /dev/sd<X>3
sudo mkfs.ext4 -L UMS /dev/sd<X>4
```

20. Unmount the microSD card and write the bootloader as follows:

```
umount /dev/sd<X>*
dd if=u-boot-sunxi/u-boot-sunxi-with-spl.bin of=/dev/sd<X> bs=1024
seek=8
```

21. After that, mount the microSD card, and copy the Linux-sunxi kernel and configuration files, such as `script.bin`, which, in most cases, are provided by the hardware vendors to the boot partition. Here is an example:

```
mkdir /mnt/sd1
mount /dev/sd<X>1 /mnt/sd1
cp linux-sunxi/arch/arm/boot/uImage /mnt/sd1
cp script.bin /mnt/sd1
sync
umount /dev/sd<X>1
```

22. Make sure that all partitions of the microSD card are unmounted as follows:

```
umount /dev/sd<X>*
```

23. Copy each Tizen image to the appropriate partition. Replace `<image>` with the Tizen image, `<X>` with the identifier of the microSD card, and `<N>` with the partition number in the following command:

```
sudo dd if=/dev/<image> of=/dev/sd<X><N> bs=1024 count=1
```

24. Optionally, you can mount the boot (FAT32) partition again and create `uEnv.txt`, which allows the hot swap of some configurations, such as the display output. Change `disp.screen0_output_type` to 1 for LCD display, 3 for HDMI, and 4 for VGA. The following is an example configuration to enable HDMI display at `uEnv.txt`:

```
console=tty0
loglevel=5
extraargs=console=ttyS0,115200 disp.screen0_output_type=3 disp.
screen0_output_mode=EDID:800x480p33 hdmi.audio=EDID:0
```

25. Unmount and unplug the microSD card from the computer. Plug into the Sunxi device, and start it to boot Tizen.

How it works

This recipe had three main ingredients: boot loader, kernel, and the Tizen image.

U-Boot is a universal boot loader for embedded devices with ARM, PowerPC, MIPS, and other processors. It is preferred for Sunxi devices, and a fork adapted for them resides at GitHub. On the second step of the recipe, the source code of U-Boot is cloned from GitHub, and it is built in the previous steps.

Linux-sunxi is the fork of the Linux kernel, which is hosted at GitHub. It is adapted for devices with Allwinner SoCs. Its build process is explained in the instructions provided from steps 6 to 8.

The final and most tricky part of the recipe is the setting up of the bootable microSD card. This starts at step 9. The first partition is with FAT32 filesystems, which means that it can easily be mounted and edited on computers with different operating systems. This is convenient, because you might want to change a binary file or edit `uEnv.txt` on a Microsoft Windows computer.

The recipe contains a lot of Linux commands. If you are unsure how they work or if you just want to see details about them, please check the corresponding Linux Man Pages. For example, type `man dd` to learn more about this command.

See also

> ▸ This recipe is based on several important sources. The information about the microSD card partitions is similar to the process for booting Tizen on PandaBoard, and more details can be found on the Tizen wiki at `https://wiki.tizen.org/wiki/Tizen_IVI_Getting_Started_Guide_For_PandaBoard`.

> ▸ The Linux-sunxi project is available in GitHub at `https://github.com/linux-sunxi/`, and more information can also be found at wiki (`http://linux-sunxi.org/Main_Page`).

> ▸ There is a community-driven initiative to port Tizen to Allwinner devices, and all resources of this project are also stored in GitHub at `https://github.com/leon-anavi/tizen-sunxi`.

> ▸ Tizen-sunxi is being developed and tested primarily on open source hardware devices manufactured by Olimex. Information about building Linux-kernel and U-Boot loader for their most popular single-board computers with Allwinner processors can be found on their blog. The following links are useful for:

>> ❑ A20-OLinuXino-MICRO (`http://olimex.wordpress.com/2013/11/05/building-the-ultimate-debian-sd-card-for-linux-with-kernel-3-4-for-a20-olinuxino-micro/`)

>> ❑ A10-OLinuXino-LIME (`http://olimex.wordpress.com/2014/06/23/a10-olinuxino-lime-debian-build-with-kernel-3-4-90/`)

>> ❑ A13-OLinuXino (`http://olimex.wordpress.com/2014/07/18/a13-olinuxino-wifi-debian-build-with-kernel-3-4-90/`)

>> ❑ A10S-OLinuXino-MICRO (`http://olimex.wordpress.com/2013/10/28/building-debian-sd-card-for-linux-with-kernel-3-4-from-scratch-for-a10s-olinuxino-micro/`)

> ▸ Additional information about Tizen, ARM devices, and porting guidelines reside on the Tizen wiki. A good starting point is `https://wiki.tizen.org/wiki/ARM`.

Hacking a tablet and booting Tizen on it

Allwinner processors can be found in numerous devices on the market. According to their product catalog, Allwinner shipped the most ARM processors for Android tablets in 2013.

The previous recipe has already proved that Tizen runs on development boards with Allwinner processors, and the next step is to boot Tizen on existing Android tablets on the market. This recipe provides guidelines on how to retrieve the binary configuration files of tablets using reverse engineering.

Getting ready

Please make sure that the following prerequisites are met:

▸ An Android tablet (or eventually smartphone) with a slot for a microSD card and an Allwinner ARMv7 compatible processor, such as A20, A13, A10, A10, and so on

▸ A computer with installed **Android Debug Bridge** (**ADB**), which comes with the Android SDK

▸ A bootable microSD card with a Tizen image prepared following the tutorial in the preceding recipe

How to do it...

Follow these guidelines to retrieve the binary configuration files of the tablet, to put them on the Tizen image, and to boot it from the microSD card on the tablet. Pay attention to the fact that the instructions are provided as is. The process is complex, and you must do it at your risk:

1. Turn on the tablet, wait until its Android stock image loads, and after that, enable **USB debugging** from **Settings | Developer options**.

2. Connect the tablet to a computer in the developer mode.

3. Enter remote shell on the tablet by executing the following command:

   `adb shell`

4. Mount and access the NAND memory of the tablet as follows:

   `mkdir /sdcard/nanda`

   `mount -t vfat /dev/block/nanda /sdcard/nanda`

5. Exit the shell, and copy `script.bin` to the computer using `adb` as follows:

   `adb pull /sdcard/nanda/script.bin .`

6. Plug the microSD card into the computer.

7. Overwrite `script.bin` on the FAT32 partition of the microSD card, and remove `uEnv.txt` if it is present.

8. Eject the microSD card from the computer.

9. Turn off the tablet.

10. Plug the microSD card into the tablet.

11. Turn on the tablet again. If everything works as expected, Tizen will be booted directly from the microSD card.

How it works

This command-line tool Android Debug Bridge is used to connect to an Android tablet with Allwinner and copy its binary configuration files. It is a client-server program that has exactly the same purpose as SDB but for Android devices.

The internal storage of Sunxi tablets, also known as their NAND flash memory, is present as a device that can be mounted as shown in step 4. After that, direct access to the files is obtained, and they can be transferred to the computer. This trick allows easy reverse engineering of configuration files and simplifies the booting process of other platforms such as Tizen and Linux distributions such as Debian.

The ADB command `pull` is used to download `script.bin` from the Android tablet to the computer. The first argument of the `pull` command is the location of the file on the device, and the second argument is the destination on the computer where it must be saved.

There's more...

To read its configurations, the binary file that has been copied from Android must be converted to a `fex` file. The open source project Linux-sunxi, which is hosted at GitHub, provides a simple command-line tool for this job. Perform the following simple operations to convert `script.bin` to the `fex` file:

1. Download the source code of sunxi-tools using `git` as follows:

    ```
    git clone https://github.com/linux-sunxi/sunxi-tools.git
    ```

2. Build from the source `bin2fex` as follows:

    ```
    make bin2fex
    ```

3. Run `bin2fex` to convert `script.bin` to `script.fex`, for example:

    ```
    ./bin2fex script.bin > script.fex
    ```

See also

▶ This recipe was inspired by the article about A10 devices available at `http://elinux.org/Hack_A10_devices`

▶ More information about Android Debug Bridge and its commands is available at `http://developer.android.com/tools/help/adb.html`

Index

Symbols

3D acceleration
enabling 308-311
3D objects
creating, with WebGL 79-88
.tpk file 49

A

A10 devices
URL 322
Active Secure profile
setting 22-24
add() function 182
alarm
setting 199
Alarm API 39
Allwinner devices
Tizen, booting on 313-318
Android application package file (APK) 49
Android apps
porting, to Tizen 262-264
Android Debug Bridge (ADB)
about 28, 320
pull command 321
URL 322
using 321
Android Development Tools (ADT) 20
Android Open Source Project (AOSP) 264
Android UI
porting, to Tizen UI Framework 264-267
Android UI components
AlertDialog 266
Button 265
CheckBox 265

DatePicker 266
EditText 265
Spinner 265
TimePicker 266
Toast 266
ToggleButton 265
API keys, Directions API
URL 235, 239, 243
application
running, in Tizen Emulator 276, 278
running, in Tizen Simulator 274-276
running, on Tizen device 278
Application API 39, 41
Application Compatibility Layer (ACL) 262
app life cycle
about 34
steps 35
apps
publishing, to Tizen Store 52, 53
asserts methods, QUnit 291
authorization grant, creating in Tizen web applications
authorization code 151
implicit 151
autodividers widget 58

B

bindClick() function 183
bindListItem() function 162
Bluetooth
about 212
data, connecting 213-218
data, discovering 213-218
data, exchanging 213-218
specifications, URL 218
using 213-218

Bluetooth API
about 40
privileges 212
references 218
Bookmark API 40
bootable USB memory stick
creating 312
buttons
creating 60-62
working 62, 63
button widget 58

C

CalendarAlarm interface
about 200
DISPLAY option 200
SOUND option 200
Calendar API
about 40, 176
alarm, setting 199
event, creating 195
event, deleting 196
events, retrieving 197, 198
task, creating 190-193
task, deleting 194
tasks, retrieving 187, 188
CalendarEvent 193
CalendarItem 193
calendar.read privilege 199
CalendarTask 193
calendar.write privilege 187
call history
browsing 210-212
URL 212
CallHistory API, Tizen
about 40
implementing 210, 211
URL 212
canvas
text, drawing on 76-79
text, writing on 76-79
CentOS
development tools, installing 300, 301
certificate
generating, through Tizen IDE 23
checkbox widget 58

checkDistance() function 245
components, SDB
client 28
daemon 28
server 28
configuration, Gatekeeper
on Mac OS X 14
Connection Explorer View 22
Contact API 40
contacts
adding 178-181
deleting 182-185
exporting, to vCard 185, 186
retrieving 176-178
Contacts API
about 176
contact, adding 178-181
contact, deleting 182-185
contact, exporting to vCard 185, 186
contacts, retrieving 176, 177
contactsRemoved() function 185
Content API 40, 124
convertToString() function 186
Cordova
installing 258, 259
web application, creating with 259-261
Cordova applications
deploying, to Tizen Emulator 261, 262
deploying, to Tizen device 261, 262

D

data
retrieving, from Web SQL Database 112-116
Data Control API 39
data manipulation methods, web storage
clear() 106
getItem(key) 105
key(n) 105
removeItem(key) 106
setItem(key, value) 105
data storage
data, retrieving from Web SQL Database 112
files, downloading 100
files, reading 92
files, writing 90
IndexedDB, using 116

simple text editor, creating 95
SQL queries, executing in Web
    SQL Database 111
Web SQL Database, creating 109
web storage, using 105
Data Synchronization API 40
Debian
  development tools, installing in 297, 298
  URL 314
decode() method 144
deleteEvent() function 196
deleteTask() function 194, 195
DENSO 140
development tools, installing
  in CentOS 300, 301
  in Debian 297, 298
  in Fedora 300, 301
  in openSUSE 299, 300
  in Ubuntu 297, 298
  URL 298-302
device motion
  detecting 245-247
  working 246
device orientation
  detecting 247-249
distance
  calculating 243-245
Download API
  about 40, 100
  URL 105
draw() function
  URL 79
Dynamic Analysis phase 53

E

e-mail messages
  displaying 206-208
  receiving 206-208
  sending 204-206
Emulator Manager 35
error() function 188, 198
Event Injector
  about 25
  URL 278
events, Tizen Emulator
  battery 277

call 277
creating 195
deleting 196
earjack 277
location 277
motion 277
NFC 277
retrieving 197, 198
RSSI (Received signal strength
    indication) 277
SD card 277
sensor 277
SMS 277
USB 277
extendable list widget 58
extension packages
  managing 19

F

Facebook apps
  developing, in Tizen 148-151
  references 151
Facebook Chat API
  URL 162
Facebook friends list
  obtaining 154, 156
Facebook Graph API
  URL 162, 165
Facebook messages
  reading 158-162
Facebook news feed
  fetching 152-154
  references 154
Facebook notifications
  retrieving 162-164
Facebook profile information
  accessing 156-158
Facebook status
  references 165
  updating 164, 165
fast scroll widget 58
features, SDB 28
Fedora
  development tools, installing 300, 301
files
  downloading 100-104

opening, modes 90
reading 92
text, reading with stream 93, 94
text, saving with Tizen Filesystem API 91, 92
writing 90
Filesystem API
about 40
used, for accessing files 90
find() function 128, 184
findImages() function 134
flip toggle widget 58
footer widget 58
friends list, Facebook
obtaining 154-156
references 156

G

gallery 3D widget 58
gallery widget 58
Gatekeeper
configuring, on Mac OS X 14
generateQrCode() function 141
geocoding 239, 240
Geocoding API keys
URL 241
getFacebookMessages() function 162
getFacebookNotifications() function 164
getUnifiedCalendar() function 188
Git Build System (GBS) 305
git config command 297
GNU/Linux installation, Tizen
troubleshooting 18
Google Developers Console
URL 235
Google Directions API
about 235
references 238
using 235-238
Google Geocoding API
URL 243
used, for retrieving geographic coordinates
address 239, 240
Google Maps Geocoding API
using 241-243

H

handler widget 58
header widget 58
Hello World web application
creating 36-38
running, on Tizen device 36-38
HTML block widget 59
hybrid application 34

I

IndexedDB
URL 119
using 116-119
info tags. *See* **NFC tags**
Initial Inspection phase 53
installable applications, Tizen
hybrid applications 34
native applications 34
web applications 34
installation, Tizen SDK
about 10
network installation 11
offline installation 12
on Mac OS 13, 14
on Ubuntu 14-17
on Windows 12, 13
Intel NUC
Tizen, booting on 311-313
Inter-Process Communication (IPC) 264

J

Java archive (JAR) 24
JavaScript bugs
references 288
tracking 285, 286
JavaScript function
implementing, for sending SMS
messages 202, 203
Jest
URL 292
jQuery() function
URL 62

jsqrcode
  download link 143
  usage 144

K

kickstart file
  URL, for downloading 304

L

launchVideoPlayer() function 131
Leaflet
  URL 243
LESS
  about 73
  URL 74
linear barcodes, multimedia apps
  generating 135, 137
  one-dimensional (1D) barcodes 135
  scanning 137-139
  two-dimensional (2D) barcodes 135
LinkedIn app
  developing, in Tizen 169-172
  references 172
  URL 169
LinkedIn updates
  network-update-types, URL 174
  references 174
  retrieving 173, 174
Linux-sunxi project, GitHub
  URL 319
list divider widget 59
list views
  about 63
  creating 64, 65
  working 65
list widget 59
loadFile() function 97
loadImage() function 134
loadVideos()function 128
local audio files, multimedia apps
  playing 122, 123
local video files, multimedia apps
  playing 124-128
location
  displaying, with location-based
     services 230-235

Log View 22
lthor tool 306

M

Mac OS
  Tizen SDK, installing on 13, 14
Mac OS X
  Gatekeeper, configuring on 14
makefile 315
Mali DDK versions, for Tizen 2 310
mediaItems() function 128
MeeGo Image Creator (MIC) 305
Message port API 40
messages, Facebook
  reading 158-162
Messaging API
  about 40
  references 206
mobile device
  Tizen image, flashing to 306-308
multimedia apps
  creating 121
  linear barcodes, generating 135-137
  linear barcodes, scanning 137-139
  local audio files, playing 122, 123
  local video files, playing 124-128
  photo, capturing 132-134
  QR codes, generating 140-142
  QR codes, scanning 143, 144
  video, launching in external player 129-131
multimedia view widget 59

N

namespaces, Tizen native framework
  reference link 46
native application
  about 34
  creating 46-48
  packaging 49, 50
  programming 45
NDEF message
  receiving 222-224
  references 222
  sending 221, 222

NDEFRecord interface
  URL 224
Near Field Communication. *See* **NFC**
Network Bearer Selection API 40
news feed, Facebook
  fetching 152-154
NFC
  about 218-220
  using, categories 218
NFC API
  about 40
  URL 221
NFC Data Exchange Format (NDEF) 221
NFC tags
  about 218
  URL 223
Nokia HERE 229
Notification API 40
notifications, Facebook
  references 164
  retrieving 162-164
notification types, Tizen
  ONGOING 69
  PROGRESS 69
  SIMPLE 69
  THUMBNAIL 69
notification widget 59
npm (Node Package Manager) 258

O

one-dimensional (1D) barcodes 135
openDatabase() function 110
openDatabaseSync() function 110
OpenGL
  enabling 308-311
OpenMobile
  URL 263, 264
openStream() function 94
OpenStreetMap
  about 229, 230
  advantages 243
  reverse geocoding 242
openSUSE
  development tools, installing 299, 300
OSP (Open Service Platform) 46

P

Packages API 39
PandaBoard
  booting on, URL 319
panels, Tizen Simulator
  application configuration 276
  communications 276
  download 276
  geolocation 276
  network management 276
  notification 275
  orientation and zooming 275
  packages and applications 276
  power manager 276
  sensors 276
  system summary 275
peer-to-peer connection
  establishing, between two NFC-enabled
      devices 219, 220
PhoneGap
  about 258
  installing 258, 259
  URL 261
  web application, creating with 259-261
PhoneGap applications
  deploying, to Tizen Emulator 261, 262
  deploying, to Tizen device 261, 262
photo, multimedia apps
  capturing 132-134
platform development environment
  setting up 294-297
pop ups
  displaying 66, 67
  types, URL 68
  working 68
Power API 40
printError() function 185
privileges, NFC
  URL 219
profile information, Facebook
  accessing 156-158
  references 158
progress bar widget 59
progress widget 59
Project Explorer View 21
Properties View 21

Push API 40
push notifications
  receiving 225-227

Q

qmake 272
QR codes
  about 140
  generating 140-142
  scanning 143, 144
Qt
  about 267
  setting 267-271
Qt 5
  URL 272
Qt applications
  deploying, on Tizen 271, 272
Qt Creator
  installing 269
  Tizen SDK, integrating into 270
  URL, for downloading 269
Quick Emulator (QEMU) 25
Quick Response. *See* QR codes
QUnit
  URL 292
  used, for unit testing 288-292

R

radio-frequency identification (RFID) 218
Rapid Development Support (RDS)
  about 282
  URL 282
readAsText() function 94
readFile() function 94
readNDEF() method 223
Red Hat Enterprise Linux (RHEL) 300
Remote Inspector
  about 280
  URL 283
remove() function 194, 197
removeProgressNotification() function 72
retrieveContacts() function 177
retrieveData() function 116
retrieveEvents() function 198
retrieveTasks() function 188
reverse geocoding 241

Review and Final Confirmation phase 53
Ripple-UI Framework 24
runProgressDemo() function 72

S

Samsung Remote Test Lab (Samsung RTL)
  about 274, 283
  technical requirements 283
  URL 284, 285
  using 284, 285
Sass 73
saveContact() function 181
saveTask() function 193
SDB
  about 9, 30, 50
  adding, to environmental path of
    Windows 7 29
  components 28
  enabling 30
  features 28
  URL, for Linux distribution package 28
  using 30
SDB commands
  connect <host>[:<port>] 31
  devices 31
  disconnect <host>[:<port>] 31
  dlog [option] [<filter-spec>] 31
  forward <local> <remote> 31
  get-serialno 32
  get-state 31
  help 31
  install <path_to_tpk> 31
  kill-server 31
  pull <remote> [<local>] 31
  push <local> <remote> [-with-utf8] 31
  root <on|off> 32
  shell 31
  shell <command> 31
  start-server 31
  status-window 32
  uninstall <appid> 31
  use cases 32
  version 31
sdb push command 122
search filter bar widget 59
Secure Element API 40

secure profile 22
selectVideo() function 128
Selenium
  URL 274
sensors
  device motion, detecting 245
  device orientation, detecting 247
  distance between locations, calculating 243
  geocoding 239
  Google Directions API, using 235
  location-based services, using 230
  reverse geocoding 241
  Vibration API, using 250
Service Discovery Protocol (SDP) 213
setReceiveNDEFListener() method 224
setTagListener() method 221
setupColors() function 82
showError() function 248
showEvents() function 198
showMessages() function 162
showTasks() function 188
showThread() function 162
simple text editor
  creating 95-99
  working 99, 100
slider widget 59
Smart Development Bridge. *See* SDB
smart tags. *See* NFC tags
SMS messages
  privileges 202
  sending 201-203
split view widget 59
SQLite
  URL 115, 116
SQL queries
  executing, in Web SQL Database 111, 112
SSH, for Gerrit access
  configuring 294-296
  URL 295
start() function 105
status, Facebook
  updating 164, 165
stream
  used, for reading text from files 93-95
swipe widget 59
System information API 40
system of units (SI) 246

System setting API 40

T

tab bar widget 59
tablet
  hacking 320, 321
  Tizen, booting on 320, 321
tasks
  creating 190-193
  deleting 194
  retrieving 187, 188
text
  drawing, on canvas 76-79
  writing, on canvas 76-79
Time API 40
time widget 58
Tizen
  Android apps, porting to 264
  booting, on Allwinner devices 313-319
  booting, on Intel NUC 311-313
  booting, on tablet 320, 321
  Calendar API 176
  Contacts API 176
  Facebook apps, developing 148-151
  installable applications 34
  LinkedIn app, developing in 169-172
  reference, for wiki article 19
  reference link, for documentation 48
  references 305
  URL 77
Tizen APIs
  references 39
Tizen applications
  debugging, with Tizen Emulator 280
Tizen, ARM devices
  URL 319
Tizen developer tools repository
  URL 299
Tizen development tools
  URL, for installation guide 268
Tizen device
  application, running on 278
  debugging on 281
  PhoneGap applications,
    deploying to 261, 262
  references 279

Tizen Emulator
  application, running 276-278
  Cordova applications, deploying to 261, 262
  features 25
  limitations, compared to real Tizen device 26
  PhoneGap applications, deploying to 261, 262
  references 278
  used, for debugging Tizen applications 280
Tizen Filesystem API
  URL 100
  used, for saving text to files 91, 92
Tizen IDE
  about 262
  certificate, generating through 23
  customizing 20, 21
  views 21, 22
Tizen image
  flashing, to mobile device 306-308
  URL, for downloading 306
Tizen Manifest Editor 47
Tizen news feed
  filtering, from Twitter 166-169
  references 169
Tizen Notification API
  about 69
  URL 73
  using 69-71
  working 72, 73
Tizen package manager 50
Tizen platform images
  building 302-305
Tizen SDK
  hardware requisites 10
  installing 10-12
  installing, on Mac OS 13, 14
  installing, on Ubuntu 14-17
  installing, on Windows 12, 13
  network installation 11
  offline installation 12
  platform compatibility 10
  references 10
Tizen SDK 2.2.1
  references 27, 32
Tizen Simulator
  application, running in 274-276
  configuring 274
  debugging in 279

references 280
  URL 276
Tizen Store
  about 45
  apps, publishing to 52, 53
Tizen Store seller
  becoming 51
Tizen Store Validation Guide 52
Tizen-sunxi 319
Tizen SystemInfo API
  URL 249
Tizen UI Framework
  Android UI, porting to 264-267
  widgets 58
Tizen web application
  creating, for image download 101-104
  e-mail, sending from 205, 206
Tizen Web Emulator
  instances, creating of 26
  URL 26
Tizen Web Simulator
  about 24
  features 24
  options, for launching application 24
token text area widget 59
Twitter
  Tizen news feed, filtering from 166-169
  URL 166
TwitterOAuth
  URL 166
two-dimensional (2D) barcodes 135
Type Name Field (TNF) 224
TZDate object 200

U

Ubuntu
  about 10
  development tools, installing in 297, 298
  Tizen SDK, installing on 14-17
unit testing
  for QUnit 288-292
Universally Unique Identifier (UUID) 213
updateFacebookStatus() function 165
update() function 182
updateProgressNotification() function 72

V

Vibration API
about 250
references 251
URL 251
using 250, 251
working 250
video, multimedia apps
launching, in external player 129-131
views, Tizen IDE
Connection Explorer View 22
Console View 22
Log View 22
Project Explorer View 21
Properties View 21
virtual grid widget 59
Virtualization Technology (VTx) 26
virtual list widget 59

W

W3C specification
URL 111
web APIs, Tizen
about 39
Alarm 39
Application 39
Bluetooth 40
Bookmark 40
Calendar 40
Call History 40
Contact 40
Content 40
Data Control 39
Data Synchronization 40
Download 40
Filesystem 40
Message port 40
Messaging 40
Network Bearer Selection 40
NFC 40
Notification 40
Packages 39
Power 40
Push 40
Secure Element 40
System information 40

System setting 40
Time 40
Web setting 40
web application, Tizen
about 34
creating, with Cordova 259-261
creating, with PhoneGap 259-261
customizing 73-76
localizing 41-43
packaging 44, 45
porting 256-258
references 36
web app programming, Tizen 36
web application, file extensions
bar 256
crx 256
ipk 256
wgt 256
xap 256
xpi 256
web apps. *See* **web application, Tizen**
WebGL
URL 81
used, for creating 3D objects 79-88
Web Runtime (WRT) engine 36
Web setting API 40
Web SQL Database
about 109
creating 109, 110
data, retrieving from 112-116
SQL queries, executing in 111, 112
web storage
using 105-108
widgets
autodividers 58
button 58
checkbox 58
date 58
date time picker 58
extendable list 58
fast scroll 58
flip toggle 58
footer 58
gallery 58
gallery 3D 58
handler 58
header 58

HTML block 59
list 59
list divider 59
multimedia view 59
notification 59
overview 58, 59
pop up 59
progress 59
progress bar 59
search filter bar 59
slider 59
split view 59
swipe 59
tab bar 59
time 58
token text area 59
URL 60
virtual grid 59
virtual list 59
working 60
window.indexedDB.open() function 119
Windows
  Tizen SDK, installing on 12, 13
write() function 92

Y

Yandex 229
YUM
  used, for Tizen development tool installation
      on CentOS 301
  used, for Tizen development tool installation
      on Fedora 301

Z

Zypper 299

Thank you for buying
Tizen Cookbook

About Packt Publishing

Packt, pronounced 'packed', published its first book "*Mastering phpMyAdmin for Effective MySQL Management*" in April 2004 and subsequently continued to specialize in publishing highly focused books on specific technologies and solutions.

Our books and publications share the experiences of your fellow IT professionals in adapting and customizing today's systems, applications, and frameworks. Our solution based books give you the knowledge and power to customize the software and technologies you're using to get the job done. Packt books are more specific and less general than the IT books you have seen in the past. Our unique business model allows us to bring you more focused information, giving you more of what you need to know, and less of what you don't.

Packt is a modern, yet unique publishing company, which focuses on producing quality, cutting-edge books for communities of developers, administrators, and newbies alike. For more information, please visit our website: www.packtpub.com.

About Packt Open Source

In 2010, Packt launched two new brands, Packt Open Source and Packt Enterprise, in order to continue its focus on specialization. This book is part of the Packt Open Source brand, home to books published on software built around Open Source licenses, and offering information to anybody from advanced developers to budding web designers. The Open Source brand also runs Packt's Open Source Royalty Scheme, by which Packt gives a royalty to each Open Source project about whose software a book is sold.

Writing for Packt

We welcome all inquiries from people who are interested in authoring. Book proposals should be sent to author@packtpub.com. If your book idea is still at an early stage and you would like to discuss it first before writing a formal book proposal, contact us; one of our commissioning editors will get in touch with you.

We're not just looking for published authors; if you have strong technical skills but no writing experience, our experienced editors can help you develop a writing career, or simply get some additional reward for your expertise.

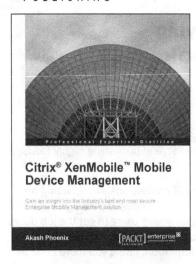

Citrix® XenMobile™ Mobile Device Management

Citrix® XenMobile™ Mobile Device Management

ISBN: 978-1-78217-214-7   Paperback: 112 pages

Gain an insight into the industry's best and most secure Enterprise Mobility Management solution

1. Deploy and manage the complete XenMobile solution.

2. Learn how to customize and troubleshoot your XenMobile apps.

3. Step-by-step instructions with relevant screenshots for better understanding.

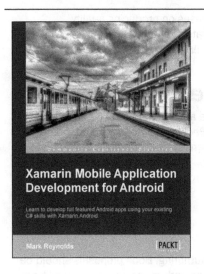

Xamarin Mobile Application Development for Android

ISBN: 978-1-78355-916-9   Paperback: 168 pages

Learn to develop full featured Android apps using your existing C# skills with Xamarin.Android

1. Gain an understanding of both the Android and Xamarin platforms.

2. Build a working multiview Android app incrementally throughout the book.

3. Work with device capabilities such as location sensors and the camera.

Please check **www.PacktPub.com** for information on our titles

Learning Dart

ISBN: 978-1-84969-742-2   Paperback: 388 pages

Learn how to program applications with Dart 1.0, a language specifically designed to produce better-structured, high-performance applications

1. Develop apps for the Web using Dart and HTML5.

2. Build powerful HTML5 forms, validate and store data in local storage, and use web components to build your own user interface.

3. Make games by drawing and integrate audio and video in the browser.

4. Learn how to develop an application with the help of a model-driven and fast-paced approach.

C++ Application Development with Code::Blocks

ISBN: 978-1-78328-341-5   Paperback: 128 pages

Develop advanced applications with Code::Blocks quickly and efficiently with this concise, hands-on guide

1. Successfully install and configure Code::Blocks for C++ development.

2. Perform rapid application development with Code::Blocks.

3. Work with advanced C++ features including code debugging and GUI toolkits.

Please check **www.PacktPub.com** for information on our titles

www.ingramcontent.com/pod-product-compliance
Lightning Source LLC
Chambersburg PA
CBHW062056050326
40690CB00016B/3107

* 9 7 8 1 7 8 3 9 8 1 9 0 8 *